D0065414

Keeping
Customers

The Harvard Business Review Book Series

Keeping Customers

Edited, with
an Introduction by
**John J. Sviokla and
Benson P. Shapiro**

A Harvard Business Review Book

Library of Congress Cataloging-in-Publication Data

Keeping customers / edited, with an introduction by John J. Sviokla
   and Benson P. Shapiro.
       p.   cm. — (The Harvard business review book series)
       "A Harvard business review book."
       Articles originally published in the Harvard Business review,
   1968–1992.
       Companion to: Seeking customers.
       Includes bibliographical references and index.
       ISBN 0-87584-333-6 (acid-free paper)
       1. Customer service—United States.   2. Consumer satisfaction—
   United States.   I. Sviokla, J. J.   II. Shapiro, Benson P.
       III. Harvard business review.   IV. Title: Seeking customers.
   V. Series
   HF5415.5.K45   1993
   658.8'12—dc20   92-39229
                                                          CIP

The *Harvard Business Review* articles in this collection are available as individual reprints. Discounts apply to quantity purchases. For information and ordering contact Operations Department, Harvard Business School Publishing Corporation, Boston, MA 02163. Telephone: (617) 495-6192, 9 a.m. to 5 p.m. Eastern Time, Monday through Friday. Fax: (617) 495-6985, 24 hours a day.

Editor's Note: Some articles in this book may have been written before authors and editors began to take into consideration the role of women in management. We hope the archaic usage representing all managers as male does not detract from the usefulness of the collection.

Contents

Most companies are better at developing new
relationships than building on existing ones. However,
most of the value in a commercial relationship is
gained after the sale. Support service contracts,
referrals, larger purchases, and repeat purchases are
among the rewards for those who concentrate on
deepening their ties with existing accounts.

Many companies have cut out layers of bureaucracy,
undertaken quality drives, and improved direct
interaction with customers only to find customer
orders falling between the cracks, profits suffering,
and organizational tensions mounting. Focusing on
the order management process provides many
opportunities for improvement, including better
pricing, superior coordination across functions, careful
prioritization, and improved communication up and
down the management chain.

Every manager wants to provide a smooth, efficient
business process that profitably meets or exceeds
customer expectations. This article shows how to chart
the sequence of internal activities required to perform
and deliver a service and map these activities against
expectations. This analysis helps service providers
visualize the current business process and pinpoint
areas for improvement.

3 How to Manage Customer Service   91
William M. Hutchison, Jr. and John F. Stolle
Many customer service efforts are managed as a
necessary evil. Customers, however, expect service to
be as much a part of what they buy as design, quality,
and price. Furthermore, the service function is
generally the most frequent and visible contact point
between the seller and the client. This classic article
suggests a program for designing customer service as a
core driver of competitiveness and profitability.

Part III   Execute with Quality

Introduction   115

**1 Competing on the Eight Dimensions
of Quality   119**
David A. Garvin
Quality is more than a means to make a better product
or service—it is a multifaceted strategic weapon.
Strategic management of quality incorporates tangible
product features, such as performance and
conformance, as well as intangibles, such as aesthetics
and reputation. Companies can improve their
competitiveness by designing the quality package that
creates the best impression in the market relative to
costs.

**2 Quality Is More Than Making a Good
Product   137**
Hirotaka Takeuchi and John A. Quelch
Managers who focus exclusively on product quality
miss many opportunities to satisfy customers. Quality
management includes keeping close tabs on changing
customer values and concentrating on after-sales
service. By paying attention to customers' evolving
quality perceptions, managers can develop long-range
programs that continue to deliver high-quality service
at the right price.

3 The Power of Unconditional Service Guarantees   151
Christopher W. L. Hart

Service guarantees are a powerful differentiator in the marketplace; they also provide valuable information on an organization's performance. In order to capture the full value of guarantees, a company should begin with a commitment to error-free service and design the organization to support it. This article offers an approach to designing guarantees that will both satisfy customers and boost profits.

Part IV   Keep the Relationship Vibrant
Introduction   169

1 Make Sure Your Customers Keep Coming Back   173
F. Stewart DeBruicker and Gregory L. Summe

Customers are new only once. Yesterday's fantastic service is today's minimum standard and tomorrow's disappointment. Those who wait for the customer to define the standard are forced into a defensive position. Sellers who anticipate their customers' evolving demands can develop product enhancement, customer service, marketing, and pricing strategies that meet customers' needs without sacrificing profits.

2 Exploit Your Product's Service Life Cycle   187
George W. Potts

Gillette made a fortune giving away razors and selling the blades. Similarly, many businesses see more profits from after-sales services than from the initial product sales. With thoughtful planning, smart management can garner profits throughout a product's service life cycle.

3 Good Product Support Is Smart Marketing   197
Milind M. Lele and Uday S. Karmarkar

Typically, product support is a reactive measure taken

only after customers complain. Diffuse responsibility for the functions that provide support leads to piecemeal management of this process. Even worse, actual service needs are often obscured by traditional measures. By analyzing the entire product support effort, managers can create the greatest impact for the least cost, setting new competitive standards.

4 The Case of the Tech Service Tangle   215
Benson P. Shapiro

How do you continue to attract sales after a new product has worked its initial magic? How should internal resources be allocated? The sales manager will want to hire more salespeople, the R&D manager will demand funds for the next new product, and the product manager argues for more technical service to discover new applications. A panel of industry experts helps clarify the substantive and political considerations in addressing these challenges.

Part V   Turn Sows' Ears into Silk Purses
Introduction   233

1 The Case of the Complaining Customer   237
Dan Finkelman and Tony Goland

Every company makes mistakes; superior companies learn from them. In the case of a lost dry cleaning order, the manager suggests that a demanding customer is not worth keeping. A panel of customer service authorities agrees that the manager's response is symptomatic of larger problems in the company's operations.

2 The Profitable Art of Service Recovery   255
Christopher W. L. Hart, James L. Heskett, and W. Earl Sasser, Jr.

In almost every business, the cost of losing customers is staggering. The natural propensity is to sweep problems under the rug, and thus miss chances to turn complaining customers into loyal ones. Rather than setting static quality standards, companies can gain significant profits and a competitive advantage by empowering employees to take action on behalf of the customer.

over time. Creating a culture of customer preservation can lead to increased customer, employee, and shareholder satisfaction.

Part VII Measure What Matters
Introduction 327

Many fortunes were created by taking the ideas of Henry Ford and applying them to every manner of product and service. Even today, comparing your practices with best practices in any industry ("benchmarking") is one of the most powerful ways to improve efficiency. When performed carefully, benchmarking provides inspiration and new insights, setting an agenda for aggressive improvements.

Poor information on product and service costs leads to unprofitable decisions. Existing cost systems frequently understate profits on high-volume products and overstate profits on specialty items. This article argues that instead of using antiquated product-based accounting systems, producers should adopt more dynamic activity-based systems, which provide a more accurate framework for determining the profitability of products and the efficiency of process technologies.

Today's measurement systems often look backward at past financial results. This article argues that a company's future performance is better managed by considering such external, customer-driven measures as quality and customer satisfaction. The challenge for management is to build these measures into the compensation and incentive systems. These efforts represent a fundamental shift in practices and priorities. The competitive implications are enormous.

Preface

John J. Sviokla and Benson P. Shapiro

In an increasingly complex and competitive business environment, having a terrific new product or service is no longer sufficient for achieving success. Technological, organizational, and institutional advances have created a marketplace where greater producer capacity chases each dollar of customer spending. Differentiating your product has become increasingly a function of the selling process itself, in addition to product features, price, and delivery schedule.

This two-volume set (*Seeking Customers* and *Keeping Customers*) focuses on improving the competitiveness with which companies attract customers and develop profitable, long-term relationships. The articles we have culled from the *Harvard Business Review* move beyond the popular rhetoric of "market orientation" as an end in itself to a philosophy that market orientation is a primary management task on the road to better corporate performance. While *Seeking Customers* addresses the challenges of competitive customer acquisition, *Keeping Customers* concentrates on developing relationships that remain profitable over time.

Efficient selling increases value to the customer (relative to price) as well as to the seller (relative to costs). At every stage in the process of seeking and keeping customers—for example, identifying prospects, initiating and cultivating relationships, setting prices, closing the sale, monitoring the order management cycle, offering postsales product support—sellers have the opportunity to add value for the customer. However, tight coordination within the selling company is necessary to ensure that the costs of investing resources in customer value creation do not outweigh the benefits of making the sale.

These two books highlight the many ways in which sellers can increase the value of their products or services efficiently. We must caution the reader that much of the advice offered in these volumes is not easy to execute. Value creation requires persistence and creativity. The process begins with understanding the needs and goals of each potential customer and demonstrating how you as the seller are best qualified to satisfy those demands. You must be aware of how the customer perceives the benefits from doing business with you rather than with your competitors. At the same time, you cannot lose sight of your interests; satisfying customers must not be pursued at the expense of long-term profitability.

Fortunately, some of the factors contributing to the complex and competitive nature of the business environment actually help sellers pursue customers more profitably. For example, information and communication technologies have vastly improved the ability to track and share important customer-related information. New distribution channels and support services enable companies to better coordinate product development, production, delivery, service, and support. Most important, today's intense competition has provided the motivation for organizational changes, such as cross-functional teams, that would have been considered impossible even a few years ago.

In this environment of rapid change and intense competition, *Seeking Customers* and *Keeping Customers* will help make the 1990s a decade of profitable customer satisfaction for your company.

Introduction

John J. Sviokla and Benson P. Shapiro

Keeping good customers should be as natural to a business as breathing is to a human being. Many businesses, however, are so oriented toward attracting new customers that they do not invest resources in sustaining long-term relationships after the sale is made. Furthermore, many suppliers are unable to identify their most profitable customers and therefore lose the opportunity to generate the greatest profits in the long term. In order to keep customers profitably, sellers must recognize that the seller-customer relationship evolves over time. The resources allocated to customer acquisition may not be sufficient to support future sales. For suppliers there is a natural tension between wanting to maintain the status quo and having to respond to customers' evolving product and service requirements. Facing these challenges requires a commitment to dynamic, long-term planning that continually creates the greatest value to customers without sacrificing profits.

The articles here provide a framework for balancing these interrelated and often conflicting goals. This collection suggests that building profitable loyal customers is a complex process involving seven management principles:

1. Put the customer at the heart of your business
2. Manage the business from the customer's point of view
3. Execute with quality
4. Keep the relationship vibrant
5. Turn sows' ears into silk purses
6. Convert customer satisfaction into profits
7. Measure what matters

The pressures of today's marketplace are forcing a renewed commitment to customer service. However, slogans such as "the decade of the customer," "total quality service," and "put the customer first" must be backed by coordinated programs at all levels of the business if suppliers expect to create a strong market orientation.

No single activity can create a customer-focused organization. Rather, keeping customers over the long term requires interconnected management actions implemented over time to build and enhance relationships with customers, while simultaneously increasing organizational efficiency. When well managed, these efforts add up to more than the sum of their parts, ultimately resulting in greater profits.

The first section, **Put the Customer at the Heart of Your Business,** establishes the bedrock philosophy on which the other sections are built. Market orientation is achieved by communicating customer concerns and demands throughout the organization. To achieve this end, managers must combat the natural tendency of organizations to draw inward over time and focus on internal goals. Instead, suppliers must be flexible and creative, recognizing that customers' needs rather than products drive the market. Technological innovation has increased the range of products and services available to consumers, who in turn have become more discerning and demanding. At the same time, however, technology has improved the ability of suppliers to recognize and respond to customers' demands.

The second principle, **Manage the Business from the Customer's Point of View** (Part II), is closely related to the first. Many businesses are designed as "functional chimneys," with management, organizational, physical, and information systems creating barriers to coordination and cooperation. Such impediments prevent companies from recognizing the potential differences between their perceptions and their customers' perceptions of value creation. Resources are invested in inefficient and inappropriate business practices that add cost, not value.

Revamping business processes that were designed in a less competitive, less global, and less technologically complex environment presents tremendous challenges. The articles in this section suggest ways for businesses to reorient their activities toward meeting customers' needs. With this fundamental orientation, companies can develop the most appropriate management actions and harness the most efficient technologies to decrease organizational tension, increase financial performance, and improve customer satisfaction.

In order to achieve these goals, suppliers must **Execute with Quality** (Part III). High quality generates brand loyalty, favorable word of mouth, and a willingness on the part of customers to pay premium prices. The concept of quality is more than simply meeting product specifications. Quality implies meeting or exceeding customers' expectations about timeliness, accuracy, responsiveness, and performance.

Competitive quality management recognizes that today's breakthrough product or service is tomorrow's undifferentiated commodity. For example, when Federal Express instituted overnight delivery, it had a unique product. Today it is locked in a price-and-feature war with several global competitors. In this rapidly changing environment, a commitment to quality at every stage of the production and service provision process allows suppliers to anticipate and meet customers' evolving demands.

The next section, **Keep the Relationship Vibrant** (Part IV), offers additional insights for staying attuned to changing expectations. Sometimes the relationship with a customer is invigorated by continual product enhancement or by technical support to find new applications for existing products. In other cases, newness is created by careful planning that embraces the entire product or service life cycle, scheduling product or service augmentations to meet the specific needs of the customers at the precise moment when these needs develop. At the same time, more value can be extracted by establishing pricing schedules that account for life cycle progression.

Even with the best planning, companies make mistakes. **Turning Sows' Ears into Silk Purses** (Part V) calls for consciously designing management policy and systems for recovery actions when the inevitable mistakes occur. Exceeding customer expectations when things go wrong is an area where a small amount of management attention can turn liabilities into assets. In fact, artful recovery often leaves a stronger positive impression than if the mistake had never occurred. Managers who create mechanisms for recovering gracefully should also monitor them to gather valuable information about the performance of their businesses. In addition, the skillful leader can use these recoveries as powerful symbols for the entire organization by spreading the stories of how individuals went the extra mile for their customers.

The sixth principle, **Convert Customer Satisfaction into Profits** (Part VI), focuses on value extraction. Many businesses oscillate from emphasizing sales volume to emphasizing profitability. This seesaw process destroys margins during downtimes and can harm customer relationships in uptimes. A consistent focus on managing profitable sales yields vastly more satisfying results, but requires constant review of customer behavior to estimate both the value of a service to the customer and the cost of providing that service. Therefore, suppliers must carefully evaluate their pricing strategy on an ongoing basis, or they may find themselves forced into providing more and more services without being able to extract this value through higher prices. In many industries, leaders and laggards alike have been swept along by following competitive offerings without reviewing the impact on profits.

In the last section, **Measure What Matters** (Part VII), we come full circle. Firms that take measurement seriously have two related challenges. First, it is difficult to create and implement control systems to track costs accurately because many existing systems are based on antiquated principles that allocate costs on the basis of direct labor and machine use—often poor proxies for customer-associated expenses. Use of these out-of-date systems can lead to systematic distortions in management information, poor management control, and faulty pricing policies.

The second challenge is to implement changes that will improve existing control systems. In particular, the time has come to include customer-based measures into the formal goals of the organization. Establishing quantitative, credible measures of satisfaction, on-time delivery, and customer retention requires a great deal of ingenuity and commitment. Putting these measures on par with return on investment, market share, and other traditional performance measures is a major senior management challenge. Nevertheless, putting customer-based measures at the heart of an organization's control systems delivers enough value to be worth the effort. First, these measures force a company to focus on responding to customers' needs. Second, they provide a more dynamic indication of the company's performance.

These seven principles create a web of activities for keeping customers (see Exhibit I). Each action by itself is not sufficient, but together they build a self-reinforcing system that keeps customers longer and extracts more value from them over the long term.

We emphasize that keeping customers is not an end in itself, but rather a means to the goal of generating profits. Establishing long-term relationships with customers increases a company's profitability along several dimensions. For example, marketing strategies

Exhibit I. The Interlocking Efforts to Keep Customers

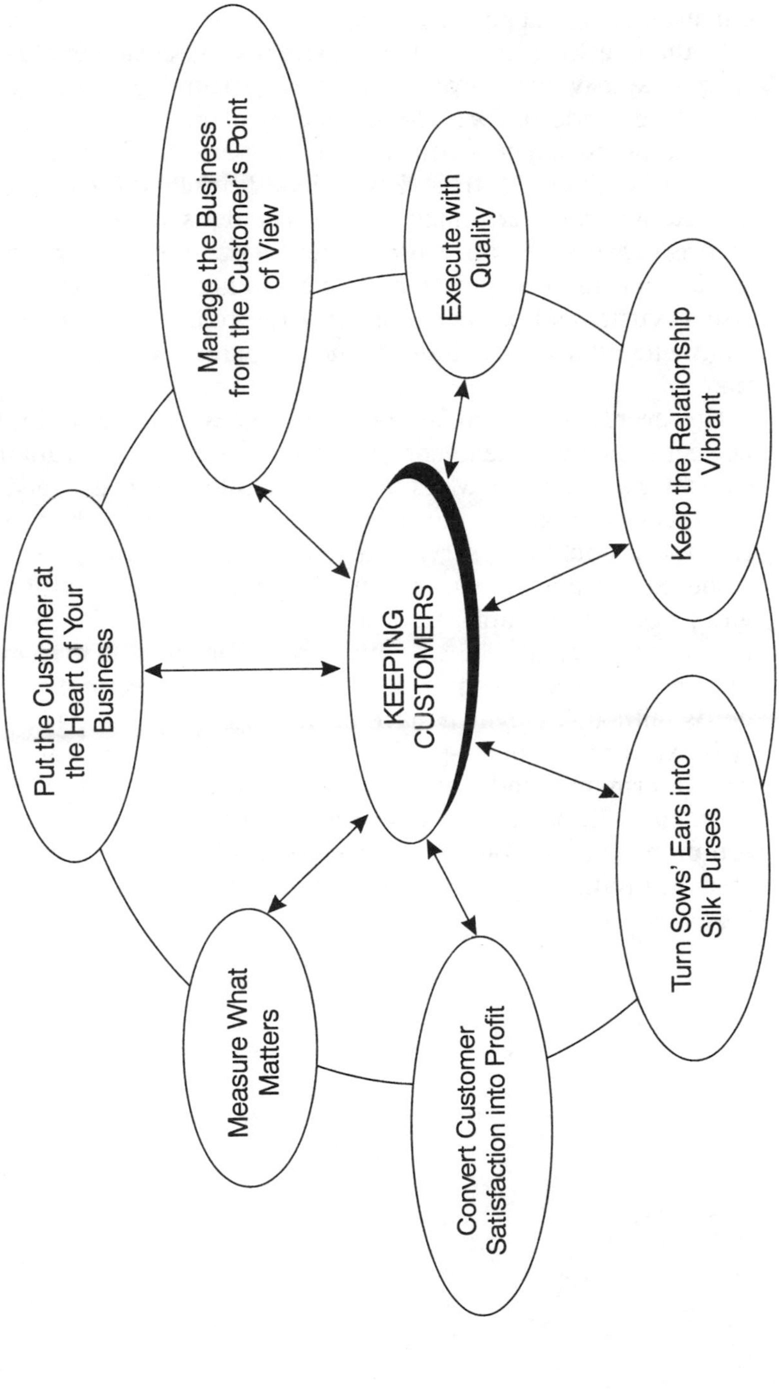

can be designed to attract existing customers to new applications, enhancements, support services, or even new products at a lower cost than seeking new customers. Long-time customers are often willing to pay higher prices to avoid incurring the expense of switching vendors. Furthermore, happy clients provide referrals.

Building customer satisfaction is at the core of achieving long-term profitability. Satisfaction is simply the difference between expectations and performance. If expectations are high and performance is average, satisfaction suffers. But when performance exceeds expectations, satisfaction soars. Since expectations tend to rise as customers become more experienced, managers must constantly monitor their abilities to meet higher thresholds of satisfaction.

However, it is easy to fall into a "business as usual" attitude and neglect to analyze the dynamic interplay between profitability and customer satisfaction. Market trends, customers' needs, and internal business practices must be scrutinized constantly to ensure that the product and service mix, the account base, and internal resource allocation are generating the greatest value relative to cost and price. For example, analysis often reveals that the "best" customers may actually be eroding profits. Or analysis may indicate that the organization's practices are no longer meeting customers' needs, although they may have been sufficient in the past.

These three themes—profits, customer satisfaction, and analysis—inform and bind together the seven principles outlined in this book. Only through focused and relentless use of analysis to guide comprehensive action can managers continue the drive for increased profitability, customer satisfaction, and competitive advantage.

PART

I

Put the Customer at the Heart of Your Business

Introduction

The first section presents the central philosophy of this book: put your customer at the heart of your business. At a *functional* level, putting the customer at the heart, or core, of your business allows you to establish the vital link between customer orientation and profitability. Simply being aware of customer needs is not enough to remain competitive. Translating knowledge about customers into profitable enduring relationships requires a flexible, creative, and dynamic approach across all company functions. At a *symbolic* level, this philosophy implies that successful selling depends on total commitment to the customer. This commitment is necessary for coordinating activities and allocating resources across functions, recognizing the most efficient means for increasing customer value, and developing a long-term vision in the face of rapidly changing market demands.

Keeping customers after the initial sale has become more important and challenging because competition has made many customers both more demanding and less loyal. As products and customers become more sophisticated, producers and suppliers must compete on the basis of service and quality as well as on product features, price, and delivery schedules. Fortunately, the new technologies are also allowing companies to track their customers' needs more directly and to develop more efficient operations to meet those needs.

In this challenging environment the rhetoric of "market orientation" is popular. But what does it mean? The first article in this collection, Benson Shapiro's "What the Hell Is Market Oriented"? addresses this fundamental question. The author first draws the distinction between *market* oriented and *marketing* oriented, where marketing as a separate function is insufficient for generating profitable sales. Market orientation exists when: (1) information on all-important buying influences permeates every corporate function; (2) strategic and tactical decisions are made interfunctionally and interdivisionally, not within myopic fiefdoms; and (3) divisions and functions are coordinated across traditional boundaries in pursuit of flawless execution. Together, these conditions turn the rhetoric of market orientation into management reality.

Satisfying these conditions lays the foundation for the customer-keeping principles that are developed throughout this book. For instance, well-planned customer orientation enables sellers to take control of the transaction, rather than letting customers push them around with unreasonable service demands or pressure to lower prices. Control of this process results in more profitable sales as well as a product mix that matches customer needs with seller capabilities.

Market orientation allows companies to identify and pursue the most profitable prospects and accounts. Selling to a new prospect is more expensive than cross-selling to an existing customer (see, for example, "Zero Defections" in Part VI). A "lost" customer may be difficult and expensive to recover; in some cases, it is necessary to wait a generation before the account has the potential to be resold. Nevertheless, many companies act as if their prospect base were infinite. The customer-focused company treats the customer as valuable raw material that must be nurtured so that benefits can be gained over a long time horizon. At the same time, intimate knowledge of the market helps sellers select the best account base: "The most important strategic decision is to choose the important customers."

The second article, "Marketing Is Everything," by Regis Mc-Kenna, further advocates the need to make every facet of the firm market-focused. "Marketing today is not a function; it is a way of doing business." Competition and technological innovation have so dramatically altered the degree of choice in the market that a fundamental shift in selling approach is needed. Instead of forcing a product on the customer, the seller must provide a product and related support that helps the customer succeed in attaining his or her own goals. This approach creates a significantly deeper relationship between customer and seller than would a simple transaction.

"Marketing Is Everything" argues that this approach depends on sensitive listening skills and attentiveness to customer needs at every opportunity. Moreover, the marketing paradigm is shifting from the static advertising monologue to a dynamic technology-enhanced dialogue between seller and customer. The winners use knowledge gained from interaction with customers to innovate, invest in core skills, and make excellent products that fill customer needs. This is not to say that selling is simply a reactive response to customer needs. When marketing permeates every company function, the company can anticipate or even create customer needs or new market niches. Dynamic product and service development allows sellers to "own" the market. Sony, for example, owns the portable stereo market because it created the first Walkman and followed it with variations, enhancements, and new products. Ownership implies high customer satisfaction and loyalty, which in turn build profitability.

A vital part of owning a market is to establish lasting relationships. The third article, "After the Sale Is Over . . ." by Theodore Levitt, argues that most of the value in a commercial relationship is created *after* the sale is made. Traditionally, internal systems have been focused on getting the sale. But in today's environment, where customers expect installation, service, support, maintenance, and enhancements over a product's life, and repeat negotiations are costly and time-consuming, the sales effort must be reoriented to account for postsale activity. During the sales and postsale process, lasting opinions about seller performance are developed; future purchase decisions are largely based on how well the seller met expectations. Meeting customer expectations throughout the process has a vital influence on customer satisfaction and profits. Referrals, larger purchases, and repeat purchases are some of the rewards for those who constantly deepen their ties with existing accounts.

From a financial point of view, selling companies tend to invest more heavily in product development and in seeking customers, expecting a revenue flow after the sale. However, "the natural tendency of relationships, whether in marriage or in business, is toward erosion of sensitivity and attentiveness . . . A healthy relationship maintains, and preferably expands, the equity and the possibilities that were created during courtship." Levitt argues that investing in longer-term relationship management will ultimately be more profitable, especially if companies establish bonds that outlive the individuals fulfilling the functions. It is the perseverance of postsale effort that extracts the maximum value from the marketing and management investment made in the initial relationship.

Overall, a philosophy of customer orientation and action is important for sustaining competitiveness. This section provides practical advice on how to achieve this focus, build relationships, and link customer orientation to profitability. This philosophy, backed by management leadership and concrete action, provides the backdrop for this volume.

1
What the Hell Is "Market Oriented"?

Benson P. Shapiro

The air hung heavy in French Lick, Indiana. A tornado watch was in effect that morning, and the sky was black. In a meeting room in one of the local resort hotels, where top management of the Wolverine Controller Company had gathered, the atmosphere matched the weather. Recent results had been poor for the Indianapolis-based producer of flow controllers for process industries like chemicals, paper, and food. Sales were off, but earnings were off even more. Market share was down in all product lines.

As the president called the meeting to order he had fire in his eyes. "The situation can't get much more serious," he proclaimed. "As you all know, over the past couple of years everything has gone to hell in a handbasket. We're in deep trouble, with both domestic and foreign competition preempting us at every turn. The only way to get out of this mess is for us to become customer driven or market oriented. I'm not even sure what that means, but I'm damn sure that we want to be there. I don't even know whether there's a difference between being market driven and customer oriented or customer driven and market oriented or whatever. We've just got to do a hell of a lot better."

"I couldn't agree with you more, Frank," the marketing vice president put in. "I've been saying all along that we've got to be more marketing oriented. The marketing department has to be more involved in everything that goes on because we represent the customer and we've got an integrated view of the company."

The CEO scowled at him. "I said *market* oriented, not marketing oriented! It's unclear to me what we get for all the overhead we have in marketing. Those sexy brochures of yours sure haven't been doing the job."

There followed a lively, often acrimonious discussion of what was wrong and what was needed. Each vice president defended his or her function or unit and set out solutions from that particular standpoint. I will draw a curtain over their heedless and profane bickering, but here are paraphrases of their positions.

Sales VP: "We need more salespeople. We're the ones who are close to the customers. We have to have more call capacity in the sales force so we can provide better service and get new product ideas into the company faster."

Manufacturing VP: "We all know that our customers want quality. We need more automated machinery so we can work to closer tolerances and give them better quality. Also, we ought to send our whole manufacturing team to Crosby's Quality College."

Research and development VP: "Clearly we could do much better at both making and selling our products. But the fundamental problem is a lack of *new* products. They're the heart of our business. Our technology is getting old because we aren't investing enough in R&D."

Finance VP: "The problem isn't not enough resources; it's too many resources misspent. We've got too much overhead. Our variable costs are out of control. Our marketing and sales expenses are unreasonable. And we spend too much on R&D. We don't need more, we need less."

The general manager of the Electronic Flow Controls Division: "We aren't organized in the right way—that's the fundamental problem. If each division had its own sales force, we would have better coordination between sales and the other functions."

Her counterpart in the Pneumatic Controls Division: "We don't need our own sales forces anywhere near as much as we need our own engineering group so we can develop designs tailored to our customers. As long as we have a central R&D group that owns all the engineers, the divisions can't do their jobs."

As the group adjourned for lunch, the president interjected a last word. "You all put in a lot of time talking past each other and defending your own turf. Some of that's all right. You're supposed to represent your own departments and sell your own perspectives. If you didn't work hard for your own organizations, you wouldn't have lasted long at Wolverine, and you couldn't have made the contributions that you have.

"But enough is enough! You aren't just representatives of your own shops. You're the corporate executives at Wolverine and you have to take a more integrated, global view. It's my job to get all of you coordinated, but it's also the job of each of you. I don't have the knowledge, and nothing can replace direct, lateral communication across departments. Let's figure out how to do that after we get some lunch."

All Right, What Is It?

Leaving the Wolverine bunch to its meal, I want to make a start in dispelling the president's uncertainty. After years of research, I'm convinced that the term "market oriented" represents a set of processes touching on all aspects of the company. It's a great deal more than the cliche "getting close to the customer." Since most companies sell to a variety of customers with varying and even conflicting desires and needs, the goal of getting close to the customer is meaningless. I've also found no meaningful difference between "market driven" and "customer oriented," so I use the phrases interchangeably. In my view, three characteristics make a company market driven.

Information on all important buying influences permeates every corporate function. A company can be market oriented only if it completely understands its markets and the people who decide whether to buy its products or services.

In some industries, wholesalers, retailers, and other parts of the distribution channels have a profound influence on the choices customers make. So it's important to understand "the trade." In other markets, nonbuying influences specify the product, although they neither purchase it nor use it. These include architects, consulting engineers, and doctors. In still other markets, one person may buy the product and another may use it; family situations are an obvious illustration. In commercial and industrial marketplaces, a professional procurement organization may actually purchase the product, while a manufacturing or operational function uses it.

To be of greatest use, customer information must move beyond the market research, sales, and marketing functions and "permeate every corporate function"—the R&D scientists and engineers, the manufacturing people, and the field-service specialists. When the technologists, for example, get unvarnished feedback on the way customers use the product, they can better develop improvements on the product and the production processes. If, on the other hand, market research or marketing people predigest the information, technologists may miss opportunities.

Of course, regular cross-functional meetings to discuss customer needs and to analyze feedback from buying influences are very important. At least once a year, the top functional officers should spend a full day or more to consider what is happening with key buying influences.

Corporate officers and functions should have access to all useful market research reports. If company staff appends summaries to regular customer surveys, like the Greenwich commercial and investment banking reports or the numerous consumer package-goods industry sales analyses, top officers are more likely to study them. That approach lets top management get the sales and marketing departments' opinions as well as those of less-biased observers.

Some companies that have customer response phones—toll-free 800 numbers that consumers or distributors call to ask questions or make comments—distribute selected cassette recordings of calls to a wide range of executives, line and staff. The cassettes stimulate new ideas for products, product improvements, packaging, and service.

Reports to read and cassettes to hear are useful—but insufficient. High-level executives need to make visits to important customers to see them using their industrial and commercial products, consuming their services, or retailing their consumer goods. When, say, top manufacturing executives understand how a customer factory uses their products, they will have a more solid appreciation of customer needs for quality and close tolerances. Trade show visits provide valuable opportunities for operations and technical people to talk with customers and visit competitors' booths (if allowed by industry custom and show rules).

In my statement on the first characteristic, I referred to "important" buying influences. Because different customers have different needs, a marketer cannot effectively satisfy a wide range of them equally. The most important strategic decision is to choose the important customers. All customers are important, but invariably some are more important to the company than others. Collaboration among the various functions is important when pinpointing the key target accounts and market segments. Then the salespeople know whom to call on first and most often, the people who schedule production runs know who gets favored treatment, and those who make service calls know who rates special attention. If the priorities are not clear in the calm of planning meetings, they certainly won't be when the sales, production scheduling, and service dispatching processes get hectic.

The choice of customers influences the way decisions are made. During a marketing meeting at Wolverine Controller, one senior marketing person said, "Sales and marketing will pick out the customers they want to do business with, and then we'll sit down with the manufacturing and technical people and manage the product mix." Too late! Once you have a certain group of customers, the product mix is pretty much set; you must make the types of products they want. If sales and marketing choose the customers, they have undue power over decisions. Customer selection must involve all operating functions.

Strategic and tactical decisions are made interfunctionally and interdivisionally. Functions and divisions will inevitably have conflicting objectives that mirror distinctions in cultures and in modes of operation. The glimpse into the meeting at French Lick demonstrates that. The customer-oriented company possesses mechanisms to get these differences out on the table for candid discussion and to make trade-offs that reconcile the various points of view. Each function and division must have the ear of the others and must be encouraged to lay out its ideas and requirements honestly and vigorously.

To make wise decisions, functions and units must recognize their differences. A big part of being market driven is the way different jurisdictions deal with one another. The marketing department may ask the R&D department to develop a product with a certain specification by a certain date. If R&D thinks the request is unreasonable but doesn't say so, it may develop a phony plan that the company will never achieve. Or R&D may make changes in the specifications and the delivery date without talking to marketing. The result: a missed deadline and an overrun budget. If, on the other hand, the two functions get together, they are in a position to make intelligent technological and marketing trade-offs. They can change a specification or extend a delivery date with the benefit of both points of view.

An alternative to integrated decision making, of course, is to kick the decision upstairs to the CEO or at least the division general manager. But though the higher executives have unbiased views, they lack the close knowledge of the specialists. An open decision-making process gets the best of both worlds, exploiting the even-handedness of the general manager and the functional skills of the specialists.

Divisions and functions make well-coordinated decisions and execute them with a sense of commitment. An open dialogue on strategic and tactical trade-offs is the best way to engender commitment to meet goals. When the implementers also do the planning, the commitment will be strong and clear.

The depth of the biases revealed at the French Lick gathering demonstrates the difficulty of implementing cross-functional programs. But there's nothing wrong with that. In fact, the strength of those biases had a lot to do with Wolverine's past success. If the R&D vice president thought like the financial vice president, she wouldn't be effective in her job. On the other hand, if each function is marching to its own drum, implementation will be weak regardless of the competence and devotion of each function.

Serial communication, when one function passes an idea or request to another routinely without interaction—like tossing a brick with a message tied to it over the wall—can't build the commitment needed in the customer-driven company. Successful new products don't, for example, emerge out of a process in which marketing sends a set of specifications to R&D, which sends finished blueprints and designs to manufacturing. But joint opportunity analysis, in which functional and divisional people share ideas and discuss alternative solutions and approaches, leverages the different strengths of each party. Powerful internal connections make communication clear, coordination strong, and commitment high.

Poor coordination leads to misapplication of resources and failure to make the most of market opportunities. At one point in the meeting at French Lick, the vice president for human resources spoke up in this fashion: "Remember how impressed everyone was in '86 with the new pulp-bleaching control we developed? Not just us, but the whole industry—especially with our fast response rate. Even though the technology was the best, the product flopped. Why? Because the industry changed its process so that the response rate was less important than the ability to handle tough operating conditions and higher temperatures and pressures. Plus we couldn't manufacture to the tight tolerances the industry needed. We wasted a lot of talent on the wrong problem."

Probably the salespeople, and perhaps the technical service people, knew about the evolving customer needs. By working together, manufacturing and R&D could have designed a manufacturable product. But the company lacked the coordination that a focused market orientation stimulates.

Action at Wolverine

Just about every company thinks of itself as market oriented. It's confident it has the strength to compete with the wolf pack, but in reality it's often weak and tends to follow the shepherd. In marketing efforts, businesses are particularly vulnerable to this delusion. Let's return to French Lick to hear of such a sheep in wolf's clothing.

"Look at Mutton Machinery," the vice president of manufacturing was saying. "They've done worse than we have. And their ads and brochures brag about them being customer oriented! At the trade show last year, they had a huge booth with the theme 'The Customer is King.' They had a sales contest that sent a salesperson and customer to tour the major castles of Europe."

The sales vice president piped up. "They should send their salespeople for technical training, not to look at castles. We interviewed two of their better people, and they didn't measure up technically. The glitzy trade show stuff and the sexy contest don't make them customer oriented."

No, slogans and glossy programs don't give a company a market orientation. It takes a philosophy and a culture that go deep in the organization. Let's take a look at Wolverine's approach.

It's unlikely that any company ever became market oriented with a bottom-up approach; to make it happen, you need the commitment and power of those at the top. In gathering everybody who mattered at French Lick, Wolverine was taking the right step at the start. And from what we have heard, clearly they were not sugarcoating their concerns.

By the end of the first day, the executives had decided that they knew too little about their own industry, particularly customers and competitors. After a mostly social dinner meeting and a good night's sleep, they began at breakfast on day two to develop a plan to learn more. They listed 20 major customers they wanted to understand better. They designated each of the ten executives at the meeting (CEO, six functional heads, and three division general managers) to visit the customers in pairs in the next two months; the sales force would coordinate the visits. All ten agreed to attend the next big trade show.

They assigned the marketing vice president to prepare dossiers on the 20 customers plus another 10, as well as prospects selected by the group. Besides data on the customer or prospect, each dossier was to include an examination of Wolverine's relationship with it.

Finally, the group singled out seven competitors for close scrutiny. The marketing vice president agreed to gather market data on them. The R&D vice president committed herself to drawing up technical reviews of them, and the financial vice president was to prepare analyses of financial performance. The seven remaining executives each agreed to analyze the relative strengths and weaknesses of one competitor.

Spurred by the president, the group concluded on day two that barriers had arisen among Wolverine's functional departments. Each was on its own little island. The human resources vice president took on the responsibility of scrutinizing cross-functional communication and identifying ways to improve it.

Back at headquarters in Indianapolis, the top brass did another smart thing: it involved all functional leadership so that line as well as staff chieftains would contribute to the effort. Top management quickly pinpointed the management information system as a major point of leverage for shaping a more integrated company view. Therefore, the president invited the MIS director to join the team.

Top management also decided that the bonus plan encouraged each function to pursue its own objectives instead of corporatewide goals. So the controller teamed up with the human resources vice president to devise a better plan, which won the approval of top management.

As a new interest in communication and cooperation developed, the president perceived the need to make changes in structure and process. Chief among these were the establishment of a process engineering department to help production and R&D move new products from design into manufacturing and the redesign of managerial reports to emphasize the total company perspective.

The management group, more sensitive now to the ways people deal with each other, awoke to the power of informal social systems. To make the salespeople more accessible to headquarters staff, the sales office at a nearby location moved to headquarters (over the objections of the vice president of sales). The effort to promote interfunctional teamwork even extended to the restructuring of the bowling league. Wolverine had divided its teams by function or division. Now, however, each team had members from various functions. Some old-timers snorted that that was taking the new market orientation too far. But in a conversation during a bowling league party, the head of technical field service and a customer-service manager came up with an idea for a program to improve customer responsiveness. Then even the skeptics began to understand.

The analyses of customers and competitors identified an important market opportunity for Wolverine. The management group diverted resources to it, and under the direction of the Pneumatic Controls Division general manager, a multifunctional task force launched an effort to exploit it. Top management viewed this undertaking as a laboratory for the development of new approaches and as a showcase to demonstrate the company's new philosophy and culture. Headquarters maintained an intense interest in the project.

As the project gained momentum, support for the underlying philosophy grew. Gradually, the tone of interfunctional relationships changed. People evinced more trust in each other and were much more willing to admit responsibility for mistakes and to expose shortcomings.

Unfortunately, some people found it difficult to change. The sales vice president resisted the idea that a big part of his job was bringing customers and data about them into the company as well as encouraging all functions to deal with customers. He became irate when the vice president of manufacturing worked directly with several major customers, and he told the president that he wouldn't stand for other people dealing with *his* customers. His colleagues couldn't alter his attitude, so the president replaced him.

Wolverine's sales and earnings slowly began to improve. The market price of its stock edged upward. Internally, decision making became more integrative. Some early victories helped build momentum. Implementation improved through cooperation very low in the ranks, where most of the real work was done.

Imitate Larry Bird

A year after Wolverine's first meeting in the French Lick hotel, the management group gathered there again. A new sales vice president was present, and the newly promoted MIS vice president/controller was also there.

This time the executives focused on two concerns. The first was how to handle the inordinate demands on the company resulting from the new push to satisfy important customers. The second was how to maintain Wolverine's momentum toward achieving a market orientation.

Attacking the first item, the group agreed to set major customer priorities. At hand was the information gathered during the year via industry analysis and executives' visits to top accounts. Available to the executives also were several frameworks for analysis.[1] Some accounts fit together in unexpected ways. In some situations, a series of accounts used similar products similarly. In others, the accounts competed for Wolverine's resources.

It took several meetings to set priorities on customers. The hardest part was resolving a dispute over whether to raise prices drastically on the custom products made for the third largest account. Wolverine was losing money on these. "Maybe not all business is good business," the R&D vice president suggested. That notion was pretty hard for the team to accept. But the CEO pushed hard for a decision. Ultimately, the group agreed to drop the account if it did not accede to price increases within the next six to eight months.

On the second matter, the management group decided it needed a way to measure the company's progress. The approach, everybody understood, had to be grounded in unrelieved emphasis on information gathering, on interfunctional decision making, and on a vigorous sense of commitment throughout the organization. They recognized how easy it is to get complacent and lose detachment when examining one's own performance. Nevertheless, the executives drew up a checklist of customer-focused questions for the organization to ask itself.

Two years after the company changed its direction, a major customer asked the president about his impressions of Wolverine's efforts to become market oriented. Here is his response:

"It's proved to be harder than I had imagined. I had to really drive people to think about customers and the corporation as a whole, not just what's good for their own departments. It's also proved to be more worthwhile. We have a different tone in our outlook and a different way of dealing with each other.

"We use all kinds of customer data and bring it into all functions. We do much more interfunctional decision making. The hardest part of all was account selection, and that really paid off for us. It also had the most impact. Our implementation has improved through what we call the three Cs, communication, coordination, and commitment. We're getting smooth, but we sure aren't flawless yet.

"Last night I watched the Pacers play the Boston Celtics on TV. The Celtics won. Sure they've got more talent, but the real edge the Celtics have is their teamwork. At one point in the game, the Indiana team got impatient with each other. They seemed to forget that the Celtics were the competition.

"That's the way we used to be too—each department competing with each other. A few years ago we had a meeting down at French Lick where everything came to a head, and I was feeling pretty desperate. There's a real irony here because French Lick is the hometown of Larry Bird.

"When I think about the Celtics and Bird, what working together means becomes clear. If each Wolverine manager only helps his or her department do its job well, we're going to lose. Back when the company was small, products were simple, competition was unsophisticated, and customers were less demanding, we could afford to work separately. But now, our individual best isn't good enough; we've got to work as a unit. Bird is the epitome. He subverts his own interest and ego for the sake of the team. That's what I want to see at Wolverine."

Note

1. They used the account profitability matrix described by Benson P. Shapiro, V. Kasturi Rangan, Rowland T. Moriarty, and Elliot B. Ross in "Manage Customers for Profits (Not Just Sales)," *Harvard Business Review*, September–October 1987, p. 101.

2
Marketing Is Everything

Regis McKenna

The 1990s will belong to the customer. And that is great news for the marketer.

Technology is transforming choice, and choice is transforming the marketplace. As a result, we are witnessing the emergence of a new marketing paradigm—not a "do more" marketing that simply turns up the volume on the sales spiels of the past but a knowledge- and experience-based marketing that represents the once-and-for-all death of the salesman.

Marketing's transformation is driven by the enormous power and ubiquitous spread of technology. So pervasive is technology today that it is virtually meaningless to make distinctions between technology and nontechnology businesses and industries: there are *only* technology companies. Technology has moved into products, the workplace, and the marketplace with astonishing speed and thoroughness. Seventy years after they were invented, fractional horsepower motors are in some 15 to 20 household products in the average American home today. In less than 20 years, the microprocessor has achieved a similar penetration. Twenty years ago, there were fewer than 50,000 computers in use; today more than 50,000 computers are purchased every day.

The defining characteristic of this new technological push is programmability. In a computer chip, programmability means the capability to alter a command, so that one chip can perform a variety of prescribed functions and produce a variety of prescribed outcomes. On the factory floor, programmability transforms the production operation, enabling one machine to produce a wide variety of models and products. More broadly, programmability is the new corporate capability to produce more and more varieties and choices for customers—even to offer each individual customer the chance to design and implement the "program" that will yield the precise product, service, or variety that is right for him or her. The technological promise of programmability has exploded into the reality of almost unlimited choice.

Take the world of drugstores and supermarkets. According to *Gorman's New Product News*, which tracks new product introductions in these two consumer-products arenas, between 1985 and 1989 the number of new products grew by an astonishing 60% to an all-time annual high of 12,055. As venerable a brand as Tide illustrates this multiplication of brand variety. In 1946, Procter & Gamble introduced the laundry detergent, the first ever. For 38 years, one version of Tide served the entire market. Then, in the mid-1980s, Procter & Gamble began to bring out a succession of new Tides: Unscented Tide and Liquid Tide in 1984, Tide with Bleach in 1988, and the concentrated Ultra Tide in 1990.

To some marketers, the creation of almost unlimited customer choice represents a threat—particularly when choice is accompanied by new competitors. Twenty years ago, IBM had only 20 competitors; today it faces more than 5,000, when you count any company that is in the "computer" business. Twenty years ago, there were fewer than 90 semiconductor companies; today there are almost 300 in the United States alone. And not only are the competitors new, bringing with them new products and new strategies, but the customers also are new: 90% of the people who used a computer in 1990 were not using one in 1980. These new customers don't know about the old rules, the old understandings, or the old ways of doing business—and they don't care. What they do care about is a company that is willing to adapt its products or services to fit their strategies. This represents the evolution of marketing to the market-driven company.

Several decades ago, there were sales-driven companies. These organizations focused their energies on changing customers' minds to fit the product—practicing the "any color as long as it's black" school of marketing.

As technology developed and competition increased, some companies shifted their approach and became customer driven. These companies expressed a new willingness to change their product to fit customers' requests—practicing the "tell us what color you want" school of marketing.

In the 1990s, successful companies are becoming market driven, adapting their products to fit their customers' strategies. These companies will practice "let's figure out together whether and how color matters to your larger goal" marketing. It is marketing that is oriented toward creating rather than controlling a market; it is based on developmental education, incremental improvement, and ongoing process rather than on simple market-share tactics, raw sales, and one-time events. Most important, it draws on the base of knowledge and experience that exists in the organization.

These two fundamentals, knowledge-based and experience-based marketing, will increasingly define the capabilities of a successful marketing organization. They will supplant the old approach to marketing and new product development. The old approach—getting an idea, conducting traditional market research, developing a product, testing the market, and finally going to market—is slow, unresponsive, and turf-ridden. Moreover, given the fast-changing marketplace, there is less and less reason to believe that this traditional approach can keep up with real customer wishes and demands or with the rigors of competition.

Consider the much-publicized 1988 lawsuit that Beecham, the international consumer products group, filed against advertising giant Saatchi & Saatchi. The suit, which sought more than $24 million in damages, argued that Yankelovich Clancy Shulman, at that time Saatchi's U.S. market-research subsidiary, had "vastly overstated" the projected market share of a new detergent that Beecham launched. Yankelovich forecast that Beecham's product, Delicare, a cold-water detergent, would win between 45.4% and 52.3% of the U.S. market if Beecham backed it with $18 million of advertising. According to Beecham, however, Delicare's highest market share was 25%; the product generally achieved a market share of between 15% and 20%. The lawsuit was settled out of court, with no clear winner or loser. Regardless of the outcome, however, the issue it illustrates is widespread and fundamental: forecasts, by their very nature, must be unreliable, particularly with technology, competitors, customers, and markets all shifting ground so often, so rapidly, and so radically.

The alternative to this old approach is knowledge-based and experience-based marketing. Knowledge-based marketing requires a company to master a scale of knowledge: of the technology in which it competes; of its competition; of its customers; of new sources of technology that can alter its competitive environment; and of its own organization, capabilities, plans, and way of doing business. Armed with this mastery, companies can put knowledge-based marketing to work in three essential ways: (1) integrating the customer into the design process to guarantee a product that is tailored not only to the customers' needs and desires but also to the customers' strategies; (2) generating niche thinking to use the company's knowledge of channels and markets to identify segments of the market the company can own; and (3) developing the infra-structure of suppliers, vendors, partners, and users whose rela-tionships will help sustain and support the company's reputation and technological edge.

The other half of this new marketing paradigm is experience-based marketing, which emphasizes interactivity, connectivity, and creativity. With this approach, companies spend time with their customers, constantly monitor their competitors, and develop a feedback-analysis system that turns this information about the mar-ket and the competition into important new product intelligence. At the same time, these companies both evaluate their own tech-nology to assess its currency and cooperate with other companies to create mutually advantageous systems and solutions. These close encounters—with customers, competitors, and internal and exter-nal technologies—give companies the firsthand experience they need to invest in market development and to take intelligent, cal-culated risks.

In a time of exploding choice and unpredictable change, mar-keting—the new marketing—is the answer. With so much choice for customers, companies face the end of loyalty. To combat that threat, they can add sales and marketing people, throwing costly resources at the market as a way to retain customers. But the real solution, of course, is not more marketing but better marketing. And that means marketing that finds a way to integrate the cus-tomer into the company, to create and sustain a relationship be-tween the company and the customer.

The marketer must be the integrator, both internally—synthe-sizing technological capability with market needs—and externally —bringing the customer into the company as a participant in the development and adaptation of goods and services. It is a funda-mental shift in the role and purpose of marketing: from manipu-lation of the customer to genuine customer involvement; from telling and selling to communicating and sharing knowledge; from last-in-line function to corporate-credibility champion.

Playing the integrator requires the marketer to command credibility. In a marketplace characterized by rapid change and potentially paralyzing choice, credibility becomes the company's sustaining value. The character of its management, the strength of its financials, the quality of its innovations, the congeniality of its customer references, the capabilities of its alliances—these are the measures of a company's credibility. They are measures that, in turn, directly affect its capacity to attract quality people, generate new ideas, and form quality relationships.

The relationships are the key, the basis of customer choice and company adaptation. After all, what is a successful brand but a special relationship? And who better than a company's marketing people to create, sustain, and interpret the relationship between the company, its suppliers, and its customers? That is why, as the demands on the company have shifted from controlling costs to competing on products to serving customers, the center of gravity in the company has shifted from finance to engineering—and now to marketing. In the 1990s, marketing will do more than sell. It will define the way a company does business.

Marketing Is Everything and Everything Is Marketing

The old notion of marketing was epitomized by the ritual phone call from the CEO to the corporate headhunter saying, "Find me a good marketing person to run my marketing operation!" What the CEO wanted, of course, was someone who could take on a discrete set of textbook functions that were generally associated with run-of-the-mill marketing. That person would immediately go to Madison Avenue to hire an advertising agency, change the ad campaign, redesign the company logo, redo the brochures, train the sales force, retain a high-powered public relations firm, and alter or otherwise reposition the company's image.

Behind the CEO's call for "a good marketing person" were a number of assumptions and attitudes about marketing: that it is a distinct function in the company, separate from and usually subordinate to the core functions; that its job is to identify groups of potential customers and find ways to convince them to buy the company's product or service; and that at the heart of it is image making—creating and projecting a false sense of the company and its offerings to lure the customer into the company's grasp. If those assumptions ever were warranted in the past, however, all three are totally unsupportable and obsolete today.

Marketing today is not a function; it is a way of doing business. Marketing is not a new ad campaign or this month's promotion. Marketing has to be all-pervasive, part of everyone's job description, from the receptionists to the board of directors. Its job is neither to fool the customer nor to falsify the company's image. It is to integrate the customer into the design of the product and to design a systematic process for interaction that will create substance in the relationship.

To understand the difference between the old and the new marketing, compare how two high-tech medical instrument companies recently handled similar customer telephone calls requesting the repair and replacement of their equipment. The first company—call it Gluco—delivered the replacement instrument to the customer within 24 hours of the request, no questions asked. The box in which it arrived contained instructions for sending back the broken instrument, a mailing label, and even tape to reseal the box. The phone call and the exchange of instruments were handled conveniently, professionally, and with maximum consideration for and minimum disruption to the customer.

The second company—call it Pumpco—handled things quite differently. The person who took the customer's telephone call had never been asked about repairing a piece of equipment; she thoughtlessly sent the customer into the limbo of hold. Finally, she came back on the line to say that the customer would have to pay for the equipment repair and that a temporary replacement would cost an additional $15.

Several days later, the customer received the replacement with no instructions, no information, no directions. Several weeks after the customer returned the broken equipment, it reappeared, repaired but with no instructions concerning the temporary replacement. Finally, the customer got a demand letter from Pumpco, indicating that someone at Pumpco had made the mistake of not sending the equipment C.O.D.

To Pumpco, marketing means selling things and collecting money; to Gluco, marketing means building relationships with its customers. The way the two companies handled two simple customer requests reflects the questions that customers increasingly ask in interactions with all kinds of businesses, from airlines to software makers: Which company is competent, responsive, and well organized? Which company do I trust to get it right? Which company would I rather do business with?

Successful companies realize that marketing is like quality—integral to the organization. Like quality, marketing is an intangible that the customer must experience to appreciate. And like quality—which in the United States has developed from early ideas like planned obsolescence and inspecting quality into more ambitious concepts like the systemization of quality in every aspect of the organization—marketing has been evolutionary.

Marketing has shifted from tricking the customer to blaming the customer to satisfying the customer—and now to integrating the customer systematically. As its next move, marketing must permanently shed its reputation for hucksterism and image making and create an award for marketing much like the Malcolm Baldrige National Quality Award. In fact, companies that continue to see marketing as a bag of tricks will lose out in short order to companies that stress substance and real performance.

Marketing's ultimate assignment is to serve customers' real needs and to communicate the substance of the company—not to introduce the kinds of cosmetics that used to typify the auto industry's annual model changes. And because marketing in the 1990s is an expression of the company's character, it necessarily is a responsibility that belongs to the whole company.

The Goal Is to Own the Market

U.S. companies typically make two kinds of mistakes. Some get caught up in the excitement and drive of making things, particularly new creations. Others become absorbed in the competition of selling things, particularly to increase their market share in a given product line.

Both approaches could prove fatal to a business. The problem with the first is that it leads to an internal focus. Companies can become so fixated on pursuing their R&D agendas that they forget about the customer, the market, the competition. They end up winning recognition as R&D pioneers but lack the more important capability—sustaining their performance and, sometimes, maintaining their independence. Genentech, for example, clearly emerged as the R&D pioneer in biotechnology, only to be acquired by Roche.

The problem with the second approach is that it leads to a market-share mentality, which inevitably translates into under-shooting the market. A market-share mentality leads a company to think of its customers as "share points" and to use gimmicks, spiffs, and promotions to eke out a percentage-point gain. It pushes a company to look for incremental, sometimes even minuscule, growth out of existing products or to spend lavishly to launch a new product in a market where competitors enjoy a fat, dominant position. It turns marketing into an expensive fight over crumbs rather than a smart effort to own the whole pie.

The real goal of marketing is to own the market—not just to make or sell products. Smart marketing means defining what whole pie is yours. It means thinking of your company, your technology, your product in a fresh way, a way that begins by defining what you can lead. Because in marketing, what you lead, you own. Leadership is ownership.

When you own the market, you do different things and you do things differently, as do your suppliers and your customers. When you own the market, you develop your products to serve that market specifically; you define the standards in that market; you bring into your camp third parties who want to develop their own compatible products or offer you new features or add-ons to augment your product; you get the first look at new ideas that others are testing in that market; you attract the most talented people because of your acknowledged leadership position.

Owning a market can become a self-reinforcing spiral. Because you own the market, you become the dominant force in the field; because you dominate the field, you deepen your ownership of the market. Ultimately, you deepen your relationship with your customers as well, as they attribute more and more leadership qualities to a company that exhibits such an integrated performance.

To own the market, a company starts by thinking of a new way to define a market. Take, for instance, the case of Convex Computer. In 1984, Convex was looking to put a new computer on the market. Because of the existing market segmentation, Convex could have seen its only choice as competing for market share in the predefined markets: in supercomputers where Cray dominated or in minicomputers where Digital led. Determined to define a market it could own, Convex created the "mini-supercomputer" market by offering a product with a price/performance ratio between Cray's $5 million to $15 million supercomputers and Digital's $300,000 to

$750,000 minicomputers. Convex's product, priced between $500,000 and $800,000, offered technological performance less than that of a full supercomputer and more than that of a minicomputer. Within this new market, Convex established itself as the leader.

Intel did the same thing with its microprocessor. The company defined its early products and market more as computers than semiconductors. Intel offered, in essence, a computer on a chip, creating a new category of products that it could own and lead.

Sometimes owning a market means broadening it; other times, narrowing it. Apple has managed to do both in efforts to create and own a market. Apple first broadened the category of small computers to achieve a leadership position. The market definition started out as hobby computers and had many small players. The next step was the home computer—a market that was also crowded and limiting. To own a market, Apple identified the personal computer, which expanded the market concept and made Apple the undeniable market leader.

In a later move, Apple did the opposite, redefining a market by narrowing its definition. Unquestionably, IBM owned the business market; for Apple, a market-share mentality in that arena would have been pointless. Instead, with technology alliances and marketing correctly defined, Apple created—and owned—a whole new market: desktop publishing. Once inside the corporate world with desktop publishing, Apple could deepen and broaden its relationships with the business customer.

Paradoxically, two important outcomes of owning a market are substantial earnings, which can replenish the company's R&D coffers, and a powerful market position, a beachhead from which a company can grow additional market share by expanding both its technological capabilities and its definition of the market. The greatest practitioners of this marketing approach are Japanese companies in industries like autos, commercial electronics, semiconductors, and computers and communications. Their primary goal is ownership of certain target markets. The keiretsu industrial structure allows them to use all of the market's infrastructure to achieve this; relationships in technology, information, politics, and distribution help the company assert its leadership.

The Japanese strategy is consistent. These companies begin by using basic research from the United States to jump-start new product development. From 1950 to 1978, for example, Japanese companies entered into 32,000 licensing arrangements to acquire foreign technology at an estimated cost of $9 billion. But the United States spent at least 50 times that much to do the original R&D. Next, these Japanese companies push out a variety of products to engage the market and to learn and then focus on dominating the market to force foreign competitors to retreat—leaving them to harvest substantial returns. These huge profits are recycled into a new spiral of R&D, innovation, market creation, and market dominance.

That model of competing, which links R&D, technology, innovation, production, and finance—integrated through marketing's drive to own a market—is the approach that all competitors will take to succeed in the 1990s.

Marketing Evolves as Technology Evolves

In a world of mass manufacturing, the counterpart was mass marketing. In a world of flexible manufacturing, the counterpart is flexible marketing. The technology comes first, the ability to market follows. The technology embodies adaptability, programmability, and customizability; now comes marketing that delivers on those qualities.

Today technology has created the promise of "any thing, any way, any time." Customers can have their own version of virtually any product, including one that appeals to mass identification rather than individuality, if they so desire. Think of a product or an industry where customization is not predominant. The telephone? Originally, Bell Telephone's goal was to place a simple, all-black phone in every home. Today there are more than 1,000 permutations and combinations available, with options running the gamut from different colors and portability to answering machines and programmability—as well as services. There is the further promise of optical fiber and the convergence of computers and communications into a unified industry with even greater technological choice.

How about a venerable product like the bicycle, which appeared originally as a sketch in Leonardo da Vinci's notebooks? According to an article in the *Washington Post*, the National Bicycle Industrial Company in Kokubu, Japan builds made-to-order bicycles on an assembly line. The bicycles, fitted to each customer's measurements, are delivered within two weeks of the order—and the company offers 11,231,862 variations on its models, at prices only 10% higher than ready-made models.

Even newspapers that report on this technology-led move to customization are themselves increasingly customized. Faced with stagnant circulation, the urban daily newspapers have begun to customize their news, advertising, and even editorial and sports pages to appeal to local suburban readers. The *Los Angeles Times*, for example, has seven zoned editions targeting each of the city's surrounding communities.

What is at work here is the predominant mathematical formula of today's marketing: variety plus service equals customization. For all of its bandying about as a marketing buzzword, customization is a remarkably direct concept—it is the capacity to deal with a customer in a unique way. Technology makes it increasingly possible to do that, but interestingly, marketing's version of the laws of physics makes it increasingly difficult.

According to quantum physics, things act differently at the micro level. Light is the classic example. When subjected to certain kinds of tests, light behaves like a wave, moving in much the way an ocean wave moves. But in other tests, light behaves more like a particle, moving as a single ball. So, scientists ask, is it a wave or a particle? And when is it which?

Markets and customers operate like light and energy. In fact, like light, the customer is more than one thing at the same time. Sometimes consumers behave as part of a group, fitting neatly into social and psychographic classifications. Other times, the consumer breaks loose and is iconoclastic. Customers make and break patterns: the senior citizen market is filled with older people who intensely wish to act youthful, and the upscale market must contend with wealthy people who hide their money behind the most utilitarian purchases.

Markets are subject to laws similar to those of quantum physics. Different markets have different levels of consumer energy, stages in the market's development where a product surges, is absorbed, dissipates, and dies. A fad, after all, is nothing more than a wave that dissipates and then becomes a particle. Take the much-discussed Yuppie market and its association with certain branded consumer products, like BMWs. After a stage of high customer energy and close identification, the wave has broken. Having been saturated and absorbed by the marketplace, the Yuppie association has faded, just as energy does in the physical world. Sensing the change, BMW no longer sells to the Yuppie lifestyle but now focuses on the technological capabilities of its machines. And Yuppies are no longer the wave they once were; as a market, they are more like particles as they look for more individualistic and personal expressions of their consumer energy.

Of course, since particles can also behave like waves again, it is likely that smart marketers will tap some new energy source, such as values, to recoalesce the young, affluent market into a wave. And technology gives marketers the tools they need, such as data base marketing, to discern waves and particles and even to design programs that combine enough particles to form a powerful wave.

The lesson for marketers is much the same as that voiced by Buckminster Fuller for scientists: "Don't fight forces; use them." Marketers who follow and use technology, rather than oppose it, will discover that it creates and leads directly to new market forms and opportunities. Take audiocassettes, tapes, and compact discs. For years, record and tape companies jealously guarded their property. Knowing that home hackers pirated tapes and created their own composite cassettes, the music companies steadfastly resisted the forces of technology—until the Personics System realized that technology was making a legitimate market for authorized, high-quality customized composite cassettes and CDs.

Rather than treating the customer as a criminal, Personics saw a market. Today consumers can design personalized music tapes from the Personics System, a revved-up jukebox with a library of over 5,000 songs. For $1.10 per song, consumers tell the machine what to record. In about ten minutes, the system makes a customized tape and prints out a laser-quality label of the selections, complete with the customer's name and a personalized title for the tape. Launched in 1988, the system has already spread to more than 250 stores. Smart marketers have, once again, allowed technology to create the customizing relationship with the customer.

Moving from Monologue to Dialogue

We are witnessing the obsolescence of advertising. In the old model of marketing, it made sense as part of the whole formula: you sell mass-produced goods to a mass market through mass media. Marketing's job was to use advertising to deliver a message to the consumer in a one-way communication: "Buy this!" That message no longer works, and advertising is showing the effects. In 1989, newspaper advertising grew only 4%, compared with 6% in 1988 and 9% in 1987. According to a study by Syracuse University's John Philip Jones, ad spending in the major media has been stalled at 1.5% of GNP since 1984. Ad agency staffing, research, and profitability have been affected.

Three related factors explain the decline of advertising. First, advertising overkill has started to ricochet back on advertising itself. The proliferation of products has yielded a proliferation of messages: U.S. customers are hit with up to 3,000 marketing messages a day. In an effort to bombard the customer with yet one more advertisement, marketers are squeezing as many voices as they can into the space allotted to them. In 1988, for example, 38% of prime-time and 47% of weekday daytime television commercials were only 15 seconds in duration; in 1984, those figures were 6% and 11%, respectively. As a result of the shift to 15-second commercials, the number of television commercials has skyrocketed; between 1984 and 1988, prime-time commercials increased by 25%, weekday daytime by 24%.

Predictably, however, a greater number of voices translates into a smaller impact. Customers simply are unable to remember which advertisement pitches which product, much less what qualities or attributes might differentiate one product from another. Very simply, it's a jumble out there.

Take the enormously clever and critically acclaimed series of advertisements for Eveready batteries, featuring a tireless marching rabbit. The ad was so successful that a survey conducted by Video Storyboard Tests Inc. named it one of the top commercials in 1990—for Duracell, Eveready's top competitor. In fact, a full 40% of those who selected the ad as an outstanding commercial attributed it to Duracell. Partly as a consequence of this confusion, reports indicate that Duracell's market share has grown, while Eveready's may have shrunk slightly.

Batteries are not the only market in which more advertising succeeds in spreading more confusion. The same thing has happened in markets like athletic footwear and soda pop, where competing companies have signed up so many celebrity sponsors that consumers can no longer keep straight who is pitching what for whom. In 1989, for example, Coke, Diet Coke, Pepsi, and Diet Pepsi used nearly three dozen movie stars, athletes, musicians, and television personalities to tell consumers to buy more cola. But when the smoke and mirrors had cleared, most consumers couldn't remember whether Joe Montana and Don Johnson drank Coke or Pepsi—or both. Or why it really mattered.

The second development in advertising's decline is an outgrowth of the first: as advertising has proliferated and become more obnoxiously insistent, consumers have gotten fed up. The more advertising seeks to intrude, the more people try to shut it out. Last year, Disney won the applause of commercial-weary customers when the company announced that it would not screen its films in theaters that showed commercials before the feature. A Disney executive was quoted as saying, "Movie theaters should be preserved as environments where consumers can escape from the pervasive onslaught of advertising." Buttressing its position, the company cited survey data obtained from moviegoers, 90% of whom said they did not want commercials shown in movie theaters and 95% of whom said they did want to see previews of coming attractions.

More recently, after a number of failed attempts, the U.S. Congress responded to the growing concerns of parents and educators over the commercial content of children's television. A new law limits the number of minutes of commercials and directs the Federal Communications Commission both to examine "program-length commercials"—cartoon shows linked to commercial product lines—and to make each television station's contribution to children's educational needs a condition for license renewal. This concern over advertising is mirrored in a variety of arenas—from public outcry over cigarette marketing plans targeted at blacks and women to calls for more environmentally sensitive packaging and products.

The underlying reason behind both of these factors is advertising's dirty little secret: it serves no useful purpose. In today's market, advertising simply misses the fundamental point of marketing—adaptability, flexibility, and responsiveness. The new marketing requires a feedback loop; it is this element that is missing from the monologue of advertising but that is built into the dialogue of marketing. The feedback loop, connecting company and customer, is central to the operating definition of a truly market-driven company: a company that adapts in a timely way to the changing needs of the customer.

Apple is one such company. Its Macintosh computer is regarded as a machine that launched a revolution. At its birth in 1984, industry analysts received it with praise and acclaim. But in retrospect, the first Macintosh had many weaknesses: it had limited, nonexpandable memory, virtually no applications software, and a black-and-white screen. For all those deficiencies, however, the Mac had two strengths that more than compensated: it was incredibly easy to use, and it had a user group that was prepared to praise Mac publicly at its launch and to advise Apple privately on how to improve it. In other words, it had a feedback loop. It was this feedback loop that brought about change in the Mac, which ultimately became an open, adaptable, and colorful computer. And it was changing the Mac that saved it.

Months before launching the Mac, Apple gave a sample of the product to 100 influential Americans to use and comment on. It signed up 100 third-party software suppliers who began to envision applications that could take advantage of the Mac's simplicity. It trained over 4,000 dealer salespeople and gave full-day, hands-on demonstrations of the Mac to industry insiders and analysts. Apple got two benefits from this network: educated Mac supporters who could legitimately praise the product to the press and invested consumers who could tell the company what the Mac needed. The dialogue with customers *and* media praise were worth more than any notice advertising could buy.

Apple's approach represents the new marketing model, a shift from monologue to dialogue. It is accomplished through experience-based marketing, where companies create opportunities for customers and potential customers to sample their products and then provide feedback. It is accomplished through beta sites, where a company can install a prelaunch product and study its use and needed refinements. Experienced-based marketing allows a company to work closely with a client to change a product, to adapt the technology—recognizing that no product is perfect when it comes from engineering. This interaction was precisely the approach taken by Xerox in developing its Docutech System. Seven months before launch, Xerox established 25 beta sites. From its prelaunch customers, Xerox learned what adjustments it should make, what service and support it should supply, and what enhancements and related new products it might next introduce.

The goal is adaptive marketing, marketing that stresses sensitivity, flexibility, and resiliency. Sensitivity comes from having a variety of modes and channels through which companies can read the environment, from user groups that offer live feedback to sophisticated consumer scanners that provide data on customer choice in real time. Flexibility comes from creating an organizational structure and operating style that permits the company to take advantage of new opportunities presented by customer feedback. Resiliency comes from learning from mistakes—marketing that listens and responds.

Blurring Distinctions

The line between products and services is fast eroding. What once appeared to be a rigid polarity now has become a hybrid: the servicization of products and the productization of services. When General Motors makes more money from lending its customers money to buy its cars than it makes from manufacturing the cars, is it marketing its products or its services? When IBM announces to all the world that it is now in the systems-integration business—the customer can buy any box from any vendor and IBM will supply the systems know-how to make the whole thing work together—is it marketing its products or its services? In fact, the computer business today is 75% services; it consists overwhelmingly of applications knowledge, systems analysis, systems engineering, systems integration, networking solutions, security, and maintenance.

The point applies just as well to less grandiose companies and to less expensive consumer products. Take the large corner drugstore that stocks thousands of products, from cosmetics to wristwatches. The products are for sale, but the store is actually marketing a service—the convenience of having so much variety collected and arrayed in one location. Or take any of the ordinary products found in the home, from boxes of cereal to table lamps to VCRs. All of them come with some form of information designed to perform a service: nutritional information to indicate the actual food value of the cereal to the health-conscious consumer; a United Laboratories label on the lamp as an assurance of testing; an operating manual to help the nontechnical VCR customer rig up the new unit. There is ample room to improve the quality of this information—to make it more useful, more convenient, or even more entertaining—but in almost every case, the service information is a critical component of the product.

On the other side of the hybrid, service providers are acknowledging the productization of services. Service providers, such as banks, insurance companies, consulting firms, even airlines and radio stations, are creating tangible events, repetitive and predictable exercises, standard and customizable packages that are product services. A frequent-flier or a frequent-listener club is a product service, as are regular audits performed by consulting firms or new loan packages assembled by banks to respond to changing economic conditions.

As products and services merge, it is critical for marketers to understand clearly what marketing the new hybrid is *not*. The service component is not satisfied by repairing a product if it breaks. Nor is it satisfied by an 800 number, a warranty, or a customer survey form. What customers want most from a product is often qualitative and intangible; it is the service that is integral to the product. Service is not an event; it is the process of creating a customer environment of information, assurance, and comfort.

Consider an experience that by now must have become commonplace for all of us as consumers. You go to an electronics store and buy an expensive piece of audio or video equipment, say, a CD player, a VCR, or a video camera. You take it home, and a few days later, you accidentally drop it. It breaks. It won't work. Now, as a customer, you have a decision to make. When you take it back to the store, do you say it was broken when you took it out of the box? Or do you tell the truth?

The answer, honestly, depends on how you think the store will respond. But just as honestly, most customers appreciate a store that encourages them to tell the truth by making good on all customer problems. Service is, ultimately, an environment that encourages honesty. The company that adopts a "we'll make good on it, no questions asked" policy in the face of adversity may win a customer for life.

Marketers who ignore the service component of their products focus on competitive differentiation and tools to penetrate markets. Marketers who appreciate the importance of the product-service hybrid focus on building loyal customer relationships.

Technology Markets Technology

Technology and marketing once may have looked like opposites. The cold, impersonal sameness of technology and the high-touch, human uniqueness of marketing seemed eternally at odds. Computers would only make marketing less personal; marketing could never learn to appreciate the look and feel of computers, data bases, and the rest of the high-tech paraphernalia.

On the grounds of cost, a truce was eventually arranged. Very simply, marketers discovered that real savings could be gained by using technology to do what previously had required expensive, intensive, and often risky, people-directed field operations. For example, marketers learned that by matching a data base with a marketing plan to simulate a new product launch on a computer, they could accomplish in 90 days and for $50,000 what otherwise would take as long as a year and cost at least several hundred thousand dollars.

But having moved beyond the simple automation-for-cost-saving stage, technology and marketing have now not only fused but also begun to feed back to each other. The result is the transformation of both technology and the product and the reshaping of both the customer and the company. Technology permits information to flow in both directions between the customer and the company. It creates the feedback loop that integrates the customer into the company, allows the company to own a market, permits customization, creates a dialogue, and turns a product into a service and a service into a product.

The direction in which Genentech has moved in its use of laptop and hand-held computers illustrates the transforming power of technology as it merges with marketing. Originally, the biotechnology company planned to have salespeople use laptops on their sales calls as a way to automate the sales function. Sales reps, working solely out of their homes, would use laptops to get and send electronic mail, file reports on computerized "templates," place orders, and receive company press releases and information updates. In addition, the laptops would enable sales reps to keep data bases that would track customers' buying histories and company performance. That was the initial level of expectations—very low.

In fact, the technology-marketing marriage has dramatically altered the customer-company relationship and the job of the sales rep. Sales reps have emerged as marketing consultants. Armed with technical information generated and gathered by Genentech, sales reps can provide a valuable educational service to their customers, who are primarily pharmacists and physicians. For example, analysis of the largest study of children with a disease called short stature is available only through Genentech and its representatives. With this analysis, which is based on clinical studies of 6,000 patients between the ages of one month and 30 years, and with the help of an on-line "growth calculator," doctors can better judge when to use the growth hormone Protropin.

Genentech's system also includes a general educational component. Sales reps can use their laptops to access the latest articles or technical reports from medical conferences to help doctors keep up to date. The laptops also make it possible for doctors to use sales reps as research associates: Genentech has a staff of medical specialists who can answer highly technical questions posed through an on-line question-and-answer template. When sales reps enter a question on the template, the e-mail function immediately routes it to the appropriate specialist. For relatively simple questions, on-line answers come back to the sales rep within a day.

In the 1990s, Genentech's laptop system—and the hundreds of similar applications that sprang up in the 1980s to automate sales, marketing, service, and distribution—will seem like a rather obvious and primitive way to meld technology and marketing. The marketer will have available not only existing technologies but also their converging capabilities: personal computers, data bases, CD-ROMs, graphic displays, multimedia, color terminals, computer-video technology, networking, a custom processor that can be built into anything anywhere to create intelligence on a countertop or a dashboard, scanners that read text, and networks that instantaneously create and distribute vast reaches of information.

As design and manufacturing technologies advance into "real time" processes, marketing will move to eliminate the gap between production and consumption. The result will be marketing workstations—the marketers' counterpart to CAD/CAM systems for engineers and product designers. The marketing workstation will draw on graphic, video, audio, and numeric information from a network of data bases. The marketer will be able to look through windows on the workstation and manipulate data, simulate markets and products, bounce concepts off others in distant cities, write production orders for product designs and packaging concepts, and obtain costs, timetables, and distribution schedules.

Just as computer-comfortable children today think nothing of manipulating figures and playing fantastic games on the same color screens, marketers will use the workstation to play both designer and consumer. The workstation will allow marketers to integrate data on historic sales and cost figures, competitive trends, and consumer patterns. At the same time, marketers will be able to create and test advertisements and promotions, evaluate media options, and analyze viewer and readership data. And finally, marketers will be able to obtain instant feedback on concepts and plans and to move marketing plans rapidly into production.

The marriage of technology and marketing should bring with it a renaissance of marketing R&D—a new capability to explore new ideas, to test them against the reactions of real customers in real time, and to advance to experience-based leaps of faith. It should be the vehicle for bringing the customer inside the company and for putting marketing in the center of the company.

In the 1990s, the critical dimensions of the company—including all of the attributes that together define how the company does business—are ultimately the functions of marketing. That is why marketing is everyone's job, why marketing is everything and everything is marketing.

3
After the Sale Is Over

Theodore Levitt

The relationship between a seller and a buyer seldom ends when a sale is made. Increasingly, the relationship intensifies after the sale and helps determine the buyer's choice the next time around. Such dynamics are found particularly with services and products dealt in a stream of transactions between seller and buyer—financial services, consulting, general contracting, military and space equipment, and capital goods.

The sale, then, merely consummates the courtship, at which point the marriage begins. How good the marriage is depends on how well the seller manages the relationship. The quality of the marriage determines whether there will be continued or expanded business, or troubles and divorce. In some cases divorce is impossible, as when a major construction or installation project is underway. If the marriage that remains is burdened, it tarnishes the seller's reputation.

Companies can avoid such troubles by recognizing at the outset the necessity of managing their relationships with customers. This takes special attention to an often ignored aspect of relationships: time.

The theory of supply and demand presumes that the work of the economic system is time-discrete and bare of human interaction—that an instantaneous, disembodied sales transaction clears the market at the intersection of supply and demand.

This was never completely accurate and has become less so as product complexity and interdependencies have intensified. Buyers of automated machinery do not, like buyers at a flea market, walk home with their purchases and take their chances. They expect installation services, application aids, parts, postpurchase repair

Exhibit I.   Purchase Cycles and Assurances

Item	Purchase cycle (in years)
Oil field installation	15 to 20
Chemical plant	10 to 15
EDP system	5 to 10
Weapons system	20 to 30
Major components of steel plant	5 to 10
Paper supply contract	5

Item	Previous assurance	Present assurance
Tankers	Spot	Charter
Apartments	Rental	Cooperative
Auto warranties	10,000 miles	100,000 miles
Technology	Buy	Lease
Labor	Hire	Contracts
Supplies	Shopping	Contracting
Equipment	Repair	Maintenance

and maintenance, retrofitted enhancements, and vendor R&D to keep the products effective and up to date for as long as possible and to help the company stay competitive.

The buyer of a continuous stream of transactions, like a frozen-food manufacturer that buys its cartons from a packaging company and its cash-management services from a bank, is concerned not only with completing transactions but also with maintaining the process. Due to the growing complexity of military equipment, even the Department of Defense makes most of its purchases in units of less than a hundred and therefore has to repeat transactions often.

Because the purchase cycles of products and major components are increasingly stretched, the needs that must be tended to have changed. Consider the purchase cycles and the changing assurances backing purchases (see Exhibit I). Under these conditions, a purchase decision is not a decision to buy an item (to have a casual affair) but a decision to enter a bonded relationship (to get married). This requires of the would-be seller a new orientation and a new strategy.

Exhibit II.   The Change from Selling to
Marketing

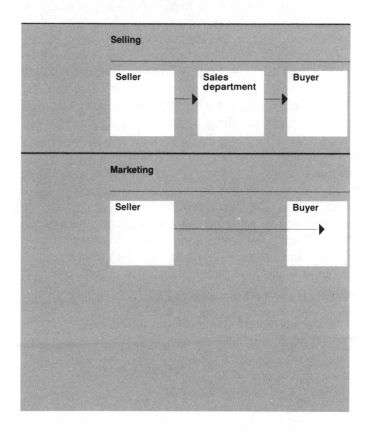

Selling by itself is no longer enough. Consider the compelling differences between the old and the new selling arrangements Exhibit II illustrates. In the selling scheme the seller is located at a distance from buyers and reaches out with a sales department to unload products on them. This is the basis for the notion that a salesperson needs charisma, because it is charisma rather than the product's qualities that makes the sale.

Consider, by contrast, marketing. Here the seller, being physically close to buyers, penetrates their domain to learn about their needs, desires, and fears and then designs and supplies the product with those considerations in mind. Instead of trying to get buyers to want what the seller has, the seller tries to have what they want. The "product" is no longer merely an item but a whole bundle of values that satisfy buyers—an "augmented" product.[1]

Thanks to increasing interdependence, more and more of the world's economic work gets done through long-term relationships between sellers and buyers. It is not a matter of just getting and then holding on to customers. It is more a matter of giving the buyers what they want. Buyers want vendors who keep promises, who'll keep supplying and standing behind what they promised. The era of the one-night stand is gone. Marriage is both necessary and more convenient. Products are too complicated, repeat negotiations too much of a hassle and too costly. Under these conditions, success in marketing is transformed into the inescapability of a relationship. Interface becomes interdependence.

Under these circumstances, being a good marketer in the conventional sense is not enough. When it takes five years of intensive work between seller and buyer to "deliver" an operating chemical plant or a telecommunications system, much more is required than the kind of marketing that simply lands the contract. The buyer needs assurance at the outset that the two parties can work well together during the long period in which the purchase gets transformed into delivery.

The seller and the buyer have different capital structures, competitive conditions, costs, and incentives driving the commitments they make to each other. The seller has made a sale that is expected to yield a profit. The buyer has bought a tool with which to produce things to yield a profit. For the seller it is the end of the process; for the buyer, only the beginning. Yet their interdependence is inescapable and profound. To make these differently motivated dependencies work, the selling company must understand the relationship and plan its management in advance of the wedding. It can't get out the marriage manual only after trouble has begun.

The Product's Changing Nature

The future will be marked by intense business relationships in all areas of marketing, including frequently purchased consumer goods. Procter & Gamble, copying General Mills's Betty Crocker

Exhibit III. **Perceptions of Product Values**

Category	Past	Present	Future
Item	Product	Augmented product	System contracts
Sale	Unit	System	System over time
Value	Feature advantages	Technology advantages	System advantages
Leadtime	Short	Long	Lengthy
Service	Modest	Important	Vital
Delivery place	Local	National	Global
Delivery phase	Once	Often	Continually
Strategy	Sales	Marketing	Relationship

advisory service, has found that the installation of a consumer hot line to give advice on its products and their uses has cemented customer brand loyalty.

In the industrial setting we have only to review changing perceptions of various aspects of product characteristics to appreciate the new emphasis on relationships (see Exhibit III). The common characteristic of the terms in the "future" column of this exhibit is time. What is labeled "item" in the first column was in the past simply a product, something that was bought for its own value. More recently that simple product has not been enough. Instead, buyers have bought augmented products.

During the era we are entering the emphasis will be on systems contracts, and buyer-seller relationships will be characterized by continuous contact and evolving relationships to effect the systems. The "sale" will be not just a system but a system over time. The value at stake will be the advantages of that total system over time. As the customer gains experience, the technology will decline in importance relative to the system that enables the buyer to realize the benefits of the technology. Services, delivery, reliability, responsiveness, and the quality of the human and organizational interactions between seller and buyer will be more important than the technology itself.

The more complex the system and the more "software" (including operating procedures and protocols, management routines, service components) it requires, the greater the customer's anxieties and expectations. People buy expectations, not things. They buy the expectations of benefits promised by the vendor. When it takes a long time to fulfill the promise (to deliver a new custom-made automated work station, for example) or when fulfillment is continual over a long period (as it is in banking services, fuel deliveries, or shipments of components for assembly operations), the buyer's anxieties build up after the purchase decision is made. Will the delivery be prompt? Will it be smooth and regular? Did we select the best vendor?

DIFFERING EXPECTATIONS

When downstream realities loom larger than up-front promises, what do you do before, during, and after the sale? Who should be responsible for what?

To answer these questions it helps to understand how the promises and behavior of the vendor before the sale is made shape the customer's expectations. It is reasonable for a customer who has been promised the moon to expect it to be delivered. But if those who make the promises are paid commissions before the customer gets everything he bargained for, they're not likely to feel compelled to ensure that the customer gets fully satisfied later. After the sale, they'll rush off to pursue other prey. If marketing plans the sale, sales makes it, manufacturing fulfills it, and service services it, who's in charge and who takes responsibility for the whole process?

Problems arise not only because those who do the selling, the marketing, the manufacturing, and the servicing have varying incentives and views of the customer but also because organizations are one-dimensional. People, with the exception of those who work in sales or marketing, seldom see beyond their company's walls. For those inside those walls, inside is where the work gets done, where the penalties and incentives are doled out, where the budgets and plans get made, where engineering and manufacturing are done, where performance is measured, where one's friends and associates gather, where things are managed and manageable. Outside "has nothing to do with me" and is where "you can't change things."

Many disjunctions exist between seller and buyer at various

Exhibit IV. *Varying Reactions and Perceptions Before and During Sale Process*

When the sale is first made	
Seller	**Buyer**
Objective achieved.	Judgment postponed; applies test of time.
Selling stops.	Shopping continues.
Focus goes elsewhere.	Focus on purchase; wants affirmation that expectations have been met.
Tension released.	Tension increased.
Relationship reduced or ended.	Commitment made; relationship intensified.

Throughout the process			
Stage of sale	**Seller**		**Buyer**
1 Before	Real hope		Vague need
2 Romance	Hot & heavy		Testing & hopeful
3 Sale	Fantasy: bed		Fantasy: board
4 After	Looks elsewhere for next sale		"You don't care"
5 Long after	Indifferent		"Can't this be made better?"
6 Next sale	"How about a new one?"		"Really?"

stages of the sales process. These may be simply illustrated, as in Exhibit IV.

After the Fact

The fact of buying changes the dynamics of the relationship. The buyer expects the seller to remember the purchase as having been a favor bestowed, not as something earned by the seller. Hence it is wrong to assume that getting an account gives you an advantage because you've got a foot in the door. The opposite is more often the case. The buyer that views the sale as a favor conferred on the

Exhibit V.　Actions That Affect Relationships

Positive actions	Negative actions
Initiate positive phone calls	Make only call backs
Make recommendations	Make justifications
Use candid language	Use accommodative language
Use phone	Use correspondence
Show appreciation	Wait for misunderstandings
Make service suggestions	Wait for service requests
Use "we" problem-solving language	Use "owe us" legal language
Get to problems	Respond only to problems
Use jargon or shorthand	Use long-winded communications
Air personality problems	Hide personality problems
Talk of "our future together"	Talk about making good on the past
Routinize responses	Fire drill/emergency responsiveness
Accept responsibility	Shift blame
Plan the future	Rehash the past

seller in effect debits the seller's account. The seller owes the buyer one. He is in the position of having to rebuild the relationship from a deficit stance.

In the absence of good management, the relationship deteriorates because both organizations tend naturally to face inward rather than outward toward each other. The natural tendency of relationships, whether in marriage or in business, is toward erosion of sensitivity and attentiveness. Inward orientation by the selling organization leads to insensitivity and unresponsiveness in customer relations. At best the company substitutes bureaucratic formalities for authentic interaction.

A healthy relationship maintains, and preferably expands, the equity and the possibilities that were created during courtship. A healthy relationship requires a conscious and constant fight against the forces of decline. It becomes important for the seller regularly and seriously to consider whether the relationship is improving or deteriorating, whether the promises are being completely fulfilled, whether he is neglecting anything, and how he stands vis-à-vis his competitors. Exhibit V compares actions that affect—for better or worse—relationships with buyers.

BUILDING DEPENDENCIES

One of the surest signs of a bad or declining relationship is the absence of complaints from the customer. Nobody is ever *that* satisfied, especially not over an extended period of time. The customer is either not being candid or not being contacted. Probably both. The absence of candor reflects the decline of trust and the deterioration of the relationship. Bad things accumulate. Impaired communication is both a symptom and a cause of trouble. Things fester inside. When they finally erupt, it's usually too late or too costly to correct the situation.

We can invest in relationships and we can borrow from them. We all do both, but we seldom account for our actions and almost never manage them. Yet a company's most precious asset is its relationships with its customers. What matters is not whom you know but how you are known to them.

Not all relationships can or need be of the same duration or at the same level of intimacy. These factors depend on the extent of the actual or felt dependency between the buyer and the seller. And of course those dependencies can be extended or contracted through various direct links that can be established between the two parties. Thus, when Bergen Brunswig, the booming drug and health care products distributor, puts computer terminals in its customers' offices to enable them to order directly and get instant feedback regarding their sales and inventory, it creates a new link that helps tie the customer to the vendor.

At the same time, however, the seller can become dependent on the buyer in important ways. Most obvious is vendor reliance on the buyer for a certain percentage of its sales. More subtle is reliance on the buyer for important information, including how the buyer's business will change, how changes will affect future purchases, and what competitors are offering in the way of substitute products or materials, at what prices and including which services. The buyer can also answer questions like these for the vendor: How well is the vendor fulfilling the customer's needs? Is performance up to promises from headquarters? To what new uses is the customer putting the product? The seller's ability to forecast the buyer's intentions rests on the quality of the overall relationship. In a good relationship the buyer shares plans and expectations with the vendor, or at least makes available relevant information. With that information the vendor can better serve the buyer. Surprises and bad forecasts are symptoms of bad relationships. In such instances, everybody—even the buyer—loses.

Thus, a system of reciprocal dependencies develops. It is up to the seller to nurture the relationship beyond its simple dollar value. In a proper relationship both the buyer and the seller will benefit or the relationship will not last.

Moreover, both parties should understand that the seller's expenses rarely end with acquisition costs. This means that the vendor should work at convincing the customer of the importance of maintaining the vendor's long-term profitability at a comfortable level instead of squeezing to get rock-bottom delivered prices. Unless the costs of the expected postpurchase services are reflected in the price, the buyer will end up paying extra in money, in delays, and in aggravation. The smart relationship manager in the selling company will help the buyer do long-term life-cycle costing to assess the vendor's offering.

Bonds That Last

Professional partnerships in law, medicine, architecture, consulting, investment banking, and advertising rate and reward associates by their client relationships. Like any other assets, these relationships can appreciate or depreciate. Their maintenance and enhancement depend not so much on good manners, public relations, tact, charm, window dressing, or manipulation as they do on management. Relationship management requires companywide maintenance, investment, improvement, and even replacement programs. The results can be spectacular.

Examine the case of the North Sea oil and gas fields. Norway and Britain urged and facilitated exploration and development of those resources. They were eager and even generous hosts to the oil companies. The companies, though they spent hundreds of millions of dollars to do the work, didn't fully nurture their relationships. When oil and gas suddenly started to flow, the host countries levied taxes exceeding 90% of the market prices. No one was more surprised than the companies. Why should they have

Exhibit VI. **Cumulative Cash Flow History of an Account**

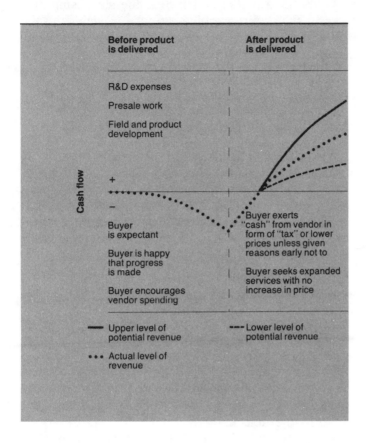

been surprised? Had they built sound relationships with the governments, the politicians, and the voters—by whatever means—so as to have created a sense of mutuality and partnership, they might have moderated the size of the taxes. What would it have been worth?

This is not an isolated occurrence. The same problem crops up in similar circumstances where vendors are required to make heavy expenditures to get accounts and develop products. Exhibit VI depicts cash flows to a vendor of this type during the life of the account. During the customer-getting and development period, cash flows are negative and the customer eagerly encourages the expenditures. When the product is delivered or the joint venture becomes operative, cumulative cash flows turn up and finally become positive. In the case of the North Sea, the surprising new high taxes represent the difference between what revenues to the oil companies might have been (the upper level of potential revenue) and what they actually became. With worse relationships they might, of course, have fallen to an even lower level of potential revenue.

Consider also the case of Gillette North America. It has four separate sales forces and special programs for major accounts to ensure Gillette's rapid and smooth response to customers' requirements. Gillette also has a vice president of business relations who has among his major duties cultivation of relationships with major retailers and distributors. He carries out that responsibility via a vast array of ceremonial activities ranging from entertainment at trade association conventions to organization of special events for major accounts in connection with the annual All-Star baseball game, the World Series, the Superbowl, and the NCAA playoffs. These activities establish bonds and affirm reciprocal obligations and benefits.

Some companies now require engineering and manufacturing people to spend time with customers and users in the field—not just to get product and design ideas or feedback regarding present products but also to get to know and to respond to customers in deep and abiding ways so as to build relationships and bonds that last. The Sperry Corporation's much-advertised "listening" campaign has included training employees to listen and communicate effectively with each other and with customers.

All too often company officials take action instead of spending time. It is all too easy to act first and later try to fix the relationship, instead of the other way around. It is all too simple to say, "We'll look into it and call you back" or "Let's get together for lunch sometime." These are tactics of diversion and delay, not of relationship building.

When a purchase cycle is long—as when a beer-making plant contracts with a can-making vendor to build a factory next door or when the U.S. Air Force commits itself to buying a jet engine with a life of 20 to 30 years—the people in the vendor organization who did the selling and those in the customer organization who did the buying will be replaced over the course of those relationships. So, in all likelihood, will the entire upper levels of management on both sides. What must the seller do to ensure continuity of good relations? What is expected of the customer when people who did the buying are changed and gone? Clearly the idea is to build bonds that last no matter who comes and goes.

MAKING IT HAPPEN

To effectively manage relationships, managers must meet four requirements.

1. *Awareness.* Understand both the problem and the opportunity areas.
2. *Assessment.* Determine where the company now stands, especially in terms of what's necessary to get the desired results.
3. *Accountability.* Establish regular reporting on individual relationships, and then on group relationships, so that these can be weighed against other measures of performance.
4. *Actions.* Make decisions and allocations and establish routines and communications on the basis of their impact on the targeted relationships. Constantly reinforce awareness and actions.

Relationship management can be institutionalized, but in the process it must also be humanized. One company has regular sensitivity sessions and role-playing seminars in which sales officials assume the buyer role. It also conducts debriefings on meetings with customers. And it requires its customer-contact people (including those who make deliveries and handle receivables) to regularly ask of various accounts the seminal questions: How are we doing in the relationship? Is it going up or down? Are we talking with the right people about the right issues? What have we not done lately?

The emphasis on "lately" is not incidental. It reflects the recognition that relationships naturally degrade and have to be reinvigorated. If I owe you a favor, I forget—but you don't. And when I've done you a favor, you feel obligated—but not for long. You ask, "What have you done for me lately?" A relationship credit must be cashed in or it expires, and it must be used soon or it depreciates.

Another way companies can institutionalize relationship management is by establishing routines that ensure the right kinds of customer contacts. A well-known Wall Street investment firm requires its security analysts and salespeople to make regular "constructive" contacts with their institutional customers. *Constructive* is defined as conveying useful information to them. The firm has set up a regular Monday-morning investment strategy "commentary" that analysts and salespeople can convey by telephone to their customers. In addition, each analyst must develop periodic industry commentaries and updates, to be mailed or telephoned to customers. Analysts and salespeople are required to keep logs of these contacts, which are compiled, counted, and communicated to all in a weekly companywide report. Those salespeople and analysts making the fewest contacts have to explain their inaction to supervisors.

The firm allocates end-of-year bonuses on the basis of not only commissions earned from the various institutions but also the number and types of contacts initiated and maintained. Meanwhile, the firm conducts regular sensitivity-training sessions to enhance the contacts and the quality of the relationships. The results, which show that the efforts have been highly successful, are analyzed and made known to all, thus reinforcing the importance of the process.

Relationship management is a special field all its own and is as important to preserving and enhancing the intangible asset commonly known as "goodwill" as is the management of hard assets. The fact that it is probably more difficult makes hard work at it that much more important.

Note

1. See my article "Marketing Success Through Differentiation—Of Anything," *Harvard Business Review*, January–February 1980, p. 83.

PART

II

Manage the Business from the Customer's Point of View

Introduction

In today's fast-paced, competitive environment, many researchers and management consultants talk about the need to redesign business processes, but few offer implementable advice on how to do it. The articles in this section provide concrete frameworks, examples, and suggestions for turning a customer-driven philosophy into profitable actions. In particular, these articles recommend rational, measurable programs for improving customer service. At the core of customer service is the ability to recognize and overcome the differences between how you and your customers perceive the value of service provision. While customer service has frequently been reduced to physical distribution or dismissed as intangible or unquantifiable, the authors of these three articles argue that service is comprised of identifiable elements, which can be analyzed and managed through programs that balance the costs of investment with the benefits of greater customer satisfaction.

"Staple Yourself to an Order," by Benson Shapiro, V. Kasturi Rangan, and John Sviokla addresses these issues by taking the *order*, not the customer or the product, as the fundamental unit of analysis. Realistically, the order management cycle (OMC) determines the customer's experience with a vendor. Every time an order is serviced, lost, or mishandled the customer receives the same treatment. Since fulfilling the OMC involves participation of many departments and functions (which often overlap, compete, or conflict), analyzing the order management process provides fertile opportunities for improvement, including better pricing, superior coordination across functions, careful prioritization, and improved communication up, down, and across the management chain.

The authors point out that while many companies have cut out layers of bureaucracy, undertaken quality drives, and concentrated on direct interaction with customers, orders are falling between the cracks and service is not necessarily being improved. "Customers want their orders handled quickly, accurately, and cost-effectively, not more people to talk to." When customers complain, organizational tensions rise. In many OMC programs, senior managers are disconnected from operational details, while those with knowledge of the real process do not have the organizationwide perspective or the political clout to effect change. Without viewing the OMC as a system, many companies perpetuate duplication and inefficiency, which eat away at potential profits.

In "Staple Yourself" the authors argue that executives should understand the OMC so thoroughly that they can anticipate problems before they occur and make investments in the system that will increase returns. The basic framework for management action consists of: (1) analysis, (2) system focus, and (3) political strategy. Analysis of the entire OMC system indicates where improvements can be made. System focus draws on the organizational structure, formal management processes, and information technology to develop an integrative design for action. Political strategy addresses the informal social network through which decisions are made and conflicts are managed. This article suggests that the rewards from evaluating your OMC will be substantial and self-reinforcing. "Staple Yourself" provides a roadmap for simultaneously increasing customer satisfaction, decreasing organizational tension, and improving financial performance.

The articles in this section illustrate how the customer's experience of a sale and the internal efforts marshalled to deliver the product or service are worlds apart. For example, the customer rarely associates filling up the gas tank with the difficulties of drilling for the oil, refining the crude, and shipping the stock to the retail outlet.

Managing from the customer's point of view allows suppliers to improve the efficiency of internal processes to meet or even exceed customer expectations. "Designing Services That Deliver," by G. Lynn Shostack, shows how to perform a detailed process analysis (a "service blueprint") that charts the sequence of internal activities required to perform and deliver a service, and maps these activities against both consumer and provider expectations of acceptable execution. Shostack's flowchart analysis provides a powerful platform for reviewing and improving a business process design, helping service providers make informed decisions that increase productivity, profits, and customer satisfaction. The blueprint is an objective measurable framework for testing new ideas and codifying successful processes. This approach to service management supports W. Edwards Deming's dictum that "workers are never to blame for flaws in a process. Process design is management's responsibility."

The link between internal business processes and external customer needs is often coordinated through the customer-service function, since service is generally the most frequent and visible contact point between the company and the client. The final article in this section, "How to Manage Customer Service," by William Hutchison and John Stolle, spotlights this critical function, offering six steps to help companies achieve cost reductions and profit gains through more efficient customer service.

Although this piece was originally published in 1968, its practical recommendations are no less applicable for today's managers. "The trend is for customers to expect service to be as much a part of what they buy as are the product's design, quality, and price. And, like these other characteristics, service consists of several elements that need to be precisely defined, specified, and *sold* to the customer." Since this article's publication, competition has increased, cycle times have shortened, and customer demands have grown. Yet, the article's fundamental message—that customer service can be designed and managed to improve profits—is still highly relevant. In fact, with the new technological capabilities to communicate more rapidly, track business processes more accurately, and codify expertise in software the potential to deliver value through customer service continues to expand. For instance, companies are increasingly empowering their customer-service personnel with data and authority to act as problem solvers on the customers' behalf (see "The Profitable Art of Sales Recovery," in Part V).

The articles in this section demonstrate that by analyzing the business from the customer's point of view, managers can drive short-term practical improvements and long-term strategic vision. Embracing the complex task of articulating and valuing customer expectations helps selling companies overcome their internal biases about "the way things work" or "what the customer really wants." Overall, these articles establish the vital link between understanding the customer and taking action to improve customer relations.

1
Staple Yourself to an Order

**Benson P. Shapiro, V. Kasturi Rangan, and
John J. Sviokla**

It's fashionable today to talk of becoming "customer oriented."
Or to focus on that moment of truth when customers experience
the actual transaction that determines whether or not they are
completely satisfied. Or to empower frontline workers so they can
delight the customer with their initiative and spunk.

None of this advice, however, focuses on the real way to harness
the customer's interests in the operation of a company. The simple
truth is that every customer's experience is determined by a company's *order management cycle* (OMC): the ten steps, from planning to postsales service, that define a company's business system.
The order management cycle offers managers the opportunity to
look at their company through a customer's eyes, to see and experience transactions the way customers do. Managers who track
each step of the OMC work their way through the company from
the customer's angle rather than their own.

In the course of the order management cycle, every time the
order is handled, the customer is handled. Every time the order
sits unattended, the customer sits unattended. Paradoxically, the
best way to be customer oriented is to go beyond customers and
products to the order; the moment of truth occurs at every step of
the OMC, and every employee in the company who affects the
OMC is the equivalent of a frontline worker. Ultimately, it is the
order that connects the customer to the company in a systematic
and companywide fashion.

Moreover, focusing on the OMC offers managers the greatest
opportunity to improve overall operations and create new competitive advantages. Managers can establish and achieve aggressive

goals—such as "improve customer fill rate from 80% to 98%," "reach 99% billing accuracy," or "cut order cycle time by 25%"—and force otherwise parochial teams to look at the entire order management cycle to discover how various changes affect customers. When the OMC substitutes for narrow functional interests, customer responsiveness becomes the overriding goal of the entire organization, and conflicts give way to systemic solutions. The best way for managers to learn this lesson and pass it on to their whole work force is, in effect, to staple themselves to an order. They can then track an order as it moves through the OMC, always aware that the order is simply a surrogate for the customer.

A Realistic Walk through the OMC

The typical OMC includes ten activities that sometimes overlap or interact (see Exhibit I). While OMCs vary from industry to industry and are different for products and services, almost every business, from the corner ice cream stand to the global computer company, has these same steps. In the following discussion, a number of important lessons will emerge that explain both the customer's experience with a company and that company's ability to achieve ambitious cost and quality goals. For example, as we "walk" an order through the OMC, note the number of times that the order or information about it physically moves horizontally from one functional department to another. Since most companies are organized along vertical functional lines, every time an order moves horizontally from one department to another it runs the risk of falling between the cracks.

In addition to these horizontal gaps, a second lesson to be learned from tracking the OMC is the likelihood of vertical gaps in knowledge. In field visits to 18 different companies in vastly different industries, we invariably found a top marketing or administrative executive who would offer a simple, truncated—and inaccurate—description of the order flow. The people at the top couldn't see the details of their OMC; the people deep within the organization saw only their own individual details. And when an order moved across departmental boundaries, from one function to another, it faded from sight; no one was responsible for it or the customer.

A third lesson concerns the importance of order selection and prioritization. In fact, not all orders are created equal; some are

Exhibit I.

simply better for the business than others. The best orders come from customers who are long-term, fit the company's capabilities, and offer healthy profits. These customers fall into the company's "sweet spot," a convergence of great customer need, high customer value, and good fit with what the company can offer. But in most companies, no one does order selection or prioritization. The sales force chooses the customers, and customer service representatives or production schedulers establish the priorities. In these cases, the OMC effectively goes unmanaged.

Finally, the fourth lesson we offer involves cost estimation and pricing. Pricing is the mediator between customer needs and company capabilities and a critical part of the OMC. But most companies don't understand the opportunity for or impact of order-based pricing. Pricing at the individual order level depends on: understanding the customer value generated by each order; evaluating the cost of filling each order; and instituting a system that enables the company to price each order based on its value and cost. While order-based pricing is difficult work that requires meticulous thinking and deliberate execution, the potential for greater profits is worth the effort. And by gaining control of their OMCs, managers can practice order-based pricing.

When we started our investigation of the order management cycle, we recognized first that the OMC, in fact, begins long before there is an order or a customer. What happens in the first step, *order planning*, already shows how and why bad customer service and fragmented operations can cripple a company: the people farthest from the customer make crucial decisions and open up deep disagreements between interdependent functions right from the start. The contention and internal gaming that we saw in order planning is an effective early warning sign of the systemwide disagreements that plague most order management cycles.

For example, people close to the customer, either in the sales force or a marketing group at company headquarters, develop a sales forecast. At the same time, a group in the operations or manufacturing function drafts a capacity plan that specifies how much money will be spent, how many people hired, and how much inventory created. And already these functional departments are at war. Lamented one production planner, "The salespeople and their forecasting 'experts' are so optimistic and so worried about late deliveries that they pad their forecasts. We have to recalculate their plans so we don't get sucked into their euphoria." From their side, marketing people counter distrust with equal distrust: "Production won't change anything, anyhow, anywhere." Ultimately, the people deepest in the organization and farthest from the customer—production planners—often develop the final forecast used to hire workers and build inventory.

The next step in the OMC is *order generation*, a stage that usually produces a gap between order generation, order planning, and later steps in the cycle. In our research, we saw orders generated in a number of ways. The sales force knocks on doors or makes cold calls. The company places advertisements that draw customers into distribution centers or retailers where they actually place an order. Or, increasingly, companies turn to direct marketing. But regardless of the specific marketing approach, the result is almost always the same: the sales and marketing functions worry about order generation, and the other functions get out of the way. Little coordination takes place across functional boundaries.

At the third step, *cost estimation and pricing*, battles erupt between engineers who do the estimating, accountants who calculate costs, a headquarters group that oversees pricing, and the field sales force that actually develops a price. Each group questions the judgment, competence, and goals of the others. Working through the organizational barriers takes time. Meanwhile, of course, the customer waits for the bid or quote, unattended.

Order receipt and entry comes next. It typically takes place in a neglected department called "customer service," "order entry," "the inside sales desk," or "customer liaison." Customer service representatives are usually either very experienced, long-term employees or totally inexperienced trainees. But regardless of their experience, customer service reps are, in fact, in daily contact with customers. At the same time, these employees have little clout in the organization and no executive-level visibility in either direction. That means customer service representatives don't know what is going on at the top of the company, including its basic strategy. And top management doesn't know much about what its customer service department—the function closest to customers—is doing.

This unlinked group of customer service reps is also often responsible for the fifth step in the OMC: *order selection and prioritization*, the process of choosing which orders to accept and which to decline. Of course, the more carefully companies think through order selection and link it to their general business strategy, the more money they stand to make, regardless of physical production capacity. In addition, companies can make important gains by the way they handle order prioritization—that is, how they decide which orders receive faster, more complete attention. However, these decisions are usually made not by top executives who articulate corporate strategy but by customer service representatives who have no idea what the strategy is. While customer service reps decide which order gets filled when, they often determine which order gets lost in limbo.

At the sixth step, *scheduling,* when the order gets slotted into an actual production or operational sequence, some of the fiercest fights erupt. Here sales, marketing, or customer service usually face off with operations or production staff. The different functional departments have conflicting goals, compensation systems, and organizational imperatives: production people seek to minimize equipment changeovers, while marketing and customer service reps argue for special service for special customers. And if the operations staff schedule orders unilaterally, both customers and their reps are completely excluded from the process. Communication between the functions is often strained at best, with customer service reporting to sales and physically separated from production scheduling, which reports to manufacturing or operations. Once again, the result is interdepartmental warfare.

Next comes *fulfillment*—the actual provision of the product or service. While the details vary from industry to industry, in almost every company this step has become increasingly complex. Sometimes, for example, order fulfillment involves multiple functions and locations: different parts of an order may be created in different manufacturing facilities and merged at yet another site, or orders may be manufactured in one location, inventoried in a second, and installed in a third. In some businesses, fulfillment includes third-party vendors. In service operations, it can mean sending individuals with different talents to the customer's site. The more complicated the assembly activity, the more coordination must take place across the organization. And the more coordination required across the organization, the greater the chance for a physical gap. The order is dropped and so is the customer. The order ends up on the floor, while different departments argue over whose fault it is and whose job it is to pick it up.

After the order has been delivered, *billing* is typically handled by people from finance who view their job as getting the bill out efficiently and making the collection quickly. In other words, the billing function is designed to serve the needs and interests of the company, not the customer. In our research, we often saw customers who could not understand a bill they had received or thought it was inaccurate. Usually the bill wasn't inaccurate, but it had been put together in a way more convenient for the billing department than for the customer. In one case, a customer acknowledged that the company provided superior service but found the billing operation a source of constant aggravation. The problem: billing insisted on sending an invoice with prices on it. But because these shipments went to subcontractors, the customer didn't want the actual prices to show. The finance function's response: how we do our invoices is none of the customer's business. Yet such a response is clearly self-serving and creates one more gap—and possibly a loss to the company—in the cycle.

In some businesses, *returns and claims* are an important part of the OMC because of their impact on administrative costs, scrap and transportation expenses, and customer relations. In the ongoing relationship with the customer, this ninth step can produce some of the most heated disagreements; every interaction becomes a zero-sum game that either the company or the customer wins. To compound the problem, most companies design their OMCs for one-way merchandise flow: outbound to the customer. That means returns and claims must flow upstream, against the current, creating logistical messes and transactional snarls—and extremely dissatisfied customers.

The last step, *postsales service*, now plays an increasingly important role in all elements of a company's profit equation: customer value, price, and cost. Depending on the specifics of the business, it can include such elements as physical installation of a product, repair and maintenance, customer training, equipment upgrading, and disposal. At this final step in the OMC, service representatives can truly get inside the customer's organization; because of the information conveyed and intimacy involved, postsales service can affect customer satisfaction and company profitability for years. But in most companies, the postsales service people are not linked to any marketing operation, internal product-development effort, or quality assurance team.

At company after company, we traced the progress of individual orders as they traveled the OMC, beginning at one end of the process where orders entered, concluding at the other end where postsales service followed up. What we witnessed was frustration, missed opportunities, dissatisfied customers, and underperforming companies. Ultimately, four problems emerged, which are tied to the four lessons discussed earlier.

> Most companies never view the OMC as a whole system. People in sales think that someone in production scheduling understands the entire system; people in production scheduling think customer service reps do. No one really does, and everyone can only give a partial description.

> Each step in the OMC requires a bewildering mix of overlapping functional responsibilities. As Exhibit II illustrates, each step is considered the primary responsibility of a specific department, and no step is the sole responsibility of any department. But given the fact that responsibilities do overlap, many disasters occur.

> To top management, the details of the OMC are invisible. Senior executives at all but the smallest operating units simply don't understand the intricacy of the OMC. And people with the most crucial information, such as customer service reps, are at the bottom of the organization and can't communicate with the top.

> The customer remains as remote from the OMC as top management. During the process, the customer's primary activities are to negotiate price, place the order, wait, accept delivery, complain, and pay. In the middle of the OMC, they are out of the picture completely.

Of course, today top managers know that customer service and customer satisfaction are critical to a company's success. In one company after another, managers pursue the same solutions to problems that crop up with customers. They try to flatten the organization to bring themselves and nonmarketing people into direct contact with customers. But while flattening the organization is a fine idea, it's not going to solve the real problem. No matter how flat an organization gets, no matter how many different functions interact with customers face to face—or phone to phone— what the customer wants is something else. Customers want their orders handled quickly, accurately, and cost-effectively, not more people to talk to.

Here's what top managers *don't* do: they don't travel horizontally through their own vertical organization. They don't consider the order management cycle as the system that ties together the entire customer experience and that can provide true customer perspec-

Exhibit II.

Why Orders Fall Through the Cracks

Customer	Steps in the OMC	Sales	Marketing	Customer Service	Engineering	Purchasing	Finance	Operations	Logistics	Top Management
plans to buy	1. Order planning	○	●	○	○	○	○	●	○	coordinates
gets sales pitch	2. Order generation	●	○	○						sometimes participates
negotiates	3. Cost estimation and pricing	○	●	○	○	○	○	○	○	sometimes participates
orders	4. Order receipt and entry	○	○	●	○			○	○	ignores this step
waits	5. Order selection and prioritization	○	○	○	○			○	○	sometimes participates
waits	6. Scheduling			○	○	○	○	●	○	ignores this step
waits	7. Fulfillment			○	○	○		●	○	ignores this step
pays	8. Billing	○		○			●		○	ignores this step
negotiates	9. Returns and claims	●	○	○			○	○	○	sometimes participates
complains	10. Postsales service	○		●				○	○	ignores this step

■ leading role ▢ supporting role

The OMC is everybody's job, but overlapping responsibilities — and lack of management involvement — often lead to confusion, delays, and customer complaints.

tive. Yet all ten steps are closely tied to customer satisfaction. Because the OMC is an intricate network that almost guarantees problems, top management's job is to understand the system so thoroughly it can anticipate those problems before they occur. That means managers must walk up and down and from side to side, every step of the way.

What's Wrong with Their OMCs?

Consider two brief case studies. One is taken from a specialty materials producer, the other from a custom capital equipment company, but both exemplify the three most common and debilitating problems that plague OMCs.

At the specialty materials company, when customers complained about order cycle time, top managers responded by increasing the work-in-process inventory. As a result, the company could meet customer specifications from semifinished goods rather than starting from scratch. At the custom capital equipment company, when customers complained about slow deliveries, this company increased its manufacturing capacity. As a result, the company always had enough capacity to expedite any order.

Both solutions pleased customers. In addition, the first solution pleased that company's marketers and the second solution pleased that company's operations department. But neither solution pleased top management because, even after several quarters, neither produced economic returns to justify the investments. In fact, both solutions only made matters worse. At the specialty materials company, marketing staff took advantage of the increased work-in-process inventory to take orders and make sales that used up that inventory but didn't generate profits. And at the capital equipment company, manufacturing staff relied on the increased capacity to meet marketing demands but allowed productivity to slide.

The next step both companies took was predictable. Top management, frustrated by the failure of its solution and concerned over continuing squabbles between departments, called on managers across the organization to rally around "making superior profits by providing top quality products and excellent service." Top management translated "top quality" and "excellent service" into catchy slogans and posters that decorated office cubicles and factory walls. It etched the "superior profit" objective into the operating budgets of higher level managers. And it formed interfunctional teams so managers could practice participative decision making in pursuit of the new, companywide goal.

At the specialty materials company, a star sales manager who had been promoted to general manager set up an interfunctional executive committee to assess quarterly revenue and profit goals. We attended one meeting of this new committee. As the general manager sat down at the head of the table to begin the meeting, he expressed concern that the division was about to miss its revenue and profit goals for the second consecutive quarter. Committee members responded by pointing at other departments or making excuses. The vice president of sales produced elaborate graphs to demonstrate that the problem was not caused by insufficient order generation. The vice president of operations produced detailed worksheets showing that many orders had come in too late in the quarter to be completed on time.

However, given their new joint responsibility for profits, both sides agreed to put aside such arguments and focus on "how to make the quarter." All agreed to ship some customer orders in advance of their due dates because those items could readily be finished from available work-in-process inventory. While this solution would delay some long cycle-time orders, the committee decided to sacrifice these orders for the moment and take them up early in the next quarter. And immediately after the meeting, committee members started executing the plan: salespeople called their customers and cajoled them to accept early delivery; manufacturing staff rescheduled the shop floor.

Because of its small size, the custom capital equipment producer didn't need such a formal mechanism for coordinating activities. The CEO simply inserted himself into the daily workings of all functional areas and insisted on hearing all customer complaints immediately. While visiting this company, we heard a customer service representative talking on the telephone to a customer who had just been told her order would be late. The customer objected and asked for an explanation. After much hemming and hawing, the rep explained that her order had been "reallocated" to another customer who needed the product more. The customer on the phone, who purchased products from the company in a relatively large volume, demanded to speak to the CEO and, under the new policy, was connected right away. When the CEO heard this important customer's complaint, he instantly plugged the order back in at the top of the priority list.

But, in spite of such heroic efforts at both companies, customer service continued to slump, and financial results did not improve. At the materials company, customers who expected later delivery of their orders received them unexpectedly early, while those who needed them early got them late. At the capital equipment company, small customers who didn't know the CEO personally or didn't understand the route to him found their orders continuously bumped. At both companies, there was no real progress toward genuine customer satisfaction, improved service, or enhanced profits. Neither company had come to terms with the three critical problems embedded in their order management cycles: horizontal and vertical gaps, poor prioritization of orders, and inaccurate cost estimation and pricing.

The specialty materials company suffered from a fundamental horizontal gap: the marketing and manufacturing departments didn't share the same priorities for customer value, order selection, and order urgency. The real solution to this problem was to encourage and reinforce an understanding between these two critical OMC elements; both the marketing and manufacturing departments needed to address how their order management cycle generated customer value and where they were dropping customer orders in the horizontal handoff. Instead the company introduced an expensive buffer to cover over the gap between the functions— a semifinished inventory—and, when that failed, it decided to sacrifice real customer service to serve its own short-term financial needs. The immediate solution, simply shipping orders based on the amount of time it would take to complete them, merely pushed the problem from one quarter to the next without addressing the system failure. When the next quarter rolls around, top management will still have to contend with horizontal gaps, a lack of order selection and prioritization, and the inability of their order flow to generate value for the customer.

The same underlying systemic problems existed at the custom capital equipment producer. However, because of the small size of the organization, this company took a simple, politically expedient solution—let the CEO decide—and superimposed it on an expensive financial solution—add manufacturing capacity. If the company suffered from vertical gaps before, where people down in the trenches failed to understand the strategy developed up in the executive suite, the CEO's intervention in customer orders only made the gaps worse. The CEO's involvement didn't address the systemic problems; he merely substituted his judgment and knowledge for that of lower level employees. The detrimental effects on employee morale more than offset any immediate gains in customer appreciation. Had the CEO invested his energy in helping employees understand how each order creates customer value, has specific costs attached, and involves a certain amount of processing time—and communicated the importance of the whole OMC—he would have generated more customer satisfaction, greater employee morale, and higher profitability without adding expensive manufacturing capacity.

How Can I Fix My OMC?

It takes hard work to improve a company's order management cycle. Most successful efforts involve three basic elements: analysis, system focus, and political strategy. Each plays a different role in overall upgrading of the OMC and requires different implementation techniques, so let's look at each in turn.

1. *Analysis: Draw your OMC—and chart the gaps.*

In the course of our research, we visited a number of companies that were actively engaged in reviewing their OMCs with an eye to improvement. But only two companies had made progress; significantly, both had begun by trying to understand the whole OMC from start to finish. And they hadn't created a diagram on a single sheet of paper or a standard report format. Rather, one of these companies had built "war rooms": two adjacent, bunker-like offices. The walls of both rooms were made of poster board coated with color-coded sheets of paper and knitting yarn that graphically charted the order flow from the first step to the last, highlighting problems, opportunities, and potential action steps. With its multiple and overlapping sheets of paper, the entire chart easily exceeded 200 feet in length.

This visual tool made it possible for different people from different functions and levels in the organization to accept the OMC as a tangible entity. Everyone could discuss the order flow with a clear and shared picture in front of them. And by representing the OMC as a visible, tangible system, the chart guaranteed that disagreements over problems would focus on facts rather than on opinions about how the OMC worked.

A second type of successful analysis requires companies to look at the OMC from the customer's point of view. For example, at one company, the in-house measurement system found that 98% of all orders went out on time. But another detailed survey noted that only 50% of customers said they were satisfied with deliveries. The company was unable to reconcile the two reports until managers looked at the issue from the customer's angle and compared it with their own point of view. For instance, the customer survey measured the date when the customer actually received the order; but the company's internal system was based on the date when it shipped the order. If an order consisted of 100 items, and the company correctly shipped 99 of the items, the internal report recorded a 99% perfect shipment. But the customer, who needed all 100 items before work could begin, recorded the order as a complete failure. And if the order contained an incorrectly shipped item, the company did not register the mistake at all. Of course, the customer did because an incorrect item could easily interfere with his or her ability to get on with the job. Once this company recognized the difference between its perspective and the customer's, it switched to the customer's view as the basis for its tracking system.

Finally, successful companies have explicitly stated that their goals are satisfied customers, higher profits, and sustainable competitive advantage without compromising any of them. One company realized that, while it currently relied on extensive competitive bidding, it would have to start tracking its own win-loss percentages by type of customer, geography, type of order, and other relevant data to meet its larger goals. Managers could then use such data to analyze the relationship between the company's prices and its competitors as well as between volume and price. That, in turn, could translate into better price and market share and less effort wasted on unattractive or unattainable business.

2. System Focus: Put the pieces together, move across boundaries.

Analyzing the order management cycle should underline this fundamental point: the OMC is a system, and executives must manage it as a system. The goal, of course, is to fit together the horizontal pieces into a unified, harmonious whole. To encourage such alignment, managers have a number of tools at their disposal. For example, through the company compensation system, managers can introduce joint reward plans that encourage employees to take a systemwide view of company performance. Or in designing performance measurements, managers can include numbers that reflect performance across boundaries or throughout the system.

Perhaps the most powerful tool managers can use is interfunctional or interdepartmental investments in projects. These expenditures not only bring different units closer together but can also result in substantial financial returns to the company. Of course, in most companies, project champions drive the decisions in the capital budgeting process. Most project champions embrace projects in their own departments or functions. Projects that cross boundaries tend to be orphans because they lack champions; even with champions, such projects require difficult, time-consuming negotiations and are often deferred or fail outright. But precisely for this reason, projects that cross department boundaries can create an integrated atmosphere. When the CEO or chief operating officer personally back investments, the whole organization gets the message that these investments reflect a new perspective. Significantly, interdepartmental projects, usually underfunded for years, often deliver the greatest returns to the company in terms of real improvements and financial results.

A company's information technology system can also play an important role. Computer technology is a crucial tool for integrating many steps of the order management cycle. Direct computer links with customers and integrated internal computer systems, for example, typically result in lower costs and better analysis. And while order processing was one of the earliest activities to be computerized in many companies, it's now time to update and reengineer such systems. When managers walk through the entire OMC, they have the opportunity to ask whether each step can be improved with a computer or, perhaps, eliminated altogether given new technology and processes. With more reliable computer systems, for instance, is manual backup still required? Or can data be captured at the source to avoid repeat entry and inevitable clerical errors?

All of these human resource, management, and information technology tools reinforce the idea, represented by the OMC, that the basic work of the company takes place across boundaries. And because obsolete or unnecessary tasks hinder coordination, all pieces of the system must fit together to meet customer needs in a seamless fashion.

3. Political Strategy: Staple yourself to an order.

Given that the order management cycle is critical to so many daily operating decisions, it is often at the center of all political maneuverings in a company. Realistically, OMC politics will never go away; working horizontally in a vertical organization is always difficult at best. In our research, we saw hard-nosed CEOs and high-ranking divisional general managers forced to admit defeat when confronted with stonewalling functional staffs. We watched young, analytically focused managers with innovative ideas face disinterest, distrust, and selfishness—and fail miserably. The only people who can succeed at interdepartmental management are usually hardened veterans who understand company politics and can cash in favors. But even they won't succeed without visible support from the top.

One way to improve the situation in any company is to "close the loop" between the service providers and the strategy setters or, in other words, to tie the company closer together through the order management cycle. Managers should try what we did in our research: we "stapled" ourselves to an order and literally followed it through each step of the OMC. When managers do this, descending from the executive heights into the organization's lower depths, they come into contact with critical people like customer service reps and production schedulers. Reps, schedulers, order processors, shipping clerks, and many others are the ones who know fine-grained information about customer needs. For example, customers might want the product delivered in a drum rather than a bag or prefer plastic wrapping to styrofoam.

For most executives in most companies, there is simply no organizational setup for listening and responding to people at all levels. The McDonald's policy of having executives regularly work behind the counter is a worthwhile example of creating such an opportunity. Requiring top managers to work as cashiers and cooks sends a message about the company's values to all staff and enables executives to experience the OMC firsthand.

However, this idea can degenerate into an empty gesture or just another management fad. Take, for example, CEO visits to customers that become official state visits in which corporate heads discuss company relationships at a level of abstraction that has little to do with reality. In most businesses, managers can learn more from salespeople, customer service representatives, production schedulers, and shippers than from a customer's CEO.

All too often, managers who try to focus on internal conflicts directly without charting the OMC find themselves thwarted by politics and recalcitrant employees. But the wall charts and interdepartmental measurements engendered by focusing on the OMC can create an overall vision that transcends vertical politics. The customer is not involved in organizational infighting, and when a company takes on the customer's perspective, politics must take a different and more productive turn.

What Happens After I Fix My OMC?

When companies improve their order management cycles, there are three important benefits. First and foremost, they will experience improved customer satisfaction. Companies will fill orders faster, become more accurate, and generally keep their promises to customers. A well-run OMC has a huge impact on customers: most OMCs perform worst when demand is greatest, which means that the largest number of customers experience service at its poorest quality. Fixing the OMC reverses that downward trend.

Second, interdepartmental problems will recede. When the OMC is not working well, it both reflects and causes monumental internal strife in a company. People in each department feel they are working hard to achieve their goals; they feel let down by other functions when customer service or financial performance fails to measure up. In the absence of unifying efforts and signs of improvement, the infighting can take on a life of its own and become even more divisive than the operating problems that started the battle. A systemic view helps everyone understand that all departments are interdependent.

Finally, companies will improve their financial performance. We saw companies lose sales, waste labor, and fumble investments because of poor order management cycles. Typically, companies throw money at their problems, building excess capacity, adding inventory, or increasing the body count, all of which are expensive and none of which solve the real problem. The simple fact is that when an OMC is poorly managed, greater sales, lower costs, higher prices, and smaller investments all seem impossible. But when the order management cycle works efficiently, a company can achieve these goals—and more.

2
Designing Services That Deliver

G. Lynn Shostack

We're all familiar with the symptoms of service failure. Your shirt comes back from the laundry with a broken button. Within a week of paying an outrageous repair bill, that ominous rattle reappears in your car's engine. A customer service representative says he'll get back to you and doesn't. An automatic teller swallows your card.

Examples of poor service are widespread; in survey after survey, services top the list in terms of consumer dissatisfaction. Ideas like H&R Block's approach to tax preparation, the McDonald's formula for fast-food service, and Walt Disney's concept of entertainment are so few and far between that they seem to be the product of genius—a brilliant flash that can never be duplicated.

Faced with service problems, we tend to become somewhat paranoid. Customers are convinced that someone is treating them badly; managers think that recalcitrant individual employees are the source of the malfunction. Thinly veiled threats by customers and managers are often first attempts to remedy the problem; if they fail, confrontation may result.

But these remedies obscure the basis for a lasting "cure." Even though services fail because of human incompetence, drawing a bead on this target obscures the underlying cause: the lack of systematic method for design and control.

The development of a new service is usually characterized by trial and error. Developers translate a subjective description of a need into an operational concept that may bear only a remote resemblance to the original idea. No one systematically quantifies the process or devises tests to ensure that the service is complete, rational, and fulfills the original need objectively. No R&D departments, laboratories, or service engineers define and oversee the design. There is no way to ensure quality or uniformity in the absence of a detailed design. What piecemeal quality controls exist address only parts of the service.

There are several reasons for the lack of analytical service systems designs. Services are unusual in that they have impact, but no form. Like light, they can't be physically stored or possessed and their consumption is often simultaneous with their production.

People confuse services with products and with good manners. But a service is not a physical object and cannot be possessed. When we buy the use of a hotel room, we take nothing away with us but the experience of the night's stay. When we fly, we are transported by an airplane but we don't own it. Although a consultant's product may appear as a bound report, what the consumer bought was mental capability and knowledge, not paper and ink. A service is not a servant; it need not be rendered by a person. Even when people are the chosen means of execution, they are only part of the process.

Outstanding service companies instill in their managers a fanatical attachment to the original service idea. Believing that this product of genius is the only thing they have going for them, they try to maintain it with considerable precision. They bring in methods engineers to quantify and make existing components more efficient. They codify the process in volumes of policies and procedures. While the outline of a great service concept may be reflected in these tools, the procedures are only fragmented views of a more comprehensive, largely undocumented phenomenon. Good and lasting service management requires much more. Better service *design* provides the key to market success, and more important, to growth.

The operations side of service management often uses work flow design and control methods such as time-motion engineering, PERT/GANTT charting, and quality-control methods derived from the work of W. Edwards Deming. These procedures provide managers with a way to visualize a process and to define and manipulate it at arm's length. What they miss is the consumer's relationship to, and interaction with, services. They make no provision for people-rendered services that require judgment and a less mechanical approach. They don't account for the service's products that must be managed simultaneously with the process. And they don't allow for special problems of market position, advertising, pricing, or distribution.

We can build on the strength of these operational systems, however, to come up with a more comprehensive and workable framework for addressing most issues of service development. We can devise a blueprint for service design that is nonsubjective and quantifiable, one which will allow developers to work out details ahead of time. Such a blueprint gives managers a context within which to deal with the management and control of the process.

Designing a Blueprint

A service blueprint allows a company to explore all the issues inherent in creating or managing a service. The process of designing a blueprint involves the consideration of several issues:

IDENTIFYING PROCESSES. The first step in creating such a blueprint is mapping the processes that constitute the service. Exhibit I maps a shoeshine parlor. As the service is simple and clear-cut, the map is straightforward. For more complex services, identifying and defining the processes involved may be difficult and result in a large, complicated diagram. Tax-return preparation or health care, for example, involves many decision points, alternative courses of action, and variable methodologies. Portfolio management, car repair, and even tailoring require contemplation and observation before diagramming.

Even within the simplest process, further definition is beneficial; in shoeshining it might be useful to specify how the proprietor will perform the step called "buff." Definition doesn't mean you must mechanize all procedures. But identifying the components of a step or action reveals the inputs needed and steps covered, and permits analysis, control, and improvement. For example, a doctor or a lawyer would do well to break down the "problem diagnosis" step.

It is important to watch out for parts of the service that the consumer does not see, like purchasing of supplies. Though invisible, these processes are important because changing them may alter the way consumers perceive the service. If, for example, a bank redesigns a computer program so that it produces a different account statement for customers, the bank may affect its image or other consumer perceptions of value. These subprocesses are integral to the success of the service.

Exhibit I. Blueprint for a Corner Shoeshine

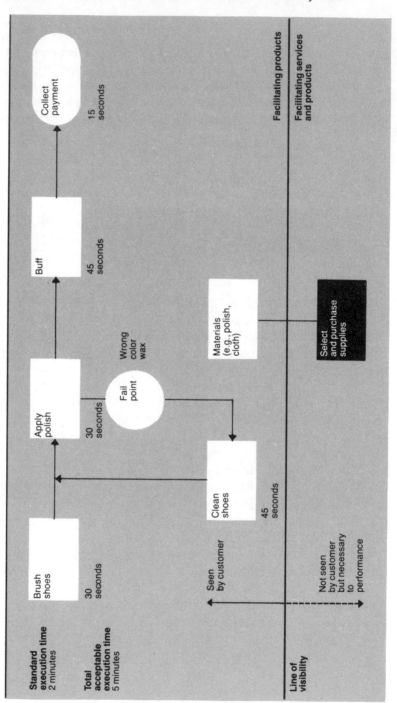

ISOLATING FAIL POINTS.   Having diagrammed the processes involved, the designer can now see where the system might go awry. The shoeshiner may pick up and apply the wrong color wax. So the designer must build in a subprocess to correct this possible error. The identification of fail points and the design of fail-safe processes are critical. The consequences of service failures can be greatly reduced by analyzing fail points at the design stage. When designers and managers think through potential problems together in advance, the quality of service execution is invariably higher.

ESTABLISHING TIME FRAME.   After diagramming a service profile, identifying processes and vulnerabilities, and building in fail-safe measures, the designer must consider the execution.

Since all services depend on time, which is usually the major cost determinant, the designer should establish a standard execution time. As a blueprint is a model, the design should also allow for deviation from standard execution time under working conditions. The amount of latitude necessary in the time frame will depend on the complexity of the delivery.

In the shoeshine example, the standard execution time is two minutes. Research showed that the customer would tolerate up to five minutes of performance before lowering his or her assessment of quality. Acceptable execution time for a shoeshine is then five minutes.

ANALYZING PROFITABILITY.   The customer can spend the three minutes between standard and acceptable execution time at the corner parlor waiting in line or during service, if an error occurs or if the shoeshiner does certain things too slowly. Whatever its source, a delay can affect profits dramatically. Exhibit II quantifies the cost of delay; after four minutes the proprietor loses money.

A service designer must establish a time-of-service-execution standard that precludes unprofitable business and maintains productivity. Such a standard not only helps measure performance and control uniformity and quality, it also serves as a model for distribution of the service to far-flung locations.

Delivering the Service

Recruiting, training, and general management are important considerations in services rendered by people, and for complex profes-

Exhibit II.   Shoeshine Profitability Analysis

		Execution time		
		2 minutes	3 minutes	4 minutes
Price		$.50	$.50	$.50
Costs	Time @ $.10 per minute	.20	.30	.40
	Wax	.03	.03	.03
	Other operating expenses	.09	.09	.09
Total costs		$.32	$.42	$.52
Pretax profit		$.18	$.08	($.02)

sional occupations such as legal, consulting, or medical services these factors are of paramount importance. But some services can be rendered mechanically, as banks have demonstrated with automatic tellers, and some can be performed by customers themselves, as at salad bars.

Implementation constantly evolves. Schools, for example, once depended entirely on teachers to render the service of education; today computers and television have an important function in the classroom. A service designer must weigh alternate means of execution, for example, by considering the merits of using a buffing machine in the process of shoeshining. The productivity and profit margin increases must be weighed against a customer's perception of lower quality. A blueprint facilitates the analysis of cost-benefit trade-offs and can be used to test the appeal of different designs to prospective customers.

A blueprint can help the service developer with other problems. For the pricing department, it provides a basis for a thorough cost analysis; for distribution, a map to be duplicated; for promotion, tangible evidence it can manage and control.

HIGHLIGHTING TANGIBLE EVIDENCE

To maintain credibility, the service must select and manage products with care. In some cases, products are optional—a consultant may not have to present a written report for instance. Consumers, however, often deduce the nature of the service from this type of circumstantial evidence. The design of a service should therefore incorporate the orchestration of tangible evidence—everything the consumer uses to verify the service's effectiveness. The setting, including color schemes, advertising, printed or graphic materials, and stationery, all proclaim a service's style. The design should not be carelessly delegated to outsiders or left to chance.

Airlines have learned this lesson. The interior and exterior decor of the plane, flight attendants' uniforms, the appearance of the reservation desk, ticket folders, baggage tags, and advertising graphics all tell the customer what kind of service to expect. They either reinforce or contradict personal experience with the airline.

MAKING PEOPLE SPECIAL

To the customer, people are inseparable parts of many services. The presence of people, however, brings a higher risk that service quality will vary. At the design stage, the developer must plan and consider every encounter between consumer and provider. The good manners and attentiveness customers associate with good personal service must be made part of the hiring, training, and performance standards of the company. Indifferent or surly execution can devalue the service.

Both the Disney organization and IBM offer outstanding examples of superior people management to provide uniform service. Airlines and fast-food chains "package" service personnel in clothes that proclaim and reinforce an overall service identity. These companies invest heavily in training and retraining at all levels.

At the beginning and end of the design cycle lies the marketing goal to which all service organizations aspire: benefiting customers. For the customer, a good shoeshine is "shiny shoes," "clean shoes," or "preservation." It goes without saying that market research throughout the design cycle is the best control mechanism to ensure that the service meets the goal.

Modifying a Service

Market research during a service's operating life enables managers to measure quality and identify needs for redesign.

Exhibit III shows how the designer may add a repeat of steps 2

Exhibit III. Modified Shoeshine Blueprint

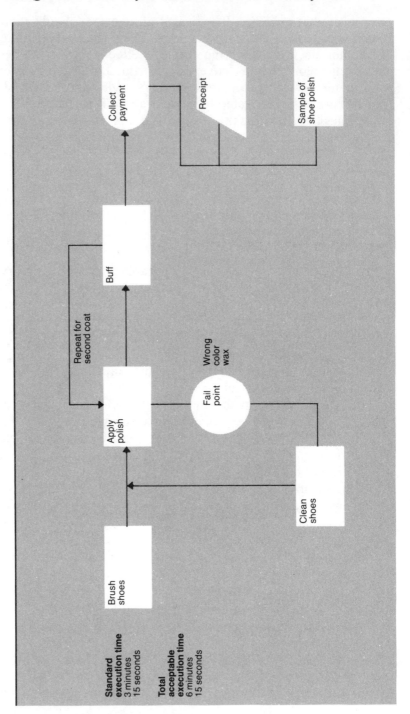

and 3 in the shoeshine service to create a two-coat shine, and justify a 20-cent price increase, thus increasing the profit margin by nearly 30%. Moreover, the shoeshiner might decide to add a receipt or a sample of shoepolish as tangible evidence of good care. Such service reminders (the shoeshiner could print his or her name and address on the shoepolish sample) could lead to a premium price for a premium service.

A designer can use a blueprint to engineer new market products or services (see Exhibit IV). A designer can do much at the drawing board, well before expensive formal market introduction of the service.

Applying the Principles

Service blueprint methods can be applied in the development of a discount brokerage service in a large money-center bank (see Exhibit V). Very little of this service is visible to customers. In fact, customers have virtually no conception of the processes that underlie most services.

Discount brokerage is not particularly complex, but the blueprint condenses and simplifies the service and omits many minor steps. For example, the step "prepare and mail statements" includes more than 12 activities, such as printing statements and stuffing and sealing envelopes.

The important fail points (F) show where the service may experience quality or consistency problems. Telephone communication, for example, is a component that is not only critical and difficult to control but also one of the most powerful influences of customer perception, since it provides the only personal contact. To deal with this potential fail point, management decided to script dialogues for various situations, to train staff thoroughly in communication and response techniques, to establish procedures making certain that calls never went unanswered, and to ensure accuracy by logging, recording, and confirming all customer instructions. While the blueprint doesn't show these processes, the system designer has diagrammed and controlled each one.

The design shows execution time standards that can be easily monitored and quantified. They allow the measurement of capacity and productivity through volume and throughput relationships. In telephone communication, for example, the brokerage set a broad

Exhibit IV.   Blueprint for More Complex Shoe Products and Services

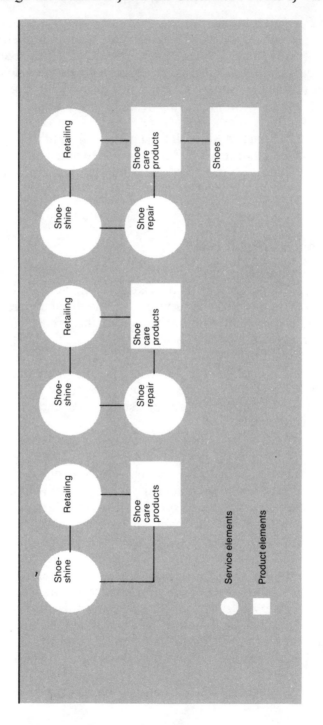

time limit for opening accounts (one-half to one hour). Execution standards can be tightened as operating experience increases.

Although the superficial aspects of services may seem the same, the design particulars involve so many alternatives and choices that no two services will have exactly the same design. Services differ from competitor to competitor in the sum of particulars. Individual aspects allow consumers to discriminate between companies offering the same product.

In its complete form, Exhibit V permits the analysis of competitive differences. The designer can then respond to unfavorable comparisons with appropriate changes. As new processes or products are added, or enhancements made, they can be mapped on the blueprint and analyzed for their impact on operations, profitability, and reliability.

Creating Better Service

A blueprint is more precise than verbal definitions and less subject to misinterpretation. It illustrates the dictum of W. Edwards Deming that workers are never to blame for flaws in a process. Process design is management's responsibility.

A service blueprint allows a company to test its assumptions on paper and thoroughly work out the bugs. A service manager can test a prototype delivery on potential customers and use the feedback to modify the blueprint before testing the procedure again.

A blueprint encourages creativity, preemptive problem solving, and controlled implementation. It can reduce the potential for failure and enhance management's ability to think effectively about new services.

The blueprint principle helps cut down the time and inefficiency of random service development and gives a higher level view of service management prerogatives. The alternative—leaving services to individual talent and managing the pieces rather than the whole—makes a company more vulnerable and creates a service that reacts slowly to market needs and opportunities. As the United States moves to a service economy, companies that gain control of the design and management process will be the companies that survive and prosper.

Exhibit V.   Blueprint for Discount Brokerage

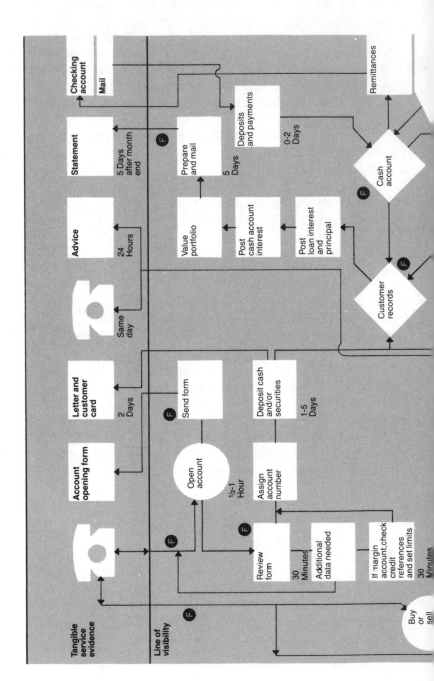

Exhibit V. (continued)

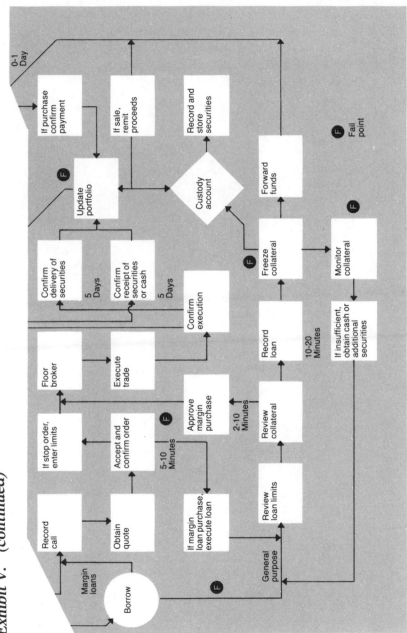

3
How to Manage Customer Service

William M. Hutchison, Jr. and John F. Stolle

Intelligent investments in customer service can pay off handsomely, as the following testimonials indicate:

> Supplier to the oil industry—"We attribute a 5% increase in sales directly to the improved delivery service and reduced number of stock shortages we achieved several months ago."

> Tool manufacturer—"The use of air freight gave us the distribution 'plus' we needed to successfully enter the consumer market."

> Food manufacturer—"Determination of our customers' *real* service requirements led to the redesign of our entire distribution system at a savings of $2 million annually."

While each of these companies obviously has taken a different tack in the management of customer service, all three have pursued courses with certain characteristics in common. Each has made a quantitative evaluation of service. Each has considered service from the customer's viewpoint. Each has evaluated the service provided by competition. Each has followed what is essentially the six-step program for customer service management described in this article.

However, it is rare for companies to give the attention to customer service that is needed to make improvements like those mentioned. Most companies fail to analyze the management of service as carefully as other functions in the manufacturing, marketing, and distribution of the product. Because service has many elements—delivery time, in-stock position, engineering assistance, and repair parts availability, to mention just a few—designing the best service package is difficult. Usually it is handled on an "experience and judgment" basis. To manage it thus is to fail to recognize its importance.

Large Stakes Involved

Today, the trend is for customers to expect service to be as much a part of what they buy as are the product's design, quality, and price. And, like these other characteristics, service consists of several elements that need to be precisely defined, specified, and *sold* to the customer.

Of course, the importance of customer service varies by industry and among companies within an industry. At one extreme, service may actually be of minor importance—for example, in the case of a women's cosmetic item in great demand. At the other extreme, service may be the prime determinant of who gets the order—for instance, in the case of a wallboard material which generally is of the same design, quality, and price as competitive wallboards. While most products lie somewhere between these extremes, they usually are more like the building material example because design, quality, and price advantages tend to be temporary in today's rapidly developing product and process technology. Thus, the level of service usually has an important effect on profits, both directly and indirectly.

DIRECT PROFIT EFFECTS

It is clear that stock-outs, excessive delivery time, and lack of repair service all result in lost sales. It is equally clear that providing a high level of service is costly and that the cost must be justified by achievement of a higher level of sales than would be the case if such service were not offered. While the sales and cost effects of customer service often have been considered as intangibles, current analysis is pointing out that:

1. They are sometimes measurable or predictable with considerable accuracy.
2. They can usually be evaluated with acceptable accuracy.
3. They are rarely so nebulous or intangible as to be imponderables.

In particular, the *cost* of different levels of service usually can be measured precisely. For example, in one large machinery-manufacturing company, the warehousing, transportation, and inventory costs of different levels of delivery service from field warehouses were precisely measured for the spare parts operations. As shown in Exhibit I, the proper level of service for this company had to be determined on the basis of the millions of dollars in annual operating costs that were involved.

While in most cases the *sales effects* of different levels of service likewise can be determined with acceptable accuracy, their measurement does present more difficulty because they are less visible. This is especially true in the case of good service. In the case of bad service, on the other hand, the effects can be pinned down with considerable concreteness. For example, when an electrical materials supplier analyzed his records and interviewed customers to measure the response to warehouse stock-outs, he found this breakdown:

25%—customers waited the required ten days for their regular warehouse to be replenished from the factory.

33%—customers waited the extra two days required for the item to be shipped from another, more distant warehouse that had stock.

42%—customers did not wait for the item but obtained it from a competitor.

The study also showed that the relative frequency of these three responses to stock-out varied considerably from warehouse to warehouse, according to the competitive situation. The response likewise varied among items in the line, depending on the acceptance that the item had with customers. This customer service information was a major input for inventory control systems and warehouse network design.

As for the sales effects of providing really good service, these usually are more difficult to measure precisely because the results are often clouded by other marketing actions of the company and of competitors. But this does not mean that they are not crucial. For example, the importance of maintenance service to computer sales has been clearly demonstrated—particularly in the more remote geographical areas where this service has varied greatly among manufacturers. In another case, a large retailer determined that when a distribution center was established, sales of white goods (washers, dryers, refrigerators, and so forth) increased immediately by about 15% in the area served, because of the greatly reduced delivery time to customers.

Recognizing the direct effect of customer service on profits, some companies are market-testing the provision of different customer service levels in much the same way that they market-test alter-

Exhibit I. Economics of Delivery Service

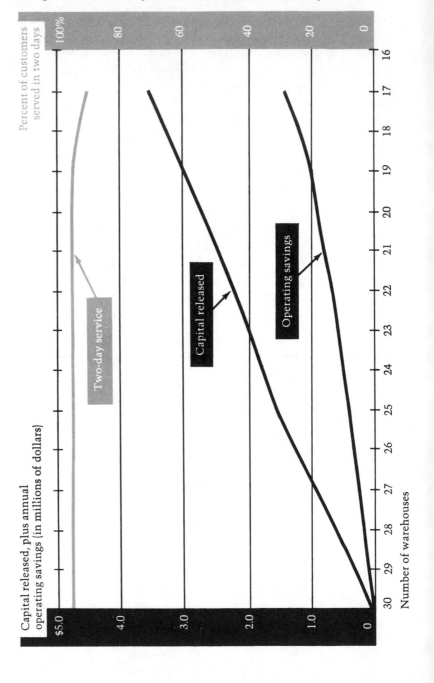

native product features, promotions, and deals. Even when an accurate appraisal of the sales effects of customer service is difficult to make, the volume/cost/profit significance of service usually can be brought into perspective with a breakeven diagram. Exhibit II shows the relative sales volume results that are required for one company to break even with the additional cost of 5 distribution centers and 20 distribution centers—and highlights the millions of dollars that are involved.

INDIRECT IMPACT

One of the best illustrations of indirect service effects is found in the marketing of grocery products to retailers. When a manufacturer's service is poorer than his competitors', the retailer most likely will continue to stock the item because his customers demand it. But the retailer will be less cooperative on promotions and much less responsive to new products of this manufacturer. Such poor service can even lead, in extreme instances, to a decrease in shelf space and to an increase in emphasis on private labels.

As this example illustrates, most instances in which indirect service effects are important occur when the customer is not the end user of the product and when the supplier is dependent on the customer's cooperation in joint marketing programs. Although the indirect effects of the level of customer service may be difficult to measure, it is no less important to consider them, for they can have a major impact on company profits.

Six Steps to Success

While individual approaches to managing customer service may differ, an examination of successful service management programs reveals six principal steps that are required. These are:

1. Define the elements of service.
2. Determine the customer's viewpoint.
3. Design a competitive service "package."
4. Develop a program to sell service.
5. Market-test the program.
6. Establish performance controls.

Exhibit II. Additional Sales Volume Required to Break Even on Local Warehousing

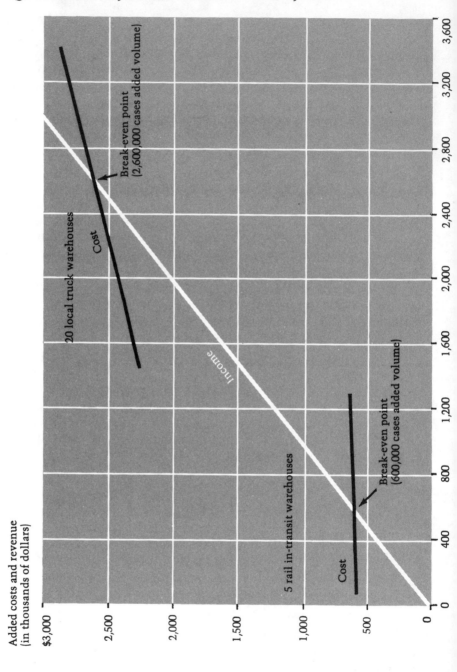

Let us examine each of these steps briefly, and then take a case example showing their application in an actual situation.

DEFINING THE ELEMENTS

The term "customer service" frequently is interpreted as involving delivery time only. This is an oversimplification. Service usually involves not one, but many, elements. It can, in fact, involve every aspect of the supplier's business.

The first step, then, is to identify specifically what the elements of customer service are. Here are some typical ones in the physical distribution area:

Order processing time—elapsed time from receipt of the customer's order until it is ready for assembly.

Order assembly time—time required to prepare the order for shipment.

Delivery time—time in transit to the customer.

Inventory reliability—stock-outs, back orders, percent of demand filled, omission rate, percent of orders shipped complete, and so on.

Order-size constraint—minimum order size and minimum frequency allowed.

Consolidation allowed—ability to consolidate items from several locations into a single shipment.

Consistency—range of variation in each of the preceding elements.

A similar list might be prepared for maintenance and repair service or for technical service.

In defining these elements, it is important to measure the level of service currently being given in each area. Managers are likely to find that the current level of service actually given differs dramatically from the level they believe the company is giving. Acquiring knowledge is a first step toward determining what is required to provide improved service.

CHECKING CUSTOMER VIEWS

One company established a nationwide network of 30 warehouses which was capable of delivering products to most customers in one-day transit time. However, the investment was wasted because the company spent an average of six days on order processing. In failing to recognize that, from the customer's point of view, service involves the total time from placement of the order to receipt of the merchandise, management made a type of mistake that is quite common. Facts detailing the customer's viewpoint are not obtained often enough. Companies spend large sums of money interviewing customers to determine their attitudes toward *products*—but their feelings concerning service are neglected.

Three important aspects of the customer's view of service should be ascertained (usually by an extensive survey):

1. *Additional elements of service that are important to the customer.* What would he like to be getting that he lacks now? Such items as these should be considered:

Frequency of a salesman's visits to check his customers' needs.

Ordering convenience (telephone, preprinted forms, and so on).

Order progress information (order acknowledgment, shipping notices, and so on).

Inventory backup during promotions, new product introductions, and competitive tests.

Format and organization of the invoice.

This group of elements indicates that, while most suppliers think of service as related to physical distribution, their customers' service needs concern every functional area of the supplier's business.

2. *The economic significance to the customer of each element of service.* A customer will almost inevitably say he wants better service or wants a service element not currently provided. However, if service is to be meaningful, it must be economically significant to the customer, in terms of either lowering his cost or increasing his selling effectiveness. The economic significance to the customer also determines whether he is willing to pay for an additional service. (For an interesting approach to this question, see the case example presented later.)

3. *The customer's rating of the service levels of the company's competitors.* Such data can be valuable in evaluating the minimum service levels required and the opportunities to use service to gain a competitive advantage. While an approximation of competitors' service usually can be made from knowledge of their facilities and

policies, the best information can be obtained from customers. Their ratings and comparisons are the truly meaningful ones.

DESIGNING A "PACKAGE"

The design of the service "package" should proceed in much the same way as the design of the product—assessing the minimum requirements for meeting customer needs, identifying the features that will have customer impact relative to competition, identifying possible trade-offs among alternatives, and accurately determining all of the economic aspects. Let us consider each of these tasks in turn.

Minimum service requirements usually can be determined with considerable accuracy, provided there is a good understanding of the economic effects of service on customers and accurate information on the service provided by competitors. For example, if failure to deliver the product within 10 days after receipt of a customer's order will shut down his plant, the minimum service level required is obvious. Similarly, if all competitors are meeting a 7-day delivery schedule, there is a strong indication that the company should do at least as well. Thus the minimum requirements are usually easy to define, given certain information.

Assessing the probable impact on customers of additional levels of service or additional service elements demands the same kind of creativity in designing the service "package" as is needed in designing the product. The use of air freight, mentioned earlier, is an example of creativity in developing a customer service "package." Other examples are telephone sales contacts, order processing, and flexibility in ordering mixed shipments. Often customer impact can be achieved at little or no cost. Sometimes better service can even be provided at lower cost—for example, by shipping part of a product line by air freight rather than using field warehouses.

Trade-off opportunities among interrelated service elements usually exist in the more complex situations. For example, delivery time might be lengthened a little in exchange for a better in-stock position. Such a trade-off must be considered when deciding on the number of warehousing locations. A system with large numbers of small warehouses will make possible shorter transit time from warehouse to customer, but the system with many small warehouses will also have frequent stock-outs; a system of a few large, well-managed warehouses, on the other hand, will require longer delivery times, but the warehouses will be much more likely to have items in stock when they are requested. Similarly, there is a direct trade-off between order processing time and delivery time, as well as many subtle interrelationships between other service elements.

Although economic analysis of service alternatives is not discussed in this article, it is important to note that, over the last 15 years, operations research and management science have provided a reservoir of management tools for designing the lowest total-cost system capable of meeting a given service requirement. Use of these tools is essential in designing the best service "package."

SELLING SERVICE

Perhaps the most discouraging experience that a company can have is to develop an outstanding new product but, because of inept marketing, fail to bring it to commercial fruition. Also very discouraging is the development of an outstanding service "package" which fails to achieve its natural impact because it is ineffectively sold.

The need to sell service is particularly important after a cost-reduction move. For example, suppose a distribution system is revised to decrease costs, and this results, for some customers, in an apparent reduction of service, such as would be the case in the closing of a local warehouse. It is almost always possible to find some positive features of the new program that offset the service decrease. If such programs are to succeed without loss of customer goodwill, it is essential to sell each customer affected in advance of the change and to direct the change so that negative reactions are avoided.

An improvement in service calls for a sales effort, too. In this case, all the principles for introducing new products or new features of existing products are applicable. A specific sales program should be planned; this should include approaches and selling methods for individual customers, identification of participating sales personnel, preparation of selling material, indoctrination of salespeople, and a step-by-step timetable. A procedure for measuring results in terms of increased sales should be installed in advance.

MARKET TESTING

When a considerable cost is involved in the service package, and when an increase in sales volume is needed to justify it, pilot area testing of both the operating and marketing programs may be desirable before the project is launched nationwide. The purpose of such testing is, of course, the same as for the market testing of new products. Similarly, management should plan procedures and controls to measure customer reaction, cost, and volume changes in order to ensure reliability of the area tests.

PERFORMANCE CONTROLS

Just as quality controls are essential to manufacturing the product itself, so control of the level of service provided is important. Such control requires management to:

Establish quantitative standards of performance for each service element.

Measure actual performance for each service element.

Analyze variance—viz., actual service versus the standard.

Take corrective action as needed to bring actual performance into line.

The difficulty in controlling service stems primarily from the fact that usually some service elements are outside the control of the company. For example, the time of actual delivery of orders to customers is often difficult to determine unless the company operates its own fleet of trucks or makes special arrangements. However, such problems can be overcome by use of statistical sampling in interviewing customers or by periodically enclosing a self-addressed postcard to be returned on arrival of merchandise. If service is worth giving, it is worth controlling.

Concepts in Practice

Now let us turn to an example of a company that improved its approach to customer service. Although no single case is likely to offer a good illustration of all six steps in managing customer service, the one described covers most of them. It is a particularly good example of the customer survey and distribution cost analysis needed to establish the proper level of service.

The company is one of the major ones in its industry. At the time of the events to be described, its annual sales were $150 million. The company sold two major product lines—one to institutional customers and one to retail customers—through 25 company-owned branches located in different parts of the nation. The retailers, about 10,000 in number, ranged from individual stores to large chains. Institutional buyers also varied in size but were, of course, fewer in number. There was strong customer acceptance of many items in both of the product lines.

The two lines differed considerably in their physical characteristics and in the manner in which they were ordered. Retailers ordered individual items of relatively high value in small quantities, thus maintaining a low inventory. Institutional buyers ordered in much larger quantities; many products in their line were bulkier and of lower value.

The branch system had been in existence for several years and was considered an important factor in the company's success. While customers in some cities could receive faster service from wholesalers, the branches generally could give "competitive service" and were in a position to give "personalized service" and special attention to emergency needs.

CAUSES OF CONCERN

Because of several factors, a number of executives had become concerned about customer service. A reorganization of the company had transferred control of all branches from the sales department to a newly formed distribution department. A number of branches had been rebuilt in suburban locations, and regular shipments to these metropolitan areas now required an extra day for delivery. A small increase in the minimum order size had just been adopted after a year's debate and with great concern that it would drive many buyers to wholesalers. However, retailers were accepting the change with apparent indifference.

Further, a cost analysis of distribution operations revealed opportunities for major savings if changes in the number and location of branches could be accomplished without negative customer reaction.

Yet, despite the great concern expressed for customer service, this company had little quantitative information on what service was actually being given. In the case of retail customers, only the number of orders delayed by stock shortages was recorded. While the policy was to process orders on the same day that they were received (some records were kept on this), no attention was given to the time required to transmit orders to branches, nor was attention given to the time of delivery from branches to customers.

An analysis showed that a large proportion of orders took more than a week from the time they were placed until the customers actually received the merchandise. Many of these customers were in metropolitan areas where salespeople believed that two-day service was required and was being given.

Service to institutional customers was much faster. However, while it was uniformly agreed that these buyers required the highest level of service on both regular and emergency bases, there were no quantitative standards of what this level should be; and, again, there was no consistent measure of what service was actually being given.

When it was pointed out that the company lacked hard facts covering what management had for a long time believed to be a vital area affecting sales, an extensive survey was conducted to determine the customers' real service needs and to learn how the company stood in relation to its competitors.

SURVEY OBJECTIVES

It was agreed that the objective of the customer survey should be to answer seven specific questions for management:

1. What actual delivery time and inventory reliability were being provided by the company and by its competitors?
2. How important were competitive service differences to customers?
3. How did delivery service and customers' appraisal of it vary with distance from the company's branches and competitors?
4. What elements other than delivery service affected the organization's success in selling an account?
5. How did the company compare with competition in respect to these other service elements?

6. How important was consistency of service relative to the service level itself?
7. What dollar value did customers place on service time and other service elements?

APPROACH TO PROBLEMS

As a first step in the design of a comprehensive nationwide survey, a few customers were interviewed on an exploratory basis. The interviews revealed some real problems in obtaining good, factual answers to service questions:

> It was often difficult to determine what actual service was being given, since the customer did not maintain records. However, this frequently did not prevent customers from commenting specifically on the service level.

> An objective ranking of competitors' service required that the company be anonymous.

> Superficial answers were given unless questions were carefully phrased. Customers tend to feel that service is never good enough, just as price is never low enough; and the question, "How good is Company X's service?" yielded an obvious answer.

> Customers' opinions in and of themselves were less important than the effect they had on actions. For example, would the customer buy less if the delivery time were two days longer? The answer is difficult to determine, particularly when the supplier is identified.

> Determining the real economic effect of service on customers requires considerable assistance from the customer and is time-consuming for the survey team.

All of the difficulties attending other types of market research were present in this case, too. Fortunately, techniques to overcome most of the problems had been developed by market researchers. A full-scale survey was planned. It had three phases:

1. A number of "friendly" customers were interviewed in depth to determine (a) what elements of service were important to them, and (b) the economic effect of these elements on their costs and profits. An effort was made to separate those elements that appeared to them as "nuisance factors" from those that had an important effect on their internal operations.

Exhibit III.   *Examples of Questions Used in Survey*

Assume the table below lists several order situations in which you, the retailer, are involved over a period of time. All orders were placed with the manufacturer's branch warehouse located in a city other than the one in which the company is located. Please consider the service provided on each order and indicate your opinion of it by placing an "x" in the proper space.

Order placed	Received	Service rating		
		Poor	Average	Good
Out-of-stock order, Monday, 8/8/67, by phone	Saturday, 8/11/67			
Stock maintenance order, Thursday, 8/25/67, by mail	Tuesday, 8/30/67			

Below is a list of 10 delivery service times from each of 5 major suppliers. All orders were placed by phone. Please give your opinion of the relative quality of service each supplier has provided by circling those which are satisfactory.

Supplier A*	Supplier B*	Supplier C*	Supplier D*	Supplier E*
4 days	3 days	1 day	3 days	4 days
4 days	1 day	1 day	2 days	7 days
5 days	5 days	6 days	3 days	3 days

*Actual suppliers' names used in questionnaire.

2. A questionnaire was then designed and used in one geographic area to quantify customers' service concerns. Some of the questions measured comparative ratings of different suppliers, while others were "tests" designed to measure a deep-rooted understanding of service importance rather than passing impressions. A few of the test questions are shown in Exhibit III.
3. After final revisions, the questionnaire was administered in five areas of the country that were chosen to represent the full range of possible sensitivity to service and competitors' strengths.

In total, 500 customers were interviewed in the survey; 25 were interviewed in depth.

VALUABLE FINDINGS

The survey produced a large amount of detailed information which proved to be of great value in subsequent marketing activities as well as in the design of a more effective physical distribution system. The principal general findings were as follows:

> *Retailers* were somewhat indifferent to delivery service time as compared to the other factors that affected their relationship with suppliers, as long as a minimum level of service was consistently given.
>
> *Institutional* buyers placed great importance on delivery service, considering it as important as any other factor affecting their relationship with suppliers.
>
> *Both* classes of customers identified the frequency of the salesman's visits as a major customer service element and considered it as important as any other aspect of service.
>
> Supplier inventory reliability (i.e., having all items in stock) was considered just as important as delivery time.

It appeared that the customer's view of service had many complex and interrelated dimensions—delivery time, order placement convenience, availability of items when ordered, and others. Most important, the overall image the customer had of the supplier from salesman contacts, trade advertising and relations, and product quality affected his reaction to delivery time. The better the customer's overall opinion of the company, the less he was concerned about delivery time. On the other hand, customers who were displeased with some other aspect of the company—pricing policy, for instance—also tended to complain about service.

Retail Customers. Information from the survey pointed to the following attitudes and requirements on the part of the company's retail customers:

> Three- to five-day delivery time was satisfactory, depending on the geographical location of customers.
>
> The company ranked first in delivery service, and second in overall service, among the five major suppliers.
>
> Greater consistency of service was worth the price of one-day longer delivery time.
>
> Complaints that suppliers were out of stock were rare in the industry.
>
> Price concessions on the order of 2% to 4% would induce customers to accept double the present service time.

Institutional Buyers. These findings came out of the study of institutional customers:

Next-day delivery was required.

The company ranked second out of five suppliers in delivery service to cities where it did not have branch warehouses, first in service to cities where it did have warehouses.

Delivery service ranked with product quality as the most important overall element of supplier choice.

The company was frequently out of stock, but made up for this deficiency in cities where it had branch warehouses by giving excellent emergency service.

On the basis of these findings, it was possible to design a customer service package that quantitatively related cost and service levels.

DESIGN OF THE "PACKAGE"

It became apparent that, because of the very different service concerns of institutional and retail customers, separate distribution systems should be considered. During the customer survey work, a complete costs analysis of the branch distribution network was made. This analysis was structured to show retail and institutional distribution costs separately and to show what the operating costs would be for a wide variety of distribution combinations. The total cost for each practical number of retail and institutional product warehouses was developed. These costs are shown in Exhibit IV.

The exhibit shows that minimum distribution cost to *retailers* can be achieved with a 10-branch system. Variable operating costs increase slowly as the number of warehouses is reduced from 26, because transportation cost increases are offset by warehousing, billing, and inventory cost decreases. But when the number of branches is reduced to less than 10, variable costs increase rapidly as transportation costs soar. Fixed costs increase steadily with the number of warehouses.

On the other hand, as Exhibit IV shows, minimum distribution cost to *institutional* customers occurs with 40 warehousing locations. Transportation and warehousing costs are relatively insensitive over a broad range of the number of warehouses. However, inventory costs increase rapidly when the number of warehouses

Exhibit IV. Total Cost for Varying Numbers of Branch Warehouses

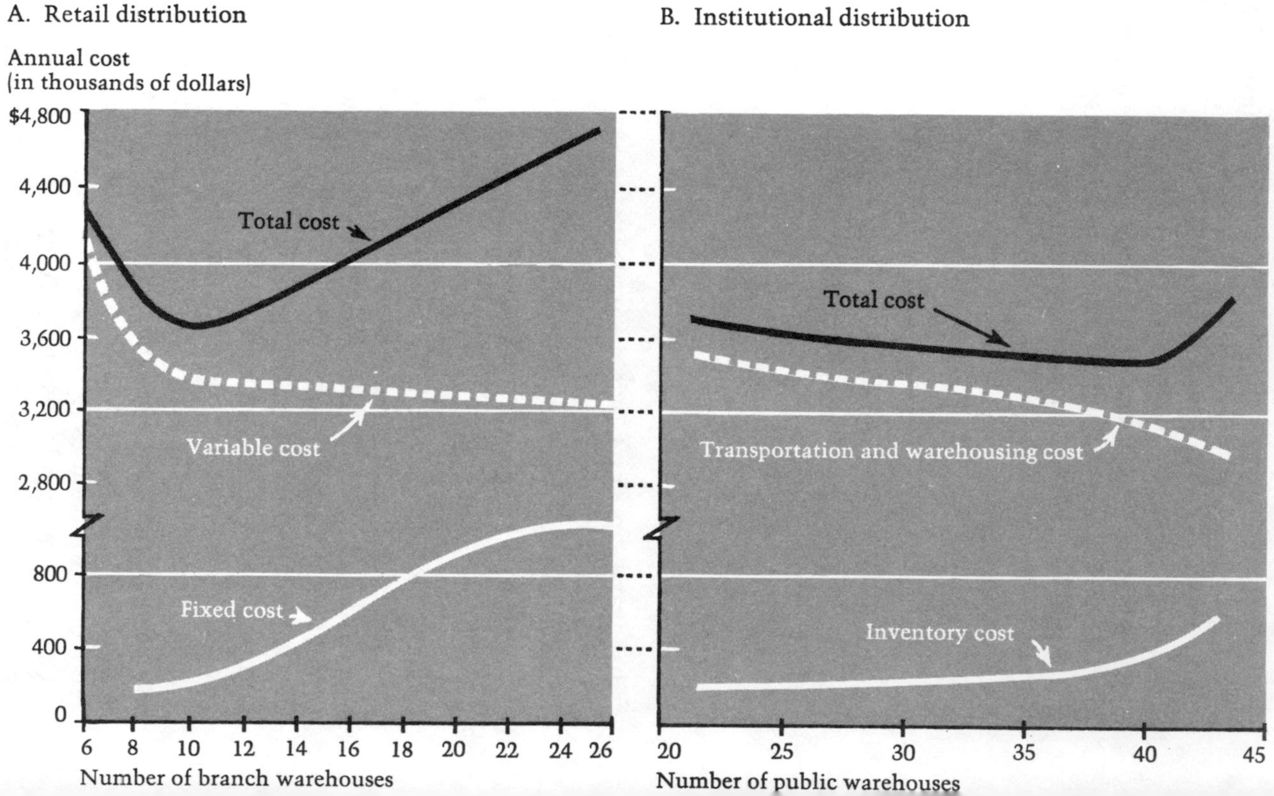
A. Retail distribution
B. Institutional distribution
Annual cost
(in thousands of dollars)
$4,800
4,400
4,000
3,600
3,200
2,800
800
400
0
Total cost
Variable cost
Fixed cost
Total cost
Transportation and warehousing cost
Inventory cost
6
8
10
12
14
16
18
20
22
24
26
Number of branch warehouses
20
25
30
35
40
45
Number of public warehouses

exceeds 40, and thus become the determining factor. Fixed costs are not involved here, since the analysis is based on the use of public warehouses for institutional products.

Service data for each number of warehouses were then developed to show the percentage of retail and institutional volume that would be served in one, two, or more days' delivery time. A chart of the variation in service pattern with changes in the number of branch warehouses is shown in Exhibit V.

Management saw that if the number of retail branches were reduced from the 25 then in operation, service would fall off slowly until a 14-branch configuration was reached. After that point, delivery service would deteriorate rapidly. If the number of institutional branches were increased from 25, service at first would improve rapidly, then more slowly. (Also, the percentage of customers beyond two days' travel time—not shown here—reached a practical minimum at 35 to 40 warehouses, the same point where the cost curve flattened out.)

What would be the best overall balance of service and cost? The company decided to distribute institutional products through 35 public warehouses in each major market, and distribute retail products through 14 highly efficient, company-owned branches. Annual savings of $1.3 million were expected with this change, while assets with a book value of over $2.0 million would be released for sale. Though the majority of these savings were achieved in branch and warehouse operating costs, savings also were realized in transportation and inventory carrying charges.

At the same time, the changes would bring a net *improvement* in service; 12% more institutional buyers—the most critical customers—would receive improved service, and while the delivery time for 8.5% of the retail customers would be increased by one day, the survey indicated that this would be of minor importance. In fact, the survey indicated that the slightly negative effect of the increased service time could be offset by making additional sales contacts with the retailer during the changeover period.

MARKET TESTING

The final step prior to nationwide installation of the program was to market-test the new service levels. The test used had several elements:

Exhibit V.　Service Patterns for Varying Branch Systems

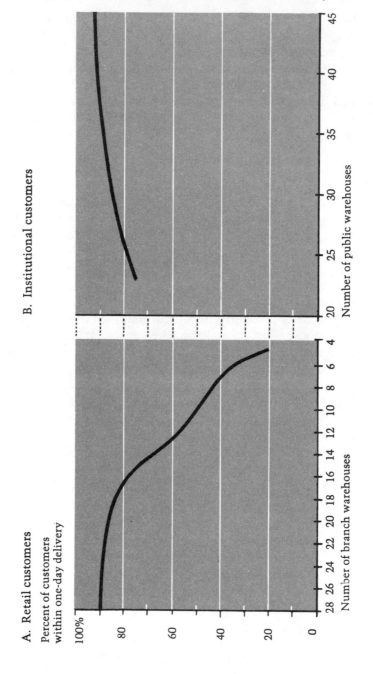

A. Retail customers

B. Institutional customers

Percent of customers
within one-day delivery

Number of branch warehouses

Number of public warehouses

Institutional products were moved into a public warehouse in a test city, and the sales department developed promotional materials to announce the improved service in the test area.

New inventory, traffic, and order-entry procedures were developed to support the public warehouse system.

A survey of institutional customers was made, ostensibly to check for any difficulties the new approach might cause, but actually to build up enthusiasm for the change.

In the retail market, before a branch was actually closed, orders were transferred to the new warehouse to test for adverse reaction. At the same time, the sales department experimented with increased promotional activity to see what additional attention from salesmen was required to cancel out the effect of a service change in areas where branches were closed.

Finally, a six-month test was run in one area of the country as a pilot project. A test area was selected in which minimum total disruption would occur; it was an area where the existing branch had severely limited facilities.

The pilot operation was also used to develop new approaches to branch operations—approaches that would take full advantage of the efficiencies obtainable in fewer, larger, and more specialized facilities.

Thus, the test series led to a complete new plan of distribution which was designed not only to achieve economies rapidly, but also to create the maximum sales impact from service improvements.

PERFORMANCE CONTROLS

Once the system was adopted, it was necessary to control operating performance. Management decided to:

Keep more complete records of back-order performance for each specific item.

Conduct regular audits to determine the lag in mail and order processing. (This was done by means of a sampling procedure similar to that used in industrial quality control.)

Audit delivery performance regularly, too. (Customer return cards were used to do this.)

Bring variations in delivery speed to the attention of the carriers—especially where products for institutional customers were concerned.

Establish a more detailed cost accounting system for distribution activities.

Prepare variance reports and review them regularly.

As a final check, make regular reviews of sales increases in different classes of trade.

Conclusion

The science of physical distribution management is now coming of age.

In its early days—in the mid-1950s—this science focused on the application of mathematics and computers to the design of physical distribution systems. While large dollar-savings opportunities were pinpointed, it was usually assumed that the status quo in the level of customer service would be maintained. Then, as work progressed, added attention was focused on questions of organization, cost reporting, and performance control.

However, until recently a quantitative, analytical approach has been lacking for the customer-service aspect of distribution. This has been an important deficiency. After all, customer service is the purpose and end result of a physical distribution system. There are clear opportunities for companies to move ahead in this area.

As we have emphasized in this article, customer service is not an intangible; each of its elements can be quantitatively expressed. Also, the approach to managing customer service is much the same as that required to determine product features. The six specific steps described can help companies to achieve meaningful cost reductions and profit improvements.

Perhaps of overriding importance is the fact that service goes far beyond the commonly recognized elements of physical distribution. In the customer's mind it involves every point of contact with the supplier—salesman's calls, order placement, engineering advice, shipping notification, processing of claims, the invoice itself, and other matters. All of these contacts produce service (or the lack of it). Service is a broad function, therefore, and management should take a broad approach to it.

PART
III

Execute with Quality

Introduction

This section emphasizes the interaction between product quality and service quality and the link between quality and profitability. Research has shown repeatedly that quality directly influences long-term profits and market share. For example, data from the Profit Impact of Market Strategy data base, which contains information from 450 companies on nearly 3,000 strategic business units, indicates that "in the long run, the most important single factor affecting a business unit's performance is the quality of its products and services relative to those of its competitors."[1] As we analyze quality, we find that there are two complementary links between quality and profits: (1) the external benefits of customer satisfaction, and (2) the internal benefits of improved production efficiency. On one level, product and service quality create a positive perception of the company, which leads to customer satisfaction, which in turn encourages customer longevity. As we see in other sections of this book (Part VI, for example) customer longevity contributes to profits by reducing customer-seeking costs and encouraging additional sales.

At the same time, however, a focus on quality delivers value internally by driving process improvements, such as tighter design and material control, more efficient use of raw materials, fewer reworks, and so on. Commitment to quality provides a framework for continuous improvement and learning that can have a substantial positive cumulative effect on efficiency, thereby lowering operating costs. The links among quality, efficiency, customer satisfaction, and profits are illustrated in Exhibit I.

The first article in this section, David Garvin's "Competing on the Eight Dimensions of Quality," argues that quality is more than a means to make a better product or service—it is a multifaceted

Exhibit I. The Benefits of Focusing on Quality

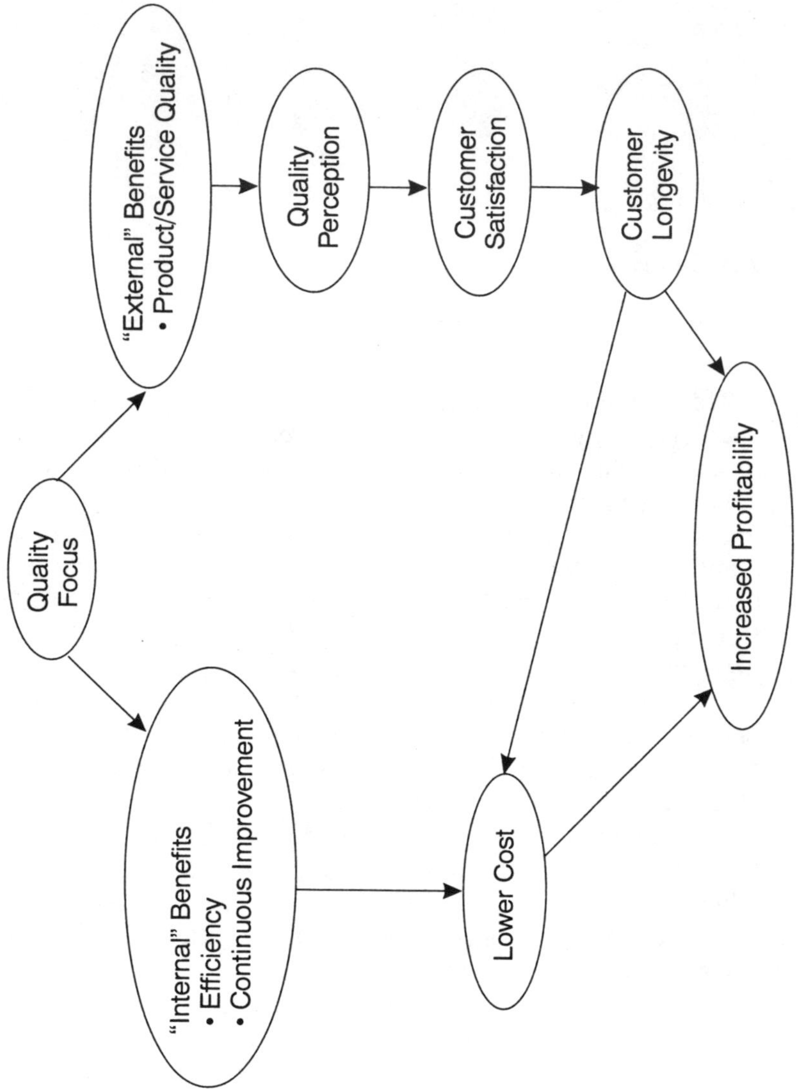

strategic weapon. Garvin contrasts today's need to compete on the basis of quality with the quality control movement of the 1950s and 1960s, which concentrated primarily on reducing product failures and monitoring design processes. Garvin argues that strategic quality management incorporates tangible product features, such as performance (a product's primary operating characteristics) and conformance (the degree to which it meets established standards), as well as intangible, more subjective features, such as aesthetics and the customers' perception of quality.

Strategic management of these quality dimensions depends on a company's ability to select a quality package that creates the best impression relative to costs. Reputation is largely a function of how customers perceive quality, regardless of a product's performance, reliability, or durability. For example, Honda and Sony have been reluctant to publicize that some of their products are manufactured in the United States because of the potential perception of lower quality. Recognizing which dimensions are important to the customer can help managers develop a competitive quality program.

The articles in this section suggest that quality is dynamic: corporate executives and consumers may have very different perceptions of quality and customer perceptions are influenced by different factors over time. In "Quality Is More Than Making a Good Product," Hirotaka Takeuchi and John Quelch argue that profitable quality management must take these changing customer perceptions into account. For example, the authors found that before purchase, the selling company's image and brand recognition are tremendously influential. At the point of purchase, performance specifications become central factors in the buying decision. After purchase, customers become increasingly concerned with service effectiveness. Given this dynamic context, the authors suggest that "quality should be primarily customer-driven, not technology-driven, production-driven, or competitor-driven." A manager who focuses exclusively on product quality will miss many opportunities to influence customer satisfaction and use quality competitively.

This attention to quality further develops the role for customer service as it was described in Part II. Customer service can be used as an intelligence mechanism to gather field data on current customer satisfaction, product performance, and changing market trends. In this way, customer service provides vital information that allows the company to make cost-effective and profitable enhancements and improvements to its products, services, and the processes for designing, producing, and delivering them.

The last article in this section, "The Power of Unconditional Service Guarantees," by Christopher Hart, provides a potent prescription for improving customer satisfaction and profits. The author argues that service providers should begin with a commitment to error-free service and design the organization to support it. A good service guarantee forces the seller to focus on customers' needs, sets performance standards, and provides valuable feedback from the market. In so doing, an unconditional guarantee is an investment in customer satisfaction and loyalty as well as in more efficient operations.

The article offers specific advice on how to craft a service guarantee that improves sales competitiveness without giving away the store. Guarantees with too many strings attached do not add value for the customer. At the same time, sellers must be willing to take some risk if they expect the costs of instituting and honoring a guarantee to result in longer-term profits and customer loyalty. A well-planned guarantee is a powerful source of competitive advantage: "one great potential of a service guarantee is its ability to change an industry's rules of the game by changing the service-delivery process as competitors conceive it." Although the examples in this article are taken primarily from service industries, the principles can be applied to the service components of product companies as well. With the increasing importance of service provision to support product sales, the potential is great for service guarantees to directly improve customer satisfaction and profitability in virtually every firm.

Note

1. Robert D. Buzzell and Bradley T. Gale, *The PIMS Principles: Linking Strategy to Performance* (New York: Free Press, 1987), p. 7.

1

Competing on the Eight Dimensions of Quality

David A. Garvin

U.S. managers know that they have to improve the quality of their products because, alas, U.S. consumers have told them so. A survey in 1981 reported that nearly 50% of U.S. consumers believed that the quality of U.S. products had dropped during the previous five years; more recent surveys have found that a quarter of consumers are "not at all" confident that U.S. industry can be depended on to deliver reliable products. Many companies have tried to upgrade their quality, adopting programs that have been staples of the quality movement for a generation: cost of quality calculations, interfunctional teams, reliability engineering, or statistical quality control. Few companies, however, have learned to *compete* on quality. Why?

Part of the problem, of course, is that until Japanese and European competition intensified, not many companies seriously tried to make quality programs work even as they implemented them. But even if companies *had* implemented the traditional principles of quality control more rigorously, it is doubtful that U.S. consumers would be satisfied today. In my view, most of those principles were narrow in scope; they were designed as purely defensive measures to preempt failures or eliminate "defects." What managers need now is an aggressive strategy to gain and hold markets, with high quality as a competitive linchpin.

Quality Control

To get a better grasp of the defensive character of traditional quality control, we should understand what the quality movement in the United States has achieved so far. How much expense on quality was tolerable? How much "quality" was enough? In 1951, Joseph Juran tackled these questions in the first edition of his *Quality Control Handbook*, a publication that became the quality movement's bible. Juran observed that quality could be understood in terms of avoidable and unavoidable costs: the former resulted from defects and product failures like scrapped materials or labor hours required for rework, repair, and complaint processing; the latter were associated with prevention, i.e., inspection, sampling, sorting, and other quality control initiatives. Juran regarded failure costs as "gold in the mine" because they could be reduced sharply by investing in quality improvement. He estimated that avoidable quality losses typically ranged from $500 to $1,000 per productive operator per year—big money back in the 1950s.

Reading Juran's book, executives inferred roughly how much to invest in quality improvement: expenditures on prevention were justified if they were lower than the costs of product failure. A corollary principle was that decisions made early in the production chain (e.g., when engineers first sketched out a product's design) have implications for the level of quality costs incurred later, both in the factory and the field.

In 1956, Armand Feigenbaum took Juran's ideas a step further by proposing "total quality control" (TQC). Companies would never make high-quality products, he argued, if the manufacturing department were forced to pursue quality in isolation. TQC called for "interfunctional teams" from marketing, engineering, purchasing, and manufacturing. These teams would share responsibility for all phases of design and manufacturing and would disband only when they had placed a product in the hands of a satisfied customer—who remained satisfied.

Feigenbaum noted that all new products moved through three stages of activity: design control, incoming material control, and product or shopfloor control. This was a step in the right direction. But Feigenbaum did not really consider how quality was first of all a strategic question for any business; how, for instance, quality might govern the development of a design and the choice of features or options. Rather, design control meant for Feigenbaum mainly preproduction assessments of a new design's manufacturability, or that projected manufacturing techniques should be debugged through pilot runs. Materials control included vendor evaluations and incoming inspection procedures.

In TQC, quality was a kind of burden to be shared—no single department shouldered all the responsibility. Top management was ultimately accountable for the effectiveness of the system; Feigenbaum, like Juran, proposed careful reporting of the costs of quality to senior executives in order to ensure their commitment. The two also stressed statistical approaches to quality, including process control charts that set limits to acceptable variations in key variables affecting a product's production. They endorsed sampling procedures that allowed managers to draw inferences about the quality of entire batches of products from the condition of items in a small, randomly selected sample.

Despite their attention to these techniques, Juran, Feigenbaum, and other experts like W. Edwards Deming were trying to get managers to see beyond purely statistical controls on quality. Meanwhile, another branch of the quality movement emerged, relying even more heavily on probability theory and statistics. This was "reliability engineering," which originated in the aerospace and electronics industries.

In 1950, only one-third of the U.S. Navy's electronic devices worked properly. A subsequent study by the Rand Corporation estimated that every vacuum tube the military used had to be backed by nine others in warehouses or on order. Reliability engineering addressed these problems by adapting the laws of probability to the challenge of predicting equipment stress.

Reliability engineering measures led to:

Techniques for reducing failure rates while products were still in the design stage.

Failure mode and effect analysis, which systematically reviewed how alternative designs could fail.

Individual component analysis, which computed the failure probability of key components and aimed to eliminate or strengthen the weakest links.

Derating, which required that parts be used below their specified stress levels.

Redundancy, which called for a parallel system to back up an important component or subsystem in case it failed.

Naturally, an effective reliability program required managers to monitor field failures closely to give company engineers the information needed to plan new designs. Effective field failure reporting also demanded the development of systems of data collection, including return of failed parts to the laboratory for testing and analysis.

Now, the proponents of all these approaches to quality control might well have denied that their views of quality were purely defensive. But what else was implied by the solutions they stressed—material controls, outgoing batch inspections, stress tests? Perhaps the best way to see the implications of their logic is in traditional quality control's most extreme form, a program called "Zero Defects." No other program defined quality so stringently as an absence of failures—and no wonder, since it emerged from the defense industries where the product was a missile whose flawless operation was, for obvious reasons, imperative.

In 1961, the Martin Company was building Pershing missiles for the U.S. Army. The design of the missile was sound, but Martin found that it could maintain high quality only through a massive program of inspection. It decided to offer workers incentives to lower the defect rate, and in December 1961, delivered a Pershing missile to Cape Canaveral with "zero discrepancies." Buoyed by this success, Martin's general manager in Orlando, Florida accepted a challenge, issued by the U.S. Army's missile command, to deliver the first field Pershing one month ahead of schedule. But he went even further. He promised that the missile would be perfect, with no hardware problems or document errors, and that all equipment would be fully operational 10 days after delivery (the norm was 90 days or more).

Two months of feverish activity followed; Martin asked all employees to contribute to building the missile exactly right the first time since there would be virtually no time for the usual inspections. Management worked hard to maintain enthusiasm on the plant floor. In February 1962, Martin delivered on time a perfect missile that was fully operational in less than 24 hours.

This experience was eye-opening for both Martin and the rest of the aerospace industry. After careful review, management concluded that, in effect, its own changed attitude had assured the project's success. In the words of one close observer: "The one time management demanded perfection, it happened!"[1] Martin management thereafter told employees that the only acceptable quality standard was "zero defects." It instilled this principle in the work force through training, special events, and by posting quality results. It set goals for workers and put great effort into giving each worker positive criticism. Formal techniques for problem solving, however, remained limited. For the most part, the program focused on motivation—on changing the attitudes of employees.

Strategic Quality Management

On the whole, U.S. corporations did not keep pace with quality control innovations the way a number of overseas competitors did. Particularly after World War II, U.S. corporations expanded rapidly and many became complacent. Managers knew that consumers wouldn't drive a VW Beetle, indestructible as it was, if they could afford a fancier car—even if this meant more visits to the repair shop.

But if U.S. car manufacturers *had* gotten their products to outlast Beetles, U.S. quality managers still would not have been prepared for Toyota Corollas—or Sony televisions. Indeed, there was nothing in the principles of quality control to disabuse them of the idea that quality was merely something that could hurt a company if ignored; that added quality was the designer's business—a matter, perhaps, of chrome and push buttons.

The beginnings of strategic quality management cannot be dated precisely because no single book or article marks its inception. But even more than in consumer electronics and cars, the volatile market in semiconductors provides a telling example of change. In March 1980, Richard W. Anderson, general manager of Hewlett-Packard's Data Systems Division, reported that after testing 300,000 16K RAM chips from three U.S. and three Japanese manufacturers, Hewlett-Packard had discovered wide disparities in quality. At incoming inspection, the Japanese chips had a failure rate of zero; the comparable rate for the three U.S. manufacturers was between 11 and 19 failures per 1,000. After 1,000 hours of use, the failure rate of the Japanese chips was between 1 and 2 per 1,000; usable U.S. chips failed up to 27 times per thousand.

Several U.S. semiconductor companies reacted to the news impulsively, complaining that the Japanese were sending only their best components to the all-important U.S. market. Others disputed the basic data. The most perceptive market analysts, however, noted how differences in quality coincided with the rapid ascendancy of Japanese chip manufacturers. In a few years the Japanese had gone from a standing start to significant market shares in both the 16K and 64K chip markets. Their message—intentional or not— was that quality could be a potent strategic weapon.

U.S. semiconductor manufacturers got the message. In 16K chips the quality gap soon closed. And in industries as diverse as machine tools and radial tires, each of which had seen its position erode in the face of Japanese competition, there has been a new seriousness about quality too. But how to translate seriousness into action? Managers who are now determined to compete on quality have been thrown back on the old questions: How much quality is enough? What does it take to look at quality from the customer's vantage point? These are still hard questions today.

To achieve quality gains, I believe, managers need a new way of thinking, a conceptual bridge to the consumer's vantage point. Obviously, market studies acquire a new importance in this context, as does a careful review of competitors' products. One thing is certain: high quality means pleasing consumers, not just protecting them from annoyances. Product designers, in turn, should shift their attention from prices at the time of purchase to life cycle costs that include expenditures on service and maintenance—the customer's total costs. Even consumer complaints play a new role because they provide a valuable source of product information.

But managers have to take a more preliminary step—a crucial one, however obvious it may appear. They must first develop a clear vocabulary with which to discuss quality as *strategy*. They must break down the word quality into manageable parts. Only then can they define the quality niches in which to compete.

I propose eight critical dimensions or categories of quality that can serve as a framework for strategic analysis: performance, features, reliability, conformance, durability, serviceability, aesthetics, and perceived quality.[2] Some of these are always mutually reinforcing; some are not. A product or service can rank high on one dimension of quality and low on another—indeed, an improvement in one may be achieved only at the expense of another. It is precisely this interplay that makes strategic quality management possible; the challenge to managers is to compete on selected dimensions.

PERFORMANCE

Of course, performance refers to a product's primary operating characteristics. For an automobile, performance would include traits like acceleration, handling, cruising speed, and comfort; for a television set, performance means sound and picture clarity, color, and the ability to receive distant stations. In service businesses—say, fast food and airlines—performance often means prompt service.

Because this dimension of quality involves measurable attributes, brands can usually be ranked objectively on individual aspects of performance. Overall performance rankings, however, are more difficult to develop, especially when they involve benefits that not every consumer needs. A power shovel with a capacity of 100 cubic yards per hour will "outperform" one with a capacity of 10 cubic yards per hour. Suppose, however, that the two shovels possessed the identical capacity—60 cubic yards per hour—but achieved it differently: one with a 1-cubic-yard bucket operating at 60 cycles per hour, the other with a 2-cubic-yard bucket operating at 30 cycles per hour. The capacities of the shovels would then be the same, but the shovel with the larger bucket could handle massive boulders while the shovel with the smaller bucket could perform precision work. The "superior performer" depends entirely on the task.

Some cosmetics wearers judge quality by a product's resistance to smudging; others, with more sensitive skin, assess it by how well it leaves skin irritation-free. A 100-watt light bulb provides greater candlepower than a 60-watt bulb, yet few customers would regard the difference as a measure of quality. The bulbs simply belong to different performance classes. So the question of whether performance differences are quality differences may depend on circumstantial preferences—but preferences based on functional requirements, not taste.

Some performance standards *are* based on subjective preferences, but the preferences are so universal that they have the force of an objective standard. The quietness of an automobile's ride is usually viewed as a direct reflection of its quality. Some people like a dimmer room, but who wants a noisy car?

FEATURES

Similar thinking can be applied to features, a second dimension of quality that is often a secondary aspect of performance. Features are the "bells and whistles" of products and services, those characteristics that supplement their basic functioning. Examples include free drinks on a plane, permanent-press cycles on a washing machine, and automatic tuners on a color television set. The line separating primary performance characteristics from secondary features is often difficult to draw. What is crucial, again, is that features involve objective and measurable attributes; objective individual needs, not prejudices, affect their translation into quality differences.

To many customers, of course, superior quality is less a reflection of the availability of particular features than of the total number of options available. Often, choice is quality: buyers may wish to customize or personalize their purchases. Fidelity Investments and other mutual fund operators have pursued this more "flexible" approach. By offering their clients a wide range of funds covering such diverse fields as health care, technology, and energy—and by then encouraging clients to shift savings among these—they have virtually tailored investment portfolios.

Employing the latest in flexible manufacturing technology, Allen-Bradley customizes starter motors for its buyers without having to price its products prohibitively. Fine furniture stores offer their customers countless variations in fabric and color. Such strategies impose heavy demands on operating managers; they are an aspect of quality likely to grow in importance with the perfection of flexible manufacturing technology.

RELIABILITY

This dimension reflects the probability of a product malfunctioning or failing within a specified time period. Among the most common measures of reliability are the mean time to first failure, the mean time between failures, and the failure rate per unit time. Because these measures require a product to be in use for a specified period, they are more relevant to durable goods than to products and services that are consumed instantly.

Reliability normally becomes more important to consumers as downtime and maintenance become more expensive. Farmers, for example, are especially sensitive to downtime during the short harvest season. Reliable equipment can mean the difference between a good year and spoiled crops. But consumers in other markets are more attuned than ever to product reliability too. Computers and copying machines certainly compete on this basis. And recent market research shows that, especially for young women, reliability has become an automobile's most desired attribute. Nor is the government, our biggest single consumer, immune. After seeing its expenditures for major weapons repair jump from $7.4 billion in fiscal year 1980 to $14.9 billion in fiscal year 1985, the Department of Defense has begun cracking down on contractors whose weapons fail frequently in the field.

CONFORMANCE

A related dimension of quality is conformance, or the degree to which a product's design and operating characteristics meet established standards. This dimension owes the most to the traditional approaches to quality pioneered by experts like Juran.

All products and services involve specifications of some sort. When new designs or models are developed, dimensions are set for parts and purity standards for materials. These specifications are normally expressed as a target or "center"; deviance from the center is permitted within a specified range. Because this approach to conformance equates good quality with operating inside a tolerance band, there is little interest in whether specifications have been met exactly. For the most part, dispersion within specification limits is ignored.

One drawback of this approach is the problem of "tolerance stack-up": when two or more parts are to be fit together, the size of their tolerances often determines how well they will match. Should one part fall at a lower limit of its specification, and a matching part at its upper limit, a tight fit is unlikely. Even if the parts are rated acceptable initially, the link between them is likely to wear more quickly than one made from parts whose dimensions have been centered more exactly.

To address this problem, a more imaginative approach to conformance has emerged. It is closely associated with Japanese manufacturers and the work of Genichi Taguchi, a prizewinning Japanese statistician. Taguchi begins with the idea of "loss function," a measure of losses from the time a product is shipped. (These losses include warranty costs, nonrepeating customers, and other problems resulting from performance failure.) Taguchi then compares such losses to two alternative approaches to quality: on the one hand, simple conformance to specifications, and on the other, a measure of the degree to which parts or products diverge from the ideal target or center.

He demonstrates that "tolerance stack-up" will be worse—more costly—when the dimensions of parts are more distant from the center than when they cluster around it, even if some parts fall outside the tolerance band entirely. According to Taguchi's approach, production process 1 in Exhibit I is better even though some items fall beyond specification limits. Traditional approaches favor production process 2. The challenge for quality managers is obvious.

Incidentally, the two most common measures of failure in conformance—for Taguchi and everyone else—are defect rates in the factory and, once a product is in the hands of the customer, the incidence of service calls. But these measures neglect other deviations from standard, like misspelled labels or shoddy construction, that do not lead to service or repair. In service businesses, measures of conformance normally focus on accuracy and timeliness and include counts of processing errors, unanticipated delays, and other frequent mistakes.

DURABILITY

A measure of product life, durability has both economic and technical dimensions. Technically, durability can be defined as the amount of use one gets from a product before it deteriorates. After so many hours of use, the filament of a light bulb burns up and the bulb must be replaced. Repair is impossible. Economists call such products "one-hoss shays" (after the carriage in the Oliver Wendell Holmes poem that was designed by the deacon to last a

Exhibit I. Two Approaches to Conformance

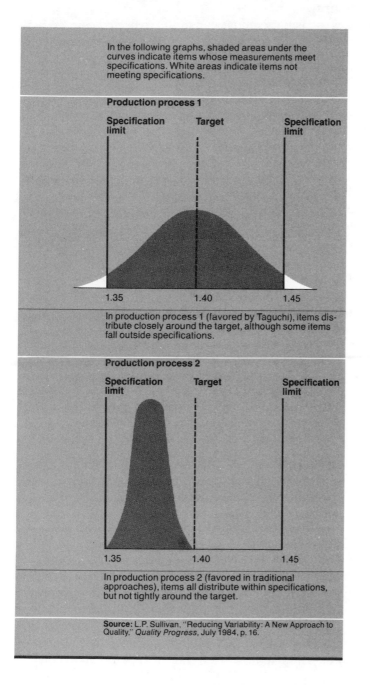

In the following graphs, shaded areas under the curves indicate items whose measurements meet specifications. White areas indicate items not meeting specifications.

Production process 1

Specification limit   Target   Specification limit

1.35   1.40   1.45

In production process 1 (favored by Taguchi), items distribute closely around the target, although some items fall outside specifications.

Production process 2

Specification limit   Target   Specification limit

1.35   1.40   1.45

In production process 2 (favored in traditional approaches), items all distribute within specifications, but not tightly around the target.

Source: L.P. Sullivan, "Reducing Variability: A New Approach to Quality," *Quality Progress*, July 1984, p. 16.

hundred years, and whose parts broke down simultaneously at the end of the century).

In other cases, consumers must weigh the expected cost, in both dollars and personal inconvenience, of future repairs against the investment and operating expenses of a newer, more reliable model. Durability, then, may be defined as the amount of use one gets from a product before it breaks down and replacement is preferable to continued repair.

This approach to durability has two important implications. First, it suggests that durability and reliability are closely linked. A product that often fails is likely to be scrapped earlier than one that is more reliable; repair costs will be correspondingly higher and the purchase of a competitive brand will look that much more desirable. Because of this linkage, companies sometimes try to reassure customers by offering lifetime guarantees on their products, as 3M has done with its videocassettes. Second, this approach implies that durability figures should be interpreted with care. An increase in product life may not be the result of technical improvements or the use of longer-lived materials. Rather, the underlying economic environment simply may have changed.

For example, the expected life of an automobile rose during the last decade—it now averages 14 years—mainly because rising gasoline prices and a weak economy reduced the average number of miles driven per year. Still, durability varies widely among brands. In 1981, estimated product lives for major home appliances ranged from 9.9 years (Westinghouse) to 13.2 years (Frigidaire) for refrigerators, 5.8 years (Gibson) to 18 years (Maytag) for clothes washers, 6.6 years (Montgomery Ward) to 13.5 years (Maytag) for dryers, and 6 years (Sears) to 17 years (Kirby) for vacuum cleaners.[3] This wide dispersion suggests that durability is a potentially fertile area for further quality differentiation.

SERVICEABILITY

A sixth dimension of quality is serviceability, or the speed, courtesy, competence, and ease of repair. Consumers are concerned not only about a product breaking down but also about the time before service is restored, the timeliness with which service appointments are kept, the nature of dealings with service personnel, and the frequency with which service calls or repairs fail to correct outstanding problems. In those cases where problems are not immediately resolved and complaints are filed, a company's complaint-handling procedures are also likely to affect customers' ultimate evaluation of product and service quality.

Some of these variables reflect differing personal standards of acceptable service. Others can be measured quite objectively. Responsiveness is typically measured by the mean time to repair, while technical competence is reflected in the incidence of multiple service calls required to correct a particular problem. Because most consumers equate rapid repair and reduced downtime with higher quality, these elements of serviceability are less subject to personal interpretation than are those involving evaluations of courtesy or standards of professional behavior.

Even reactions to downtime, however, can be quite complex. In certain environments, rapid response becomes critical only after certain thresholds have been reached. During harvest season, farmers generally accept downtime of one to six hours on harvesting equipment, such as combines, with little resistance. As downtime increases, they become anxious; beyond eight hours of downtime they become frantic and frequently go to great lengths to continue harvesting even if it means purchasing or leasing additional equipment. In markets like this, superior service can be a powerful selling tool. Caterpillar guarantees delivery of repair parts anywhere in the world within 48 hours; a competitor offers the free loan of farm equipment during critical periods should its customers' machines break down.

Customers may remain dissatisfied even after completion of repairs. How these complaints are handled is important to a company's reputation for quality and service. Eventually, profitability is likely to be affected as well. A 1976 consumer survey found that among households that initiated complaints to resolve problems, more than 40% were not satisfied with the results. Understandably, the degree of satisfaction with complaint resolution closely correlated with consumers' willingness to repurchase the offending brands.[4]

Companies differ widely in their approaches to complaint handling and in the importance they attach to this element of serviceability. Some do their best to resolve complaints; others use legal gimmicks, the silent treatment, and similar ploys to rebuff dissatisfied customers. Recently, General Electric, Pillsbury, Procter & Gamble, Polaroid, Whirlpool, Johnson & Johnson, and other com-

panies have sought to preempt consumer dissatisfaction by installing toll-free telephone hot lines to their customer relations
departments.

AESTHETICS

The final two dimensions of quality are the most subjective.
Aesthetics—how a product looks, feels, sounds, tastes, or smells—
is clearly a matter of personal judgment and a reflection of individual preference. Nevertheless, there appear to be some patterns
in consumers' rankings of products on the basis of taste. A recent
study of quality in 33 food categories, for example, found that high
quality was most often associated with "rich and full flavor, tastes
natural, tastes fresh, good aroma, and looks appetizing."[5]

The aesthetics dimension differs from subjective criteria pertain-
ing to "performance"—the quiet car engine, say—in that aesthetic
choices are not nearly universal. Not all people prefer "rich and
full" flavor or even agree on what it means. Companies therefore
have to search for a niche. On this dimension of quality, it is
impossible to please everyone.

PERCEIVED QUALITY

Consumers do not always have complete information about a
product's or service's attributes; indirect measures may be their
only basis for comparing brands. A product's durability, for example, can seldom be observed directly; it usually must be inferred
from various tangible and intangible aspects of the product. In such
circumstances, images, advertising, and brand names—inferences
about quality rather than the reality itself—can be critical. For this
reason, both Honda—which makes cars in Marysville, Ohio—and
Sony—which builds color televisions in San Diego—have been reluctant to publicize that their products are "made in America."

Reputation is the primary stuff of perceived quality. Its power
comes from an unstated analogy: that the quality of products today
is similar to the quality of products yesterday, or the quality of
goods in a new product line is similar to the quality of a company's
established products. In the early 1980s, Maytag introduced a new
line of dishwashers. Needless to say, salespeople immediately em-

phasized the product's reliability—not yet proven—because of the reputation of Maytag's clothes washers and dryers.

Competing on Quality

This completes the list of the eight dimensions of quality. The most traditional notions—conformance and reliability—remain important, but they are subsumed within a broader strategic framework. A company's first challenge is to use this framework to explore the opportunities it has to distinguish its products from another company's wares.

The quality of an automobile tire may reflect its tread-wear rate, handling, traction in dangerous driving conditions, rolling resistance (i.e., impact on gas mileage), noise levels, resistance to punctures, or appearance. High-quality furniture may be distinguished by its uniform finish, an absence of surface flaws, reinforced frames, comfort, or superior design.

Even the quality of a less tangible product like computer software can be evaluated in multiple dimensions. These dimensions include reliability, ease of maintenance, match with users' needs, integrity (the extent to which unauthorized access can be controlled), and portability (the ease with which a program can be transferred from one hardware or software environment to another).

A company need not pursue all eight dimensions simultaneously. In fact, that is seldom possible unless it intends to charge unreasonably high prices. Technological limitations may impose a further constraint. In some cases, a product or service can be improved in one dimension of quality only if it becomes worse in another. Cray Research, a manufacturer of supercomputers, has faced particularly difficult choices of this sort. According to the company's chairman, if a supercomputer doesn't fail every month or so, it probably wasn't built for maximum speed; in pursuit of higher speed, Cray has deliberately sacrificed reliability.

There are other trade-offs. Consider the following:

In entering U.S. markets, Japanese manufacturers often emphasize their products' reliability and conformance while downplaying options and features. The superior "fits and finishes" and low repair rates of Japanese cars are well known; less often recognized are their poor safety records and low resistance to corrosion.

Tandem Computers has based its business on superior reliability. For computer users that find downtime intolerable, like telephone companies and utilities, Tandem has devised a fail-safe system: two processors working in parallel and linked by software that shifts responsibility between the two if an important component or subsystem fails. The result, in an industry already well known for quality products, has been spectacular corporate growth. In 1984, after less than 10 years in business, Tandem's annual sales topped $500 million.

Not long ago, New York's Chemical Bank upgraded its services for collecting payments for corporations. Managers had first conducted a user survey indicating that what customers wanted most was rapid response to queries about account status. After it installed a computerized system to answer customers' calls, Chemical, which banking consumers had ranked fourth in quality in the industry, jumped to first.

In the piano business, Steinway & Sons has long been the quality leader. Its instruments are known for their even voicing (the evenness of character and timbre in each of the 88 notes on the keyboard), the sweetness of their registers, the duration of their tone, their long lives, and even their fine cabinet work. Each piano is built by hand and is distinctive in sound and style. Despite these advantages, Steinway recently has been challenged by Yamaha, a Japanese manufacturer that has built a strong reputation for quality in a relatively short time. Yamaha has done so by emphasizing reliability and conformance, two quality dimensions that are low on Steinway's list.

These examples confirm that companies can pursue a selective quality niche. In fact, they may have no other choice, especially if competitors have established reputations for a certain kind of excellence. Few products rank high on all eight dimensions of quality. Those that do—Cross pens, Rolex watches, Rolls-Royce automobiles—require consumers to pay the cost of skilled workmanship.

STRATEGIC ERRORS

A final word, not about strategic opportunities, but about the worst strategic mistakes. The first is direct confrontation with an industry's leader. As with Yamaha vs. Steinway, it is far preferable to nullify the leader's advantage in a particular niche while avoiding the risk of retaliation. Moreover, a common error is to introduce dimensions of quality that are unimportant to consumers. When deregulation unlocked the market for residential telephones, a number of manufacturers, including AT&T, assumed that customers equated quality with a wide range of expensive features. They were soon proven wrong. Fancy telephones sold poorly while durable, reliable, and easy-to-operate sets gained large market shares.

Shoddy market research often results in neglect of quality dimensions that *are* critical to consumers. Using outdated surveys, car companies overlooked how important reliability and conformance were becoming in the 1970s; ironically, these companies failed consumers on the very dimensions that were key targets of traditional approaches to quality control.

It is often a mistake to stick with old quality measures when the external environment has changed. A major telecommunications company had always evaluated its quality by measuring timeliness—the amount of time it took to provide a dial tone, to connect a call, or to be connected to an operator. On these measures it performed well. More sophisticated market surveys, conducted in anticipation of the industry's deregulation, found that consumers were not really concerned about call connection time; consumers assumed that this would be more or less acceptable. They were more concerned with the clarity of transmission and the degree of static on the line. On these measures, the company found it was well behind its competitors.

In an industry like semiconductor manufacturing equipment, Japanese machines generally require less set-up time; they break down less often and have few problems meeting their specified performance levels. These are precisely the traits desired by most buyers. Still, U.S. equipment can *do* more. As one U.S. plant manager put it: "Our equipment is more advanced, but Japanese equipment is more developed."

Quality measures may be inadequate in less obvious ways. Some measures are too limited; they fail to capture aspects of quality that are important for competitive success. Singapore International Airlines, a carrier with a reputation for excellent service, saw its market share decline in the early 1980s. The company dismissed quality problems as the cause of its difficulties because data on service complaints showed steady improvement during the period. Only later, after SIA solicited consumer responses, did managers see the weakness of their former measures. Relative declines in service had indeed been responsible for the loss of market share. Complaint counts had failed to register problems because the proportion of passengers who wrote complaint letters was small—they were primarily Europeans and U.S. citizens rather than Asians, the largest percentage of SIA passengers. SIA also had failed to capture data about its competitors' service improvements.

The pervasiveness of these errors is difficult to determine. Anecdotal evidence suggests that many U.S. companies lack hard data and are thus more vulnerable than they need be. One survey found that 65% of executives thought that consumers could readily name—without help—a good quality brand in a big-ticket category like major home appliances. But when the question was actually posed to consumers, only 16% could name a brand for small appliances, and only 23% for large appliances.[6] Are U.S. executives that ill-informed about consumers' perceptions? The answer is not likely to be reassuring.

Managers have to stop thinking about quality merely as a narrow effort to gain control of the production process, and start thinking more rigorously about consumers' needs and preferences. Quality is not simply a problem to be solved; it is a competitive opportunity.

Notes

1. James F. Halpin, *Zero Defects* (New York: McGraw-Hill, 1966), p. 15.
2. This framework first appeared, in a preliminary form, in my article "What Does 'Product Quality' Really Mean?" *Sloan Management Review*, Fall 1984.
3. Roger B. Yepsen, Jr., ed., *The Durability Factor* (Emmaus, Penn: Rodale Press, 1982), p. 190.
4. TARP, *Consumer Complaint Handling in America: Final Report* (Springfield, Va.: National Technical Information Service, U.S. Department of Commerce, 1979).
5. P. Greg Bonner and Richard Nelson, "Product Attributes and Perceived Quality: Foods," in *Perceived Quality*, eds. Jacob Jacoby and Jerry C. Olson (Lexington, Mass.: Lexington Books, D.C. Heath, 1985), p. 71.
6. Consumer Network, Inc., *Brand Quality Perceptions* (Philadelphia: Consumer Network, August 1983), pp. 17 and 50–51.

2
Quality Is More Than Making a Good Product

Hirotaka Takeuchi and John A. Quelch

Corporate executives and consumers have in recent years adopted divergent views of product quality. Several recent surveys indicate how wide the quality perception gap is:

> Three out of five chief executives of the country's largest 1,300 companies said in a 1981 survey that quality is improving; only 13% said it is declining.[1] Yet 49% of 7,000 consumers surveyed in a separate 1981 study said that the quality of U.S. products had declined in the past five years. In addition, 59% expected quality to stay down or decline further in the upcoming five years.[2]

> Half the executives of major American appliance manufacturers said in a 1981 survey that the reliability of their products had improved in recent years. Only 21% of U.S. consumers expressed that belief.[3]

> Executives of U.S. auto manufacturers cite internal records that show quality to be improving each year. "Ford quality improved by 27% in our 1981 models over 1980 models," said a Ford executive.[4] But surveys show that consumers perceive the quality of U.S. cars to be declining in comparison with imported cars, particularly those from Japan.

Mindful of this gap, many U.S. companies have turned to promotional tactics to improve their quality image. Such efforts are evident in two trends. The first is the greater emphasis advertisements place on the word *quality* and on such themes as reliability, durability, and workmanship. Ford, for instance, advertises that "quality is job one," and Levi Strauss proffers the notion that "quality never goes out of style." And many ads now claim that products are "the best" or "better than" competitors'.

The second trend is the move to quality assurance and extended service programs. Chrysler offers a five-year, 50,000 mile warranty; Whirlpool Corporation promises that parts for all models will be available for 15 years; Hewlett-Packard gives customers a 99% up-time service guarantee on its computers; and Mercedes-Benz makes technicians available for roadside assistance after normal dealer service hours.

While these attempts to change customer perceptions are a step in the right direction, a company's or a product's quality image obviously cannot be improved overnight. It takes time to cultivate customer confidence, and promotional tactics alone will not do the job. In fact, they can backfire if the claims and promises do not hold up and customers perceive them as gimmicks.

To ensure delivery of advertising claims, companies must build quality into their products or services. From a production perspective, this means a companywide commitment to eliminate errors at every stage of the product development process—product design, process design, and manufacturing. It also means working closely with suppliers to eliminate defects from all incoming parts.

Equally important yet often overlooked are the marketing aspects of quality-improvement programs. Companies must be sure they are offering the benefits customers seek. Quality should be primarily customer-driven, not technology-driven, production-driven, or competitor-driven.

In developing product quality programs, companies often fail to take into account two basic sets of questions. First, how do customers define quality, and why are they suddenly demanding higher quality than in the past? Second, how important is high quality in customer service, and how can it be ensured after the sale?

As mundane as these questions may sound, the answers provide essential information on how to build an effective customer-driven quality program. We should not forget that customers, after all, serve as the ultimate judge of quality in the marketplace.

The Production-Service Connection

Product performance and customer service are closely linked in any quality program; the greater the attention to product quality in production, the fewer the demands on the customer service operation to correct subsequent problems. Office equipment manufacturers, for example, are designing products to have fewer manual and more automatic controls. Not only are the products easier to operate and less susceptible to misuse but they also require little maintenance and have internal troubleshooting systems to aid in problem identification. The up-front investment in quality minimizes the need for customer service.

Besides its usual functions, customer service can act as an early warning system to detect product quality problems. Customer surveys measuring product performance can also help spot quality control or design difficulties. And of course detecting defects early spares later embarrassment and headaches.

QUALITY-IMPROVEMENT SUCCESSES

It is relevant at this point to consider two companies that have developed successful customer-driven quality programs: L.L. Bean, Inc. and Caterpillar Tractor Company. Although these two companies are in different businesses—L.L. Bean sells outdoor apparel and equipment primarily through mail-order while Caterpillar manufactures earth-moving equipment, diesel engines, and materials-handling devices, which it sells through dealers—both enjoy an enviable reputation for high quality.

Some 96.7% of 3,000 customers L.L. Bean recently surveyed said that quality is the attribute they like most about the company. Bean executes a customer-driven quality program by:

Conducting regular customer satisfaction surveys and sample group interviews to track customer and noncustomer perceptions of the quality of its own and its competitors' products and services.

Tracking on its computer all customer inquiries and complaints and updating the file daily.

Guaranteeing all its products to be 100% satisfactory and providing a full cash refund, if requested, on any returns.

Asking customers to fill out a short, coded questionnaire and explain their reasons for returning the merchandise.

Performing extensive field tests on any new outdoor equipment before listing it in the company's catalogs.

Even stocking extra buttons for most of the apparel items carried years ago, just in case a customer needs one.

Despite recent financial setbacks, Caterpillar continues to be fully committed to sticking with its quality program, which includes:

Conducting two customer satisfaction surveys following each purchase, one after 300 hours of product use and the second after 500 hours of use.

Maintaining a centrally managed list of product problems as identified by customers from around the world.

Analyzing warranty and service reports submitted by dealers, as part of a product improvement program.

Asking dealers to conduct a quality audit as soon as the products are received and to attribute defects to either assembly errors or shipping damages.

Guaranteeing 48-hour delivery of any part to any customer in the world.

Encouraging dealers to establish side businesses in rebuilding parts to reduce costs and increase the speed of repairs.

How Do Customers Define Quality?

To understand how customers perceive quality, both L.L. Bean and Caterpillar collect much information directly from them. Even with such information, though, pinpointing what consumers *really* want is no simple task. For one thing, consumers cannot always articulate their quality requirements. They often speak in generalities, complaining, for instance, that they bought "a lemon" or that manufacturers "don't make 'em like they used to."

Consumers' priorities and perceptions also change over time. Taking automobiles as an example, market data compiled by SRI International suggest that consumer priorities shifted from styling in 1970 to fuel economy in 1975 and then to quality of design and performance in 1980.[5] (See Exhibit I.)

In addition, consumers perceive a product's quality relative to competing products. As John F. Welch, chairman and chief executive of General Electric Company, observed, "The customer . . . rates us better or worse than somebody else. It's not very scientific, but it's disastrous if you score low."[6]

Exhibit I.   *Changes in the Importance to Customers of U.S. Automobile Characteristics*

	1970	1975	1980
1	Styling	Fuel economy	Quality
2	Value for money	Styling	How well-made
3	Ease of handling and driving	Prior experience with the make	Fuel economy
4	Fuel economy	Size and weight	Value for money
5	Riding comfort	Ease of handling and driving	Riding comfort

One of the major problems facing U.S. automobile manufacturers is the public perception that imported cars, particularly those from Japan, are of higher quality. When a 1981 *New York Times*–CBS News poll asked consumers if they thought that Japanese-made cars are usually better quality than those made here, about the same, or not as good, 34% answered better, 30% said the same, 22% said not as good, and 14% did not know. When the Roper Organization asked the same question in 1977, only 18% said better, 30% said the same, 32% said not as good, and 20% did not know.[7]

Further, consumers are demanding high quality at low prices. When a national panel of shoppers was asked where it would like to see food manufacturers invest more, the highest-rated response was "better quality for the same price."[8] In search of such value, some consumers are even chartering buses to Cohoes Manufacturing Company, an apparel specialty store located in Cohoes, New York that has a reputation for offering high-quality, designer-label merchandise at discount prices.

Consumers' perceptions of product quality are influenced by various factors at each stage of the buying process. Some of the major influences are listed in Exhibit II.

WATCHING FOR KEY TRENDS

What should companies do to improve their understanding of customers' perspectives on quality? We know of no other way than

Exhibit II.   Factors Influencing Consumer Perception of Quality*

Before purchase	At point of purchase	After purchase
Company's brand name and image	Performance specifications	Ease of installation and use
Previous experience	Comments of salespeople	Handling of repairs, claims, warranty
Opinions of friends	Warranty provisions	Spare parts availability
Store reputation	Service and repair policies	Service effectiveness
Published test results	Support programs	Reliability
Advertised price for performance	Quoted price for performance	Comparative performance

*Not necessarily in order of importance.

to collect and analyze internal data and to monitor publicly available information.

Internally generated information is obtained principally through customer surveys, interviews of potential customers (such as focus group interviews), reports from salespeople, and field experiments. Recall how L.L. Bean and Caterpillar use these approaches to obtain data on how their current and potential customers rate their products' quality versus those of competitors'.

Publicly available information of a more general nature can be obtained through pollsters, independent research organizations, government agencies, and the news media. Such sources are often helpful in identifying shifts in societal attitudes.

Companies that try to define their customers' attitudes on product and service quality often focus too narrowly on the meaning of quality for their products and services; an understanding of changing attitudes in the broader marketplace can be equally valuable.

Toward the end of the last decade, too many U.S. companies failed to observe that the optimism of the mid-1970s was increasingly giving way to a mood of pessimism and restraint because of deteriorating economic conditions. Several polls taken during the 1970s indicated the nature and extent of this shift;[9] for instance,

Gallup polls showed that while only 21% of Americans in the early 1970s believed "next year will be worse than this year," 55% held this pessimistic outlook by the end of the 1970s.

Pessimistic about what the future held, consumers began adjusting their life-styles. The unrestrained desire during the mid-1970s to buy and own more gave way to more restrained behavior, such as "integrity" buying, "investment" buying, and "life-cycle" buying.

Integrity purchases are those made for their perceived importance to society rather than solely for personal status. Buying a small, energy-efficient automobile, for example, can be a sign of personal integrity. Investment buying is geared toward long-lasting products, even if that means paying a little more. The emphasis is on such values as durability, reliability, craftsmanship, and longevity. In the apparel business, for example, more manufacturers have begun stressing the investment value of clothing. And life-cycle buying entails comparing the cost of buying with the cost of owning. For example, some might see a $10 light bulb, which uses one-third as much electricity and lasts four times as long as a $1 conventional light bulb, as the better deal.

These changes in buying behavior reflect the pessimistic outlook of consumers and their growing emphasis on quality rather than quantity: "If we're going to buy less, let it be better."

By overlooking this fundamental shift in consumer attitudes, companies missed the opportunity to capitalize on it. If they had monitored the information available, managers could have identified and responded to the trends earlier.

Ensuring Quality after the Sale

As we suggested earlier, the quality of customer service after the sale is often as important as the quality of the product itself. Of course, excellent customer service can rarely compensate for a weak product. But poor customer service can quickly negate all the advantages associated with delivering a product of superior quality.

At companies like L.L. Bean and Caterpillar, customer service is not an afterthought but an integral part of the product offering and is subject to the same quality standards as the production process. These companies realize that a top-notch customer service operation can be an effective means of accomplishing the following three objectives:

1. *Differentiating a company from competitors.* As more customers seek to extend the lives of their durable goods, the perceived quality of customer service becomes an increasingly important factor in the purchase decision. Whirlpool Corporation promises to stand by its products rather than hide behind its distribution channels; it has parlayed a reputation for effective customer service into a distinct competitive advantage that reinforces its image of quality.

2. *Generating new sales leads and discouraging switches to alternative suppliers.* Keeping in regular contact with customers so as to deliver new information to them and gather suggestions for product improvements can ensure the continued satisfaction of existing customers and improve the chances of meeting the needs of potential purchasers.

3. *Reinforcing dealer loyalty.* Companies with strong customer service programs can also broaden their distribution channels more easily to include outlets that may not be able to deliver high levels of postpurchase customer service on their own.

THE CUSTOMER SERVICE AUDIT

To be effective, a customer service operation requires a marketing plan. Customer services should be viewed as a product line that must be packaged, priced, communicated, and delivered to customers. An evaluation of a company's current customer service operation—a customer service audit—is essential to the development of such a plan. A customer service audit asks managers the following questions:

What are your customer service objectives? Many companies have not established objectives for their customer service operations and have no concept of the role customer service should play in their business and marketing strategies. Every company should know what percentage of its revenue stream it expects to derive from service sales and whether the goal is to make a profit, break even, or—for reasons of competitive advantage—sustain a loss.

What services do you provide? It is useful to develop a grid showing which services your company provides or could provide for each of the products in your line. These might include customer education, financing arrangements, order confirmation and tracing, predelivery preparation, spare-parts inventory, repair service, and claims and complaints handling.

How do you compare with the competition? A similar grid can be used to chart the customer services your competitors provide. Through customer surveys, you can identify those areas of customer service in which your company rates higher or lower than the competition. In areas where your company is weak, can you invest to improve your performance? Where you are strong, how easy is it for competitors to match or exceed your performance?

What services do your customers want? There is little value in developing superior performance in areas of customer service most customers consider only marginally important. An essential ingredient of the audit is, therefore, to understand the relative importance of various customer services to current and potential customers. Distinct customer segments can often be identified according to the priorities they attach to particular services.

What are your customers' service demand patterns? The level and nature of customer service needed often change over the product's life. Services that are top priority at the time of sale may be less important five years later. Companies must understand the patterns and timing of demand for customer services on each of their products. These they can graph, as Exhibit III shows.

Product A in the exhibit is a security control system, an electronics product with few moving parts. A high level of service is needed immediately following installation to train operators and debug the system. Thereafter, the need for service quickly drops to only periodic replacement of mechanical parts, such as frequently used door switches.

Product B is an automobile. Service requirements are significant during the warranty period because of customer sensitivity to any aesthetic and functional defects and also because repairs are free (to the customer). After the warranty period, however, service requirements beyond basic maintenance will be more extensive for B than for A, since there are more mechanical parts to wear out.

What trade-offs are your customers prepared to make? Excellent service can always be extended—at a price. You should know the costs to your company of providing assorted customer services through various delivery systems (an 800 telephone number, a

*Exhibit III. Postpurchase Service Demands
for Two Products*

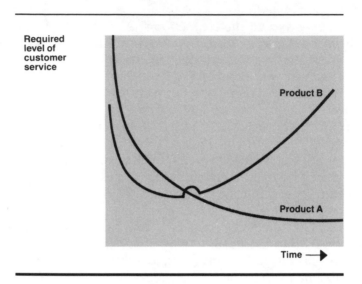

Required
level of
customer
service

Product B

Product A

Time ⟶

customer service agent, a salesperson) at different levels of performance efficiency. At the same time, you should establish what value your customers place on varying levels of customer service, what level of service quality they are prepared to pay for, and whether they prefer to pay for services separately or as part of the product purchase price.

Customers are likely to differ widely in price sensitivity. A printing press manufacturer, for example, has found that daily newspaper publishers, because of the time sensitivity of their product, are willing to pay a high price for immediate repair service, whereas book publishers, being less time pressured, can afford to be more price conscious.

The Customer Service Program

The success of the marketing program will depend as much on effective implementation as on sound analysis and research. After reviewing several customer service operations in a variety of industries, we believe that managers should concentrate on the following seven guidelines for effective program implementation:

1. *Educate your customers*. Customers must be taught both how to use and how not to use a product. And through appropriate training programs, companies can reduce the chances of calls for highly trained service personnel to solve simple problems. General Electric recently established a network of product education centers that purchasers of GE appliances can call toll free. Many consumer problems during the warranty period can be handled at a cost of $5 per call rather than the $30 to $50 cost for a service technician to visit a consumer's home.

2. *Educate your employees*. In many organizations, employees view the customer with a problem as an annoyance rather than as a source of information. A marketing program is often needed to change such negative attitudes and to convince employees not only that customers are the ultimate judge of quality but also that their criticisms should be respected and acted on immediately. The internal marketing program should incorporate detailed procedures to guide customer-employee interactions.

3. *Be efficient first, nice second*. Given the choice, most customers would rather have efficient resolution of their problem than a smiling face. The two, of course, are not mutually exclusive, but no company should hesitate to centralize its customer service operation in the interests of efficiency. Federal Express, for example, recently centralized its customer service function to improve quality control of customer-employee interactions, to more easily monitor customer service performance, and to enable field personnel to concentrate on operations and selling. The fear that channeling all calls through three national centers would depersonalize service and annoy customers used to dealing with a field office sales representative proved unwarranted.

4. *Standardize service response systems*. A standard response mechanism is essential for handling inquiries and complaints. L.L. Bean has a standard form that customer service personnel use to cover all telephone inquiries and complaints. As noted earlier, the documented information is immediately fed into a computer and updated daily to expedite followthrough. In addition, most companies should establish a response system to handle customer problems in which technically sophisticated people are called in on problems not solved within specific time periods by lower-level employees.

5. *Develop a pricing policy.* Quality customer service does not necessarily mean free service. Many customers even prefer to pay for service beyond a minimum level. This is why long warranty periods often have limited appeal; customers recognize that product prices must rise to cover extra warranty costs, which may principally benefit those customers who misuse the product.[10] More important to success than free service is the development of pricing policies and multiple-option service contracts that customers view as equitable and easy to understand.

Because a separate market exists for postsale service in many product categories, running the customer service operation as a profit center is increasingly common. But the philosophy of "selling the product cheap and making money on the service" is likely to be self-defeating over the long term, since it implicitly encourages poor product quality.

6. *Involve subcontractors, if necessary.* To ensure quality, most companies prefer to have all customer services performed by in-house personnel. When effectiveness is compromised as a result, however, the company must consider subcontracting selected service functions to other members of the distribution channel or to other manufacturers. Otherwise the quality of customer service will decline as an aftermath of cost-cutting or attempts to artificially stimulate demand for customer service to use slack capacity. Docutel, the automated teller manufacturer, for example, transferred responsibility for customer service operations to Texas Instruments because servicing its small base of equipment dispersed nationwide was unprofitable.

7. *Evaluate customer service.* Whether the customer service operation is treated as a cost center or a profit center, quantitative performance standards should be set for each element of the service package. Do an analysis of variances between actual and standard performances. American Airlines and other companies use such variances to calculate bonuses to service personnel. In addition, many companies regularly solicit customers' opinions about service operations and personnel.

In conclusion, we must stress that responsibility for quality cannot rest exclusively with the production department. Marketers must also be active in contributing to perceptions of quality. Marketers have been too passive in managing quality. Successful businesses of today will use marketing techniques to plan, design, and implement quality strategies that stretch beyond the factory floor.

Notes

1. Results of a *Wall Street Journal*–Gallup survey conducted in September 1981, published in *The Wall Street Journal*, October 12, 1981.

2. Results of a survey conducted by the American Society for Quality Control and published in the *Boston Globe*, January 25, 1981.

3. 1981 survey data from *Appliance Manufacturer*, April 1981.

4. John Holusha, "Detroit's New Stress on Quality," *New York Times*, April 30, 1981.

5. Norman B. McEachron and Harold S. Javitz, "Managing Quality: A Strategic Perspective," SRI International, Business Intelligence Program Report No. 658 (Stanford, Calif.: 1981).

6. John F. Welch, "Where Is Marketing Now That We Really Need It?," a speech presented to The Conference Board's 1981 Marketing Conference, New York City, October 28, 1981.

7. Holusha, "Detroit's New Stress on Quality."

8. Bill Abrams, "Research Suggests Consumers Will Increasingly Seek Quality," *The Wall Street Journal*, October 15, 1981.

9. Daniel Yankelovich, *New Rules* (New York: Random House, 1981), p. 182.

10. For evidence of this fact, see John R. Kennedy, Michael R. Pearce, and John A. Quelch, *Consumer Products Warranties: Perspectives, Issues, and Options*, report to the Canadian Ministry of Consumer and Corporate Affairs, 1979.

3

The Power of Unconditional Service Guarantees

Christopher W. L. Hart

When you buy a car, a camera, or a toaster oven, you receive a warranty, a guarantee that the product will work. How often do you receive a warranty for auto repair, wedding photography, or a catered dinner? Virtually never. Yet it is here, in buying services, that the assurance of a guarantee would presumably count most.

Many business executives believe that, by definition, services simply can't be guaranteed. Services are generally delivered by human beings, who are known to be less predictable than machines, and they are usually produced at the same time they are consumed. It is one thing to guarantee a camera, which can be inspected before a customer sets eyes on it and which can be returned to the factory for repairs. But how can you preinspect a car tune-up or send an unsuccessful legal argument or bad haircut back for repair? Obviously you can't.

But that doesn't mean customer satisfaction can't be guaranteed. Consider the guarantee offered by "Bugs" Burger Bug Killers (BBBK), a Miami-based pest-extermination company that is owned by S.C. Johnson & Son.

Most of BBBK's competitors claim that they will reduce pests to "acceptable levels"; BBBK promises to eliminate them entirely. Its service guarantee to hotel and restaurant clients promises:

> You don't owe one penny until all pests on your premises have been eradicated.
>
> If you are ever dissatisfied with BBBK's service, you will receive a refund for up to 12 months of the company's services—plus fees for another exterminator of your choice for the next year.

If a guest spots a pest on your premises, BBBK will pay for the guest's meal or room, send a letter of apology, and pay for a future meal or stay.

If your facility is closed down due to the presence of roaches or rodents, BBBK will pay any fines, as well as all lost profits, *plus* $5,000.

In short, BBBK says, "If we don't satisfy you 100%, we don't take your money."

How successful is this guarantee? The company, which operates throughout the United States, charges up to ten times more than its competitors and yet has a disproportionately high market share in its operating areas. Its service quality is so outstanding that the company rarely needs to make good on its guarantee (in 1986 it paid out only $120,000 on sales of $33 million—just enough to prove that its promises aren't empty ones).

A main reason that the "Bugs" Burger guarantee is a strong model for the service industry is that its founder, Al Burger, began with the concept of the unconditional guarantee and worked backward, designing his entire organization to support the no-pests guarantee—in short, he started with a vision of error-free service. In this article, I will explain why the service guarantee can help your organization institutionalize superlative performance.

What a Good Service Guarantee Is

Would you be willing to offer a guarantee of 100% customer satisfaction—to pay your dissatisfied customer to use a competitor's service, for example? Or do you believe that promising error-free service is a crazy idea?

Not only is it not crazy, but *committing* to error-free service can help force a company to *provide* it. It's a little like skiing. You've got to lean over your skis as you go down the hill, as if willing yourself to fall. But if you edge properly, you don't fall or plunge wildly; you gain control while you pick up speed.

Similarly, a strong service guarantee that puts the customer first doesn't necessarily lead to chaos and failure. If designed and implemented properly, it enables you to get control over your organization—with clear goals and an information network that gives you the data you need to improve performance. BBBK and other service companies show that a service guarantee is not only possible—it's a boon to performance and profits and can be a vehicle to market dominance.

Most existing service guarantees don't really do the job: they are limited in scope and difficult to use. Lufthansa guarantees that its customers will make their connecting flights *if* there are no delays due to weather or air-traffic control problems. Yet these two factors cause fully 95% of all flight delays. Bank of America will refund up to six months of checking-account fees if a customer is dissatisfied with any aspect of its checking-account service. However, the customer must close the account to collect the modest $5 or $6 per month fee. This guarantee won't win any prizes for fostering repeat business—a primary objective of a good guarantee.

A service guarantee loses power in direct proportion to the number of conditions it contains. How effective is a restaurant's guarantee of prompt service *except* when it's busy? A housing inspector's guarantee to identify all potential problems in a house *except for* those not readily apparent? Squaw Valley in California guarantees "your money back" to any skier who has to wait more than ten minutes in a lift line. But it's not that easy: the skier must first pay $1 and register at the lodge as a beginner, intermediate, or expert; the guarantee is operative only if *all* lifts at the skier's skill level exceed the ten minutes in any half-hour period; and skiers must check with a "ski hostess" at the end of the day to "win" a refund. A Squaw Valley spokesperson said the resort had made just one payout under the guarantee in a year and a half. No wonder!

What is a good service guarantee? It is (1) unconditional, (2) easy to understand and communicate, (3) meaningful, (4) easy (and painless) to invoke, and (5) easy and quick to collect on.

UNCONDITIONAL. The best service guarantee promises customer satisfaction unconditionally, without exceptions. Like that of L.L. Bean, the Freeport, Maine retail store and mail-order house: "100% satisfaction in every way. . . ." An L.L. Bean customer can return a product at any time and get, at his or her option, a replacement, a refund, or a credit. Reputedly, if a customer returns a pair of L.L. Bean boots after ten years, the company will replace them with new boots and no questions. Talk about customer assurance! Customers shouldn't need a lawyer to explain the "ifs, ands, and buts" of a guarantee—because ideally there shouldn't be any conditions; a customer is either satisfied or not.

If a company cannot guarantee all elements of its service unconditionally, it should unconditionally guarantee the elements that it can control. Lufthansa cannot promise on-time arrival, for example, but it could guarantee that passengers will be satisfied with its airport waiting areas, its service on the ground and in the air, and its food quality—or simply guarantee overall satisfaction.

EASY TO UNDERSTAND AND COMMUNICATE.   A guarantee should be written in simple, concise language that pinpoints the promise. Customers then know precisely what they can expect and employees know precisely what's expected of them. "Five-minute" lunch service, rather than "prompt" service, creates clear expectations, as does "no pests," rather than "pest control."

MEANINGFUL.   A good service guarantee is meaningful in two respects. First, it guarantees those aspects of your service that are important to your customers. It may be speedy delivery. Bennigan's, a restaurant chain, promises 15-minute service (or you get a free meal) at lunch, when many customers are in a hurry to get back to the office, but not at dinner, when fast service is not considered a priority to most patrons.

In other cases, price may be the most important element, especially with relatively undifferentiated commodities like rental cars or commercial air travel. By promising the lowest prices in town, stereo shops assuage customers' fears that if they don't go to every outlet in the area they'll pay more than they ought to.

Second, a good guarantee is meaningful financially; it calls for a significant payout when the promise is not kept. What should it be—a full refund? An offer of free service the next time? A trip to Monte Carlo? The answer depends on factors like the cost of the service, the seriousness of the failure, and customers' perception of what's fair. A money-back payout should be large enough to give customers an incentive to invoke the guarantee if dissatisfied. The adage "Let the punishment fit the crime" is an appropriate guide. At one point, Domino's Pizza (which is based in Ann Arbor, Michigan but operates worldwide) promised "delivery within 30 minutes or the pizza is free." Management found that customers considered this too generous; they felt uncomfortable accepting a free pizza for a mere 5- or 15-minute delay and didn't always take advantage of the guarantee. Consequently, Domino's adjusted its guarantee to "delivery within 30 minutes or $3 off," and customers appear to consider this commitment reasonable.

EASY TO INVOKE. A customer who is already dissatisfied should not have to jump through hoops to invoke a guarantee; the dissatisfaction is only exacerbated when the customer has to talk to three different people, fill out five forms, go to a different location, make two telephone calls, send in written proof of purchase with a full description of the events, wait for a written reply, go somewhere else to see someone to verify all the preceding facts, and so on.

Traveler's Advantage—a division of CUC International—has, in principle, a great idea: to guarantee the lowest price on the accommodations it books. But to invoke the guarantee, customers must prove the lower competing price by booking with another agency. That's unpleasant work. Cititravel, a subsidiary of Citicorp, has a better approach. A customer who knows of a lower price can call a toll-free number and speak with an agent, as I did recently. The agent told me that if I didn't have proof of the lower fare, she'd check competing airfares on her computer screen. If the lower fare was there, I'd get that price. If not, she would call the competing airline. If the price was confirmed, she said, "We'll refund your money so fast, you won't believe it—because we want you to be our customer." That's the right attitude if you're offering a guarantee.

Similarly, customers should not be made to feel guilty about invoking the guarantee—no questioning, no raised eyebrows, or "Why me, Lord?" looks. A company should encourage unhappy customers to invoke its guarantee, not put up roadblocks to keep them from speaking up.

EASY TO COLLECT. Customers shouldn't have to work hard to collect a payout, either. The procedure should be easy and, equally important, quick—on the spot, if possible. Dissatisfaction with a Manpower temporary worker, for instance, results in an immediate credit to your bill.

What you should *not* do in your guarantee: don't promise something your customers already expect; don't shroud a guarantee in so many conditions that it loses its point; and don't offer a guarantee so mild that it is never invoked. A guarantee that is essentially risk free to the company will be of little or no value to your customers—and may be a joke to your employees.

Why a Service Guarantee Works

A guarantee is a powerful tool—both for marketing service quality and for achieving it—for five reasons.

First, it pushes the entire company to focus on customers' definition of good service—not on executives' assumptions. Second, it sets clear performance standards, which boost employee performance and morale. Third, it generates reliable data (through payouts) when performance is poor. Fourth, it forces an organization to examine its entire service-delivery system for possible failure points. Last, it builds customer loyalty, sales, and market share.

A guarantee forces you to focus on customers. Knowing what customers want is the sine qua non in offering a service guarantee. A company has to identify its target customers' expectations about the elements of the service and the importance they attach to each. Lacking this knowledge of customer needs, a company that wants to guarantee its service may very well guarantee the wrong things.

British Airways conducted a market study and found that its passengers judge its customer services on four dimensions:[1]

1. Care and concern (employees' friendliness, courtesy, and warmth).
2. Initiative (employees' ability and willingness to jockey the system on the customer's behalf).
3. Problem solving (figuring out solutions to customer problems, whether unusual or routine—like multiflight airline tickets).
4. Recovery (going the extra yard, when things go wrong, to handle a particular problem—which includes the simple but often overlooked step of delivering an apology).

British Airways managers confessed that they hadn't even thought about the second and fourth categories. Worse, they realized that if *they* hadn't understood these important dimensions of customer service, how much thought could their employees be giving to them?

A guarantee sets clear standards. A specific, unambiguous service guarantee sets standards for your organization. It tells employees what the company stands for. BBBK stands for pest elimination, not pest control; Federal Express stands for "absolutely, positively by 10:30 A.M.," not "sometime tomorrow, probably." And it forces the company to define each employee's role and responsibilities in delivering the service. Salespeople, for example, know precisely what their companies can deliver and can represent that accurately—the opposite of the common situation in which salespeople promise the moon and customers get only dirt.

This clarity and sense of identity have the added advantage of creating employee team spirit and pride. Mitchell Fromstein, president and CEO of Manpower, says, "At one point, we wondered what the marketing impact would be if we dropped our guarantee. We figured that our accounts were well aware of the guarantee and that it might not have much marketing power anymore. Our employees' reaction was fierce—and it had a lot less to do with marketing than with the pride they take in their work. They said, 'The guarantee is proof that we're a great company. We're willing to tell our customers that if they don't like our service for any reason, it's our fault, not theirs, and we'll make it right.' I realized then that the guarantee is far more than a simple piece of paper that puts customers at ease. It really sets the tone, externally and, perhaps more important, internally, for our commitment to our customers and workers."

A payout that creates financial pain when errors occur is also a powerful statement, to employees and customers alike, that management demands customer satisfaction. A significant payout ensures that both middle and upper management will take the service guarantee seriously; it provides a strong incentive to take every step necessary to deliver. A manager who must bear the full cost of mistakes has ample incentive to figure out how to prevent them from happening.

A guarantee generates feedback. A guarantee creates the goal; it defines what you must do to satisfy your customers. Next, you need to know when you go wrong. A guarantee forces you to create a system for discovering errors—which the Japanese call "golden nuggets" because they're opportunities to learn.

Arguably the greatest ailment afflicting service companies is a lack of decent systems for generating and acting on customer data. Dissatisfied service customers have little incentive to complain on their own, far less so than unhappy product owners do. Many elements of a service are intangible, so consumers who receive poor service are often left with no evidence to support their complaints.

(The customer believes the waiter was rude; perhaps the waiter will deny it.) Second, without the equivalent of a product warranty, customers don't know their rights. (Is 15 minutes too long to wait for a restaurant meal? 30 minutes?) Third, there is often no one to complain to—at least no one who looks capable of solving the problem. Often, complaining directly to the person who is rendering poor service will only make things worse.

Customer comment cards have traditionally been the most common method of gathering customer feedback on a company's operations, but they, too, are inadequate for collecting valid, reliable error data. In the first place, they are an impersonal form of communication and are usually short (to maximize the response rate). Why bother, people think, to cram the details of a bad experience onto a printed survey form with a handful of "excellent—good—fair" check-off boxes? Few aggrieved customers believe that completing a comment card will resolve their problems. Therefore, only a few customers—usually the most satisfied and dissatisfied—provide feedback through such forms, and fewer still provide meaningful feedback. As a broad gauge of customer sentiment, cards and surveys are useful, but for specific information about customer problems and operational weaknesses, they simply don't fill the bill.

Service companies thus have a hard time collecting error data. Less information on mistakes means fewer opportunities to improve, ultimately resulting in more service errors and more customer dissatisfaction—a cycle that management is often unaware of. A guarantee attacks this malady by giving consumers an incentive and a vehicle for bringing their grievances to management's attention.

Manpower uses its guarantee to glean error data in addition to allaying customer worries about using an unknown quantity (the temporary worker). Every customer who employs a Manpower temporary worker is called the first day of a one-day assignment or the second day of a longer assignment to check on the worker's performance. A dissatisfied customer doesn't pay—period. (Manpower pays the worker, however; it assumes complete responsibility for the quality of its service.) The company uses its error data to improve both its work force and its proprietary skills-testing software and skills data base—major elements in its ability to match worker skills to customer requirements. The information

Manpower obtains before and after hiring enables it to offer its guarantee with confidence.

A guarantee forces you to understand why you fail. In developing a guarantee, managers must ask questions like these: What failure points exist in the system? If failure points can be identified, can their origins be traced—and overcome? A company that wants to promise timely service delivery, for example, must first understand its operation's capability and the factors limiting that capability. Many service executives, lacking understanding of such basic issues as system throughput time, capacity, and process flow, tend to blame workers, customers, or anything *but* the service-delivery process.

Even if workers *are* a problem, managers can do several things to "fix" the organization so that it can support a guarantee—such as design better recruiting, hiring, and training processes. The pest-control industry has historically suffered from unmotivated personnel and high turnover. Al Burger overcame the status quo by offering higher than average pay (attracting a higher caliber of job candidate), using a vigorous screening program (making those hired feel like members of a select group), training all workers for six months, and keeping them motivated by giving them a great deal of autonomy and lots of recognition.

Some managers may be unwilling to pay for an internal service-delivery capability that is above the industry average. Fine. They will never have better than average organizations, either, and they will therefore never be able to develop the kind of competitive advantage that flows from a good service guarantee.

A guarantee builds marketing muscle. Perhaps the most obvious reason for offering a strong service guarantee is its ability to boost marketing: it encourages consumers to buy a service by reducing the risk of the purchase decision, and it generates more sales to existing customers by enhancing loyalty. In the last ten years, Manpower's revenues have mushroomed from $400 million to $4 billion. That's marketing impact.

Keeping most of your customers and getting positive word of mouth, though desirable in any business, are particularly important for service companies. The net present value of sales forgone from lost customers—in other words, the cost of customer dissatisfaction—is enormous. In this respect, it's fair to say that many service companies' biggest competitors are themselves. They frequently spend huge amounts of money to attract new customers without ever figuring out how to provide the consistent service they promise to their existing customers. If customers aren't satisfied, the marketing money has been poured down the drain and may even engender further ill will. (See appendix, "Maximizing Marketing Impact.")

A guarantee will only work, of course, if you start with commitment to the customer. If your aim is to minimize the guarantee's impact on your organization but to maximize its marketing punch, you won't succeed. In the long run, you will nullify the guarantee's potential impact on customers, and your marketing dollars will go down the drain.

Phil Bressler, owner of 18 Domino's Pizza franchises in the Baltimore, Maryland area, demonstrates the right commitment to customers. He got upset the time his company recorded its highest monthly earnings ever because, he correctly figured, the profits had come from money that should have been paid out on the Domino's guarantee of "delivery within 30 minutes or $3 off." Bressler's unit managers, who have bottom-line responsibility, had pumped up their short-term profits by failing to honor the guarantee consistently. Bressler is convinced that money spent on guarantees is an investment in customer satisfaction and loyalty. He also recognizes that the guarantee is the best way to identify weak operations, and that guarantees not acted on are data not collected.

Compare Bressler's attitude with that of an owner of several nationally franchised motels. *His* guarantee promises that the company will do "everything possible" to remedy a customer's problem; if the problem cannot be resolved, the customer stays for free. He brags that he's paid, on average, refunds for only two room guarantees per motel per year—a minuscule percentage of room sales. "If my managers are doing their jobs, I don't have to pay out for the guarantee," he says. "If I do have to pay out, my managers are not doing their jobs, and I get rid of them."

Clearly, more than two guests of *any* hotel are likely to be dissatisfied over the course of a year. By seeking to limit payouts rather than hear complaints, this owner is undoubtedly blowing countless opportunities to create loyal customers out of disgruntled ones. He is also losing rich information about which of his motels need improvement and why, information that can most easily be obtained from customer complaints. You have to wonder why he offers a guarantee at all, since he completely misses the point.

Why You May Need a Guarantee Even If You Don't Think So

Of course, guarantees may not be effective or practicable for all service firms. Four Seasons Hotels, for example, could probably not get much marketing or operational mileage from a guarantee. With its strong internal vision of absolute customer satisfaction, the company has developed an outstanding service-delivery system and a reputation to match. Thus it already has an implicit guarantee. To advertise the obvious would produce little gain and might actually be perceived as incongruent with the company's prestigious image.

A crucial element in Four Seasons's service strategy is instilling in all employees a mission of absolute customer satisfaction and empowering them to do whatever is necessary if customer problems do occur. For example, Four Seasons's Washington hotel was once asked by the State Department to make room for a foreign dignitary. Already booked to capacity, Four Seasons had to tell four other customers with reservations that they could not be accommodated. However, the hotel immediately found rooms for them at another first-class hotel, while assuring them they would remain registered at the Four Seasons (so that any messages they received would be taken and sent to the other hotel). When rooms became available, the customers were driven back to the Four Seasons by limousine. Four Seasons also paid for their rooms at the other hotel. It was the equivalent of a full money-back guarantee, and more.

Does this mean that every company that performs at the level of a Four Seasons need not offer a service guarantee? Could Federal Express, for example, drop its "absolutely, positively" assurance with little or no effect? Probably not. Its guarantee is such a part of its image that dropping the guarantee would hurt it.

In general, organizations that meet the following tests probably have little to gain by offering a service guarantee: the company is perceived by the market to be the quality leader in its industry; every employee is inculcated with the "absolute customer satisfaction" philosophy; employees are empowered to take whatever corrective action is necessary to handle complaints; errors are few; and a stated guarantee would be at odds with the company's image.

It is probably unnecessary to point out that few service companies meet these tests.

External Variables. Service guarantees may also be impractical where customer satisfaction is influenced strongly by external forces the service provider can't control. While everybody thinks their businesses are in this fix, most are wrong.

How many variables are truly beyond management's control? Not the work force. Not equipment problems. Not vendor quality. And even businesses subject to "acts of God" (like weather) can control a great deal of their service quality.

BBBK is an example of how one company turned the situation around by analyzing the elements of the service-delivery process. By asking, "What obstacles stand in the way of our guaranteeing pest elimination?" Al Burger discovered that clients' poor cleaning and storage practices were one such obstacle. So the company requires customers to maintain sanitary practices and in some cases even make physical changes to their property (like putting in walls). By changing the process, the company could guarantee the outcome.

There may well be uncontrollable factors that create problems. As I noted earlier, such things as flight controllers, airport capacity, and weather limit the extent to which even the finest airline can consistently deliver on-time service. But how employees respond to such externally imposed problems strongly influences customer satisfaction, as British Airways executives learned from their market survey. When things go wrong, will employees go the extra yard to handle the problem? Why couldn't an airline that has refined its problem-handling skills to a science ensure absolute customer satisfaction—uncontrollable variables be damned? How many customers would invoke a guarantee if they understood that the reasons for a problem were completely out of the airline's control—if they were treated with warmth, compassion, and a sense of humor, and if the airline's staff communicated with them honestly?

Cheating. Fear of customer cheating is another big hurdle for most service managers considering offering guarantees. When asked why Lufthansa's guarantee required customers to present written proof of purchase, a manager at the airline's U.S. headquarters told me, "If we didn't ask for written proof, our customers would cheat us blind."

But experience teaches a different lesson. Sure, there will be cheats—the handful of customers who take advantage of a guarantee to get something for nothing. What they cost the company amounts to very little compared to the benefits derived from a strong guarantee. Says Michael Leven, a hotel industry executive, "Too often management spends its time worrying about the 1% of people who might cheat the company instead of the 99% who don't."

Phil Bressler of Domino's argues that customers cheat only when *they* feel cheated: "If we charge $8 for a pizza, our customers expect $8 worth of product and service. If we started giving them $7.50 worth of product and service, then they'd start looking for ways to get back that extra 50 cents. Companies create the incentive to cheat, in almost all cases, by cutting costs and not providing value."

Where the potential for false claims is high, a no-questions-asked guarantee may appear to be foolhardy. When Domino's first offered its "delivery within 30 minutes or the pizza is free" guarantee, some college students telephoned orders from hard-to-find locations. The result was free pizza for the students and lost revenue for Domino's. In this environment, the guarantee was problematic because some students perceived it as a game against Domino's. But Bressler takes the view that the revenue thus lost was an investment in the future. "They'll be Domino's customers for life, those kids," he says.

High Costs. Managers are likely to worry about the costs of a service-guarantee program, but for the wrong reasons. Quality "guru" Philip Crosby coined the phrase "quality is free" (in his 1979 book, *Quality Is Free*) to indicate *not* that quality-improvement efforts cost nothing but that the benefits of quality improvement—fewer errors, higher productivity, more repeat business—outweigh the costs over the long term.

Clearly, a company whose operations are slipshod (or out of control) should not consider offering an unconditional guarantee; the outcome would be either bankruptcy from staggering payouts or an employee revolt stemming from demands to meet standards that are beyond the organization's capability. If your company is like most, however, it's not in that shape; you will probably only need to buttress operations somewhat. To be sure, an investment of financial and human resources to shore up weak points in the delivery system will likely cause a quick, sharp rise in expenditures.

How sharp an increase depends on several factors: your company's weaknesses (how far does it have to go to become good?), the nature of the industry, and the strength of your competition, for example. A small restaurant might simply spend more on employee recruiting and training, and perhaps on sponsoring quality circles; a large utility company might need to restructure its entire organization to overcome years of bad habits if it is to deliver on a guarantee.

Even though a guarantee carries costs, bear in mind that, as Crosby asserts, a badly performed service also incurs costs—failure costs, which come in many forms, including lost business from disgruntled consumers. In a guarantee program, you shift from spending to mop up failures to spending on preventing failures. And many of those costs are incurred in most organizations anyway (like outlays for staff time spent in planning meetings). It's just that they're spent more productively.

Breakthrough Service

One great potential of a service guarantee is its ability to change an industry's rules of the game by changing the service-delivery process as competitors conceive it.

BBBK and Federal Express both redefined the meaning of service in their industries, performing at levels that other companies have so far been unable to match. (According to the owner of a competing pest-control company, BBBK "is number one. There is no number two.") By offering breakthrough service, these companies altered the basis of competition in their businesses and put their competitors at a severe disadvantage.

What are the possibilities for replicating their success in other service businesses? Skeptics might claim that BBBK's and Federal Express's success is not widely applicable because they target price-insensitive customers willing to pay for superior service—in short, that these companies are pursuing differentiation strategies.

It is true that BBBK's complex preparation, cleaning, and checkup procedures are much more time consuming than those of typical pest-control operators, that the company spends more on pesticides than competitors do, and that its employees are well compensated. And many restaurants and hotels are willing to pay BBBK's higher prices because to them it's ultimately cheaper: the cost of "errors" (guests' spotting roaches or ants) is higher than the cost of error prevention.

But, because of the "quality is free" dictum, breakthrough service does not mean you must become the high-cost producer. Manpower's procedures are not radically more expensive than its competitors'; they're simply better. The company's skills-testing methods and customer-needs diagnoses surely cost less in the long run than a sloppy system. A company that inadequately screens and trains temporary-worker recruits, establishes no detailed customer specifications, and fails to check worker performance loses customers.

Manpower spends heavily on ways to reduce errors further, seeing this spending as an investment that will (a) protect its market position; (b) reduce time-consuming service errors; and (c) reinforce the company's values to employees. Here is the "absolute customer satisfaction" philosophy at work, and whatever cost increase Manpower incurs it makes up in sales volume.

Organizations that figure out how to offer—and deliver—guaranteed, breakthrough service will have tapped into a powerful source of competitive advantage. Doing so is no mean feat, of course, which is precisely why the opportunity to build a competitive advantage exists. Though the task is difficult, it is clearly not impossible, and the service guarantee can play a fundamental role in the process.

Appendix

MAXIMIZING MARKETING IMPACT

The odds of gaining powerful marketing impact from a service guarantee are in your favor when one or more of the following conditions exist:

The price of the service is high. A bad shoe shine? No big deal. A botched $1,000 car repair is a different story; a guarantee is more effective here.

The customer's ego is on the line. Who wants to be seen after getting a bad haircut?

The customer's expertise with the service is low. When in doubt about a service, a customer will choose one that's covered by a guarantee over those that are not.

The negative consequences of service failure are high. As consumers' expected aggravation, expense, and time lost due to service failure increase, a guarantee gains power. Your computer went down? A computer-repair service with guaranteed response and repair times would be the most logical company to call.

The industry has a bad image for service quality—like pest-control services, security guards, or home repair. A guard company that guarantees to have its posts filled by qualified people would automatically rank high on a list of prospective vendors.

The company depends on frequent customer re-purchases. Can it exist on a never-ending stream of new triers (like small service businesses in large markets), or does it have to deal with a finite market? If the market is finite, how close is market saturation? The smaller the size of the potential market of new triers, the more attention management should pay to increasing the loyalty and re-purchase rate of existing customers—objectives that a good service guarantee will serve.

The company's business is affected deeply by word of mouth (both positive and negative). Consultants, stockbrokers, restaurants, and resorts are all good examples of services where there are strong incentives to minimize the extent of customer dissatisfaction—and hence, negative word of mouth.

Note

1. See British Airways study cited in Karl Albrecht and Ron Zemke, *Service America!* (Homewood, Ill.: Dow Jones-Irwin, 1985), pp. 33–34.

PART

IV

Keep the Relationship Vibrant

Introduction

Vibrant relationships depend on high-quality execution today; at the same time tomorrow's demands must be considered. Skillful anticipation of changing market conditions and customer needs results in higher profits over the long term. As industries, products, services, and customer needs evolve, suppliers must decide where to invest time and resources in building enduring relationships. Those who effectively balance long-term investments (such as research and development) against short-term policies (such as hiring more salespeople), while gauging current customer needs against market dynamics, create happier customers and stronger, more profitable relationships. This section provides useful advice on how to maximize the return on these interrelated investments.

The first article, "Make Sure Your Customers Keep Coming Back," by F. Stewart DeBruicker and Gregory Summe, provides a framework for developing marketing strategies to meet customers' changing needs. The authors describe how early in the life of a highly differentiated product (such as the IBM personal computer when it was launched in the early 1980s) buyers are "inexperienced generalists," who take a long time to make purchasing decisions and demand a great deal of support. Over time, products become less differentiated and customers become "experienced specialists," willing to take risks they once deferred to the vendor. At this point, price and availability are more important purchasing criteria than support services or superlative quality. Firms that plan for this dynamic of customer learning can develop marketing, product enhancement, customer service, and pricing strategies that reflect the conditions of the market. "Successful companies choose and manage their customers with the same care they put into choosing and managing their products." Sellers who anticipate customers' evolving demands will be able to sustain their competitiveness and profitability over a longer period.

Another important way to boost profitability, while building customer satisfaction, is to "Exploit Your Product's Service Life Cycle," as advocated by George Potts. Using the computer industry as an example, the author illustrates how the life cycle of support services lags behind the product life cycle: as a product is reaching maturity, its service cycle is only beginning. When the service cycle is carefully managed, its profits can exceed those gained through product sales. The author stresses the importance of careful analysis and planning, because each phase of the service cycle requires a different set of skills and material resources. For example, early in the service life cycle, excellent technological support is important. Later, when the installed service base is large, inventory control and efficient service execution are the primary skills. Inappropriate resource allocation will result in escalating costs and dissatisfied customers. This article provides excellent advice for developing service programs that generate profits long after the initial sale.

The next article, "Good Product Support Is Smart Marketing," by Milind Lele and Uday Karmarkar, outlines a straightforward approach for developing the most effective support strategy. Typically, product support is a reactive measure taken only after customers complain about product failure. Moreover, sales of high-quality products may suffer because suppliers fail to offer a support program that meets customers' expectations. The authors argue that *proactive* support strategies will result in greater customer satisfaction and more efficient resource allocation in the long run.

Designing the best support strategy, however, requires thorough analysis and commitment on the part of the supplier. Many companies have inefficient and uncompetitive support policies because they lack an explicit, cross-functional, and coordinated strategy; consider support needs late in the product development cycle; and focus more on internal, rather than customer-driven measures (e.g., engineering reliability or parts availability, rather than downtime per failure or service response time). Furthermore, customers' support needs are often measured with faulty techniques. "While conceptually straightforward, translation of expectations into measurable terms is complicated by the fact that many customer expectations regarding support are nonlinear, support effectiveness is measured by many different variables, and statistical averages [such as hours of downtime per year] are misleading."

By accounting for all these variables, building support into the development process, and sharing support responsibility across functions, suppliers can develop a matrix that measures alternative support strategies against suppliers' costs and customers' benefits. In this way, suppliers can segment customers by support needs, establish support programs that balance costs with customer value, and anticipate changes in support needs over the course of a product life cycle. This approach gives the supplier a competitive edge: "If customers and competitors perceive the company as a leader in identifying and meeting support needs, management can set the pace at which support effectiveness is improved."

The final article in this section, "The Case of the Tech Service Tangle," by Benson Shapiro, takes on the pervasive and challenging issue of sustaining growth and profitability after a high-quality product has matured. In this case study the vice president of marketing for an industrial chemicals company is faced with the following strategic options: (1) finance additional technical service, (2) hire more salespeople, or (3) support R&D in search of the next big product. Short-term customer satisfaction and increased sales might result from the first two options. In the long term, the third option might yield greater benefit, but it is riskier. In extending the competitiveness of the product, each option has important implications for current and future customer relationships. While there are no easy answers to the complex trade-offs involved in the alternative investments, a careful analysis, following the principles presented in this section, can help improve the chances of optimizing both customer satisfaction and profitability.

1

Make Sure Your Customers Keep Coming Back

F. Stewart DeBruicker and Gregory L. Summe

Jerry Evans, a sales applications engineer for Polyplastics, a plastic resin manufacturer, expected a rewarding day. For the better part of two years he had been calling on Universal Electric's new product design group. In the last year his efforts had paid off in hefty orders, as the group included several of his modified-nylon resins in their specifications for a promising new line of home appliances.

True, he now seemed to be spending increasing amounts of time with the procurement manager rather than with his original benefactor, the design group's leader. But the project leader had specifically asked to meet with him today. Jerry welcomed the chance to talk over some of the new applications he had in mind.

Jerry's optimism was short-lived. The design group leader greeted him with the announcement that the team was winding up its current assignment and members were being reassigned to various new projects in the company. In the future, he said, reorders of the modified nylon Jerry sold would be handled exclusively by the procurement manager.

Later, meeting alone with the procurement manager, Jerry tried to establish rapport and stimulate interest in his product. He mentioned how much he had enjoyed working with the design group and began to describe ideas for other product applications. "We appreciate that, Jerry—we do," the procurement manager interrupted, "but I'll have to be honest with you. I'm looking for three things: price, price, and price. What can you do for us?"

Surprised at the manager's bluntness, Jerry floundered, joking lamely, "Well, as you know, we're not exactly the Chevrolet of the industry." Even as the words were coming out, he could see his customer's interest slipping. Later, when walking to his car, Jerry had the uneasy feeling that he was losing the account—worth more than half a million dollars in annual orders. It had all happened so suddenly.

Jerry Evans is a hypothetical salesman, but his problem is real and increasingly common. He has confronted the industrial marketing phenomenon of evolving customer experience. That is, his customer has evolved from an inexperienced buyer that leaned heavily on the support and services Jerry's company offered to an experienced buyer more interested in other benefits—in this case, price.

Jerry walked away with an empty order sheet because his marketing department had not prepared him for this predictable change in customer behavior. Had he been alert to the change, he would have noticed some telling signals: the increasing participation of a purchasing agent in the buying decision and the dwindling interest of the team in his application suggestions.

Jerry's problem illustrates a marketing strategy issue that affects all manufacturers of products sold to other businesses. Whether the product is a standard industrial product like sheet steel or a high-tech item like telecommunications equipment, the company will confront customer changes that result from this customer experience effect. Understood in its relation to the product life cycle, this effect provides insight into the customer's needs and serves as a guide for planning marketing strategies.

The Customer Experience Effect

As customers gain familiarity with a product, they find a manufacturer's support programs to be of declining value. Their buying decisions become increasingly price-sensitive. They unbundle into components the products they once purchased as systems and open their doors to suppliers who sell on price and offer little in the way of product support. Even the most remote observer, once instructed, can spot this pattern.

THE INEXPERIENCED GENERALIST

Naturally, when a product family is at the beginning of its life cycle, most customers are inexperienced. Even as the product matures, it will continue to attract inexperienced customers. Novice customers are distinguished by two characteristics: they are generalists, and they place a premium on technical and applications support in making purchases.

They are generalists because companies dealing with a new product usually assign responsibility to people who are competent in traditional skills and trustworthy in dealing with uncertainties. In some cases, these people will be, by default, members of general management. There may be no other member of the organization who will take on the political risk of being associated with a bad decision.

Other inexperienced customers will be design engineers, systems analysts, and other "professional" generalists who are rewarded for introducing major new products and processes and for moving their companies into new businesses.

Inexperienced customers place strong emphasis on product support. They are attracted by a bundle of vendor-supplied benefits and proven technology. Their decision processes are slow and they rely on vendors for guidance throughout.

In such a market situation, vendors with strong marketing and account management resources compete most effectively. Companies that are unwilling or unable to manage prolonged decision processes and to provide turnkey solutions to problems will fail with this type of customer.

A look at the history of the mainframe computer industry's environment tells us much about inexperienced customers and the strategies that serve them. This industry got off the ground in the 1960s, when a few large corporations decided to remain a jump ahead of competitors (and get a better handle on working capital) by computerizing the enormous task of record keeping.

Since the purchase decision involved changes in internal information flows and procedures and large financial commitments, it was usually made by a committee of senior managers—each with a functional ax to grind. Decision making took 18 to 24 months.

IBM dominated this market from the outset because it had tailored its marketing strategy to the inexperienced buyer. Its marketing program included complete systems of reliable (rather than technologically advanced) hardware and software; a wide product line permitting future upgrading; extensive human resources for installation, education, service, and account management; rental options with liberal system-upgrading privileges and fees quoted on a whole-system basis; and a pricing strategy that yielded margins much higher than systems offered by smaller competitors.

IBM's was a formidable strategy, not so much because of the enormous resources behind it but because it was tailored to a market of inexperienced generalists.

Similarly, the robotics industry today confronts a market in which most customers are inexperienced and risk-averse. Buyers are less interested in the performance-price ratios of component robots than in proven, comprehensive, packaged solutions. Only companies that offer complete systems and products with unassailable reputations for reliability will succeed in this environment. Strong marketing resources are much more important than low price.

In short, inexperienced generalists buy systems, and they take a long time to reach a decision. Any strategy that offers them less than a complete, systematic solution is unlikely to succeed.

THE EXPERIENCED SPECIALIST

The initially successful vendor will falter, however, if it fails to respond to the growing sophistication and self-confidence of its customer base.

As companies become more familiar with a product and more confident of their ability to make judgments about it, they shift the purchasing responsibility from general management or support professionals to either functional specialists with detailed knowledge of the product or purchasing agents, who base the buying decision on standard specifications. In robotics purchasing, for example, the corporate-level committee at Fisher Body has in recent years been replaced by a smaller group of manufacturing and production specialists. They are more knowledgeable about component performance and system applications and rely much less on the guidance of manufacturers' account management teams.

Product experience emboldens customers to assume certain risks they once deferred to the vendor. No longer do they look for a comprehensive bundle of benefits. The bundle's components can be seen, sorted, and valued. Some of those components may be purchased from the original systems vendor, others are likely to be made by the customers themselves, and still others bought from specialist suppliers. When this unbundling takes place, customers tend to base buying decisions not on strong support from the account manager or on turnkey systems but on price-performance trade-offs. Decision making is less time-consuming. (The few exceptions are products with complex component interfaces, such as integrated office systems and flexible manufacturing systems.)

Customers in the telecommunications industry have already embarked on the transition. Prodded by AT&T's divestiture and industry deregulation to make their own choices of equipment and long-distance service vendors, businesses are beginning to develop in-house staffs to manage their telecommunications needs. As these staffs become more experienced, they will increasingly unbundle telecommunications products. They will buy some components of equipment from one vendor and some from another, and select more carefully between service vendors. They will *build* their systems using the products and services offering the best price-performance benefits.

The point of transition from inexperienced generalist to experienced specialist is, of course, rarely as clear-cut as in the hypothetical situation described at the outset of this article. But certainly inexperienced and experienced customers base their buying decisions on quite different factors.

Customer Sophistication and Product Maturity

How does the customer's evolution relate to the product life cycle? The two can evolve in parallel, as in the telecommunications industry today, but the transition from inexperienced to experienced customer often takes place independent of product maturation. Product market evolution, in other words, is driven by customer forces as well as by product forces. The engineering plastics story with which we started illustrates the point: as the customers mature, purchase decisions are made first by applications engineers, later by purchasing agents, and then, in some cases, by the many thousands of operators of molding companies that process resins into finished plastic parts. Other factors, such as the length of time required to make the purchase decision and

Exhibit I.   Effects of Customer Experience in the Engineering Plastics Industry

	Customer groups	
	Inexperienced customers	**Experienced customers**
Decision-making unit	Applications engineers	Purchasing agents
Decision-making process	New task, two years	Routine repurchase, four to five per year
Marketing policy areas:		
Dominant product benefits	Technical assistance, applications, support	Performance, availability, price
Price/value considerations	Enhanced competitive position	Low cost
Sales program	Account management via industry specialists	Field sales on a geographical basis
Key success factors	Account management and technology	Low cost of goods sold, low or parity prices

the benefits sought, also change as the customer gains experience (see Exhibit I). No wise marketer makes the mistake of assuming that customer evolution parallels a company's product life cycle.

The patterns of product benefits customers desire are definable and predictable. As Exhibit II shows, a product's market will be a mosaic of four customer profiles. These four possible stages (no customer goes through all four) can provide the basis for targeted marketing programs:

1. Early in the development of an industry, customers can be expected to reward vendors who provide not only reliable new technology but also high levels of technical and applications support. These first-purchase decisions, while potentially rewarding, are risky, and customers proceed cautiously for fear of failure. Customers may be attracted to promising new products, but the so-called FUD factor—fear, uncertainty, and doubt—will predispose them to pay a premium price for a product of known reliability

Exhibit II. Product Benefit Profiles

	Customers →	
	Inexperienced generalists	**Experienced specialists**
High	**1** Applications support / Technical support / Product performance	**2** Product performance / Applications support
Low	**3** Technical support / Service / Price	**4** Price / Acceptable quality / Availability

Product differentiation (High → Low)

coupled with effective support. Products whose markets currently fit this profile include aseptic packaging (which is familiar to consumers as the latest packaging for beverages), fiber optics, and powdered metals.

2. As customers gain knowledge, they purchase the product primarily for its performance characteristics. However, the vendor can still deliver value by helping develop new applications. For example, polycarbonates now face a market composed largely of experienced buyers, as do industrial robots (while many buyers of robots are inexperienced, most of the volume in that market is presently controlled by experienced buyers).

3. Customers entering the market late will be influenced by the availability of substitute products. Since competing vendors may have lower product development costs (by virtue of their later entry) and lower application costs (because they can imitate the

innovating company), they are likely to offer lower prices. Customers in this environment, while seeking technical support and responsive service, will also tend to be price-sensitive. Portions of the electric switch-gear and long-distance telephone service markets fall into this category.

4. Under the pressure of customer and competitive forces, most of the market will eventually assume the profile of the experienced customer buying an undifferentiated product. At this stage, customers will unbundle the original product-benefit package and strip away the benefits not directly related to their dominant buying needs. They will seek adequate rather than superlative quality, assured availability to ensure stable production planning and efficient use of related resources, and the lowest possible price. Polyvinylchloride, sheet steel, and glass containers are among the commodity products that fit this profile.

Marketing Strategy Implications

Once a good customer relationship has been established, the seller tends to cherish and sustain the status quo. But as customer needs change over time, sellers can be left holding an empty bag. Conversely, a competitive advantage exists for the vendor who understands and anticipates the customer experience effect and who designs strategies based on the benefits a given group of customers desires.

These benefits can be provided in many ways to the advantage of both buyer and seller. Four primary approaches, outlined in Exhibit III, are as follows.

ACCOUNT MANAGEMENT STRATEGIES

As long as most competitors fail to duplicate a product's core technology, the principal evolution in the product-market environment takes place on the customer side. In industries with a brisk rate of new product development, the vendor can slow this evolution by emphasizing account management—strengthening the account management representation and perhaps even adding top management to the team. This strategy is designed to keep purchasing decisions under the regular review of general managers in

Exhibit III. **Marketing Strategies That Recognize Customer Experience***

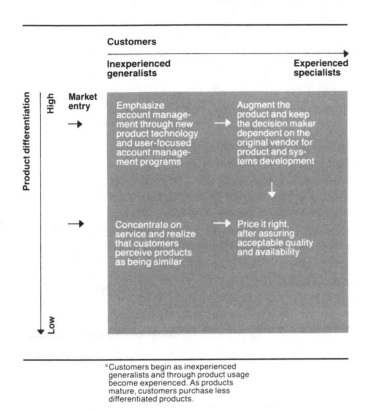

Customers

Inexperienced generalists → **Experienced specialists**

Product differentiation — High / Low

Market entry

→ Emphasize account management through new product technology and user-focused account management programs → Augment the product and keep the decision maker dependent on the original vendor for product and systems development

→ Concentrate on service and realize that customers perceive products as being similar → Price it right, after assuring acceptable quality and availability

*Customers begin as inexperienced generalists and through product usage become experienced. As products mature, customers purchase less differentiated products.

senior positions, thereby limiting the impact of experienced specialists on important decisions. Its purpose is to sustain the vendor's influence and block competitive inroads into the account.

IBM used this strategy to great advantage in the computer industry. The company inhibited customers' transitions from inexperienced to experienced buyers by using a multilevel team account management approach. Including both high-level managers and data processing specialists in the decision-making unit ensured the continued involvement of inexperienced generalists in the decision-making process. These moves enabled IBM to retain most of its customer base over the long term. Not until recently was IBM forced to address the price-sensitive needs of experienced customers.

In high-tech industries, the fast pace of product and systems development makes account management a feasible strategy, even when customers have achieved some sophistication. Making the strategy work, however, requires an enormous commitment to support skilled marketing resources. And to succeed, the strategy must add real value; in other words, the involvement of higher level managers must result in superior responsiveness based on a genuine commitment to meet the customer's needs efficiently and economically.

PRODUCT AUGMENTATION STRATEGIES

Advanced products eventually spawn imitations, and inexperienced customers become experienced specialists. Theodore Levitt has suggested that at this point "it makes sense to embark on a systematic program of customer-benefiting, and therefore customer-keeping, product augmentation."[1] In other words, sellers should emphasize a particular benefit—say, new applications support—that they know the customer is seeking. The thrust of this strategy is to keep differentiating the product in the customer's eyes, thereby drawing attention away from the price appeal of competing products. To do so, the vendor identifies the customer's product needs and adapts offerings to serve them. A supplier who can identify an associated product need and fill it through a unique service of continuing value to the customer will not be forced to compete on the basis of price.

In the industrial market for converted paper products, for example, one U.S. producer is differentiating its product on the basis of reliability and specialization. Its paper products, which are considered a mature line, account for a very small percentage of the cost of the customer's final product. But when they fail, the end product usually suffers costly damage. Having tested all the competitive offerings, this producer took steps to lower its failure rate through design and manufacturing changes. Next the company began working with its major customers to design products with superior loading characteristics for their particular applications. It is now changing its sales emphasis from customer relationships to applications expertise.

With its new augmentation strategy, this company expects to provide a product that commands both a significant premium and a large share of the market. The supplier benefits by slowing the movement of its product into the commodity category, where purchase decisions are based mainly on price. The customer receives real value through increased reliability of its end product.

CUSTOMER SERVICE STRATEGIES

Sellers seeking to attract inexperienced customers who enter the market late in the product life cycle may find a service strategy to be appropriate. The presence of substitute products in the market will make even first-time decision makers aware of how few differences exist between the offerings of competing suppliers, rendering product performance characteristics less important than they would be early in the cycle. Customer interest will likely focus not on product but on service—the distribution, customer education, and aftermarket support elements of the marketing mix.

Consider the situation in the microcomputer industry. Dozens of competitors have entered the market, with most products based on the same Intel 8088 chip. Their products are virtually identical in performance capabilities. This proliferation of vendors with similar products has affected end-user decisions by shifting the purchase decision away from issues of technical product capability. Some vendors—notably Apple Computer—have followed a product augmentation strategy for experienced users by developing extensive software for particular customer applications. Apple, along with others, targeting the inexperienced customer, have emphasized service areas: training, product maintenance, and related support. Still others, targeting the inexperienced customer, has emphasized service areas: training, product maintenance, and related support. Still

The telecommunications industry provides another example. A current AT&T ad has this lead: "Our products come with the following standard equipment: technical consultant, account executive, systems technician." In other words, the strategy is service, and it is targeted toward the great mass of companies, inexperienced with large telecommunications systems, that can now select among competitive products.

PRICING STRATEGIES

Eventually, customer and competitive forces combine to drive a marketplace into a highly price-sensitive mode. If the vendor is to protect its market position, strategies that emphasize account management, product augmentation, and customer service must give way to a strategy based at least partly on price.

A Supplier's Strategic Evolution

Companies can use an aggressive market-development strategy to respond to the mosaic of customer profiles that prevail at any given time. The experience of one company—a major producer of engineering plastics in Europe—illustrates how to do so successfully.

Historically, this company used strongly differentiated products and extensive customer-support programs to attract customers who were insensitive to price. The company simply avoided markets that had become price-sensitive as products aged and users became sophisticated.

Through the late 1970s, the company's sales growth and profit margins outpaced the industry's. But by 1982, as one of the company's products, a branded resin, was maturing, several other companies had entered the market. These competitors sold standard grades of the resin at prices 10% to 20% less than the European company's. None of the newcomers offered comparable customer-support programs, but by concentrating on price-sensitive customers they succeeded in establishing positions in the industry.

Using customer-experience and product-differentiation analyses as guidelines (segmenting customers according to knowledge of the product and products according to intensity of the competition), the company discovered that its strategy of avoiding experienced, price-sensitive users no longer made sound strategic sense. It learned via interviews with former customers that while its applications development efforts were still expanding the market, the company was losing many customers who were switching to less differentiated, standard grades. Further, it was giving aid and comfort to price-cutting competitors by avoiding price-sensitive business. Management finally concluded that the price-sensitive segment was the largest and fastest-growing segment in a slow-growing market and that its market leadership would be jeopardized if the company let its customers slip away by failing to recognize both their experience and the commodity nature of the product.

Based on its customer-experience analysis, the company revised its strategy in three ways. First, it decided to continue the traditional strategy of developing new products for designated industries. It expected this portion of the overall strategy to be a vigorous generator of net income in the near term but to diminish in the longer term due to technical limits.

Second, the company elected to reduce prices on products for which the total contribution from price-sensitive customers (experienced specialists) was greater than performance-sensitive customers (inexperienced generalists). To preserve margins, it also cut back on the support resources allocated to these products internally.

Third, the company took steps to slow the passage of the remaining customers who were experienced but still performance-sensitive to the price-sensitive category. These actions included active pursuit of legal protection of patent and licensing rights, development of new product grades, and the further augmentation of the product by offering associated services, such as computer-aided design.

This story stands in sharp contrast to our opening anecdote. Two things, however, are clear from both: the effect of customer experience is a potent factor in the marketplace and does not exist in isolation from the product life cycle. The two forces are interactive elements in the evolution of a market. Companies have often ignored the customer-experience factor because it is not readily measured—it is a concept that pertains to the forest, not to the trees. But successful companies choose and manage their customers with the same care they put into choosing and managing their products. Anticipating the patterns of evolution in customer decision making is as vital to success as is the most technically sophisticated product development program. In their final product-market choices, customers are as important as products.

Note

1. Theodore Levitt, "Marketing Success through Differentiation—of Anything," *Harvard Business Review*, January–February 1980, p. 83.

2

Exploit Your Product's Service Life Cycle

George W. Potts

> "It is the capacity for maintenance which is the best test for the vigor and stamina of a society. Any society can be galvanized for a while to build something, but the will and the skill to keep things in good repair day in, day out are fairly rare."—Eric Hoffer in *Working and Thinking on the Waterfront* (1969).

By Eric Hoffer's measure, the United States is a vigorous culture. Repair services for electronic products alone are estimated to cost more than $60 billion annually and employ 400,000 people. The computer industry by itself generates more than $20 billion a year in maintenance service revenues. When including everything serviced in the private sector—elevators, construction machinery, typewriters, vending machines, autos, machine tools, cameras, airplanes, home appliances, industrial controls, turbines, trucks, and so on—the number grows to almost $200 billion, or about 6% of the GNP.

Service operations, however, do not always enjoy the same depth and quality of managerial controls found in the manufacturing environment. As a result, product management tools are often transferred unaltered to the service side. When a product is maturing in its life cycle, for instance, its service cycle is only beginning to generate steam. If a service manager uses this product life-cycle notion unthinkingly, the result can be an excessive spare parts inventory buildup, a self-defeating service pricing strategy, misallocation of field manpower resources, or a premature shutdown of product improvement programs.

In this article I explore a way to look at maintenance control for products that have fairly long lives and require a good deal of service. This service life-cycle approach has been a fixture at Data General Corporation for several years.

The service life cycle covers the installed base of products needing maintenance. The installed base consists of the difference between total shipments and total "decay"—that is, the reduction in numbers still in use caused by product wear and discard, the customer's upgrading or switching to a substitute, or cannibalization of the product for spare parts.

Estimating the decay rate is very similar to calculating depreciation. Once a product is shipped to a customer there are measurable odds, in each year thereafter, that it will remain in the installed base. Data General found through experience that decay probabilities are reasonably stable by product class. By spreading the projected rate of decay of hardware shipped during the years of the product life cycle, Data General's forecasters could construct a good approximation of the total decay that would take place.

The difference between the cumulative shipments and this aggregated decay is in effect the service cycle. As Exhibit I shows, whereas the typical computer may reach its peak in shipments after only two or three years, the service cycle can easily last 15 years. An elevator may have a product cycle of only 10 years but a service cycle of 100 years!

At Data General, the service life cycle falls naturally into four phases:

1. Rapid growth—from the first shipment to the peak in the product cycle.
2. Transition—from the peak in the product cycle to the peak in the service cycle.
3. Maturity—from the peak in the service cycle to the last shipment.
4. End of life—from the last shipment through the last unit in the installed base.

Almost 70% of service revenues for this product came in the last two phases. Four factors determined this phenomenon: distribution and installation delays, which combined to postpone service revenue flow well beyond that for products; the compounding effect of service price increases; product upgrade purchases, often producing more servicing opportunities and, therefore, more revenue; and

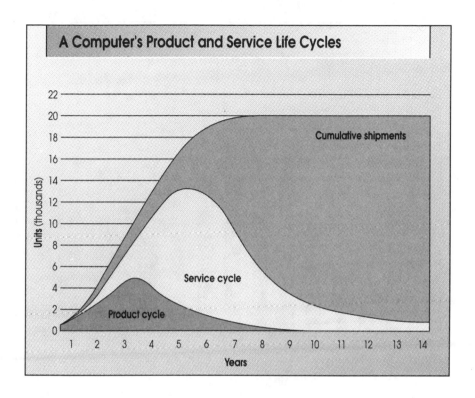

A Computer's Product and Service Life Cycles

certain service options (at premium prices) available later in the cycle.

For generation of service *profits* from installations, the last two phases were even more productive: more than 95% came during that period, which began two years after the product cycle had peaked. A main reason for this, of course, was the high revenue flow in those two phases. (See Exhibit II.)

Other factors were the front-end loading of many service costs, including repairer training, the product launch, and purchase of spare parts, and the sparse installation density of products (higher fixed costs per unit) in the early part of the service life cycle. In other words, about the time that manufacturing, development, and product marketing are leaving the scene, the service profit annuity is just beginning to kick in.

Often, however, there are forces working against this back-end

Exhibit II.

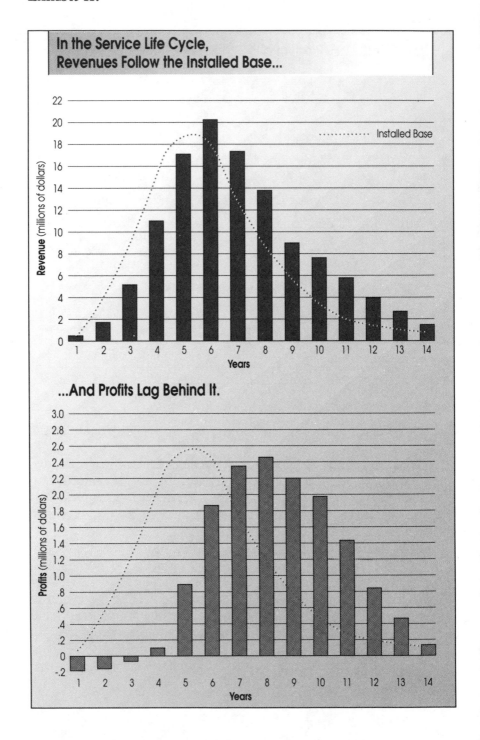

loading of profitability. They include: (1) higher failure rates toward the end of a product's economic life, particularly for mechanical and electromechanical products; (2) the annual compounding effect of wage hikes for field repair personnel, particularly hikes not offset by service price increases; (3) mismanagement of spare parts acquisition, distribution, or repair; and (4) the loss, through neglect and field-force attrition, of repair skills.

In the following pages I take up the four phases of the service life cycle.

RAPID GROWTH

At the outset, of course, expansion of the rate and extension of the length of the product sales surge are everybody's goals. There are many ways to gain an advantage through service at this time.

One way is by being very service-price aggressive against major competitors. The new product is perhaps being evaluated on a cost-of-ownership basis, so a trivial service price disadvantage can turn into a big sales headache. It is generally inadvisable to raise service prices during this phase.

A recently rediscovered wrinkle for many companies is the longer warranty, like Chrysler's seven years or 70,000 miles for its cars. These warranties appear to reduce service costs to zero during the period when discounting rates are the lowest in the cost-of-ownership analysis. (Obviously, the service cost is often buried in the product price anyway.) Such a ploy can also help the corporate image by carrying the implicit promise of high product quality.

During this period of product "infant mortality," ensure on-time distribution of enough spare parts to make prompt repairs. Vigorous stocking of field inventory can help build the reputation of the product and maintain the goodwill of "pioneering" customers.

Be ready to respond to complaints of product design or manufacturing process flaws. An effective early-warning system after the product launch will bring great rewards if it leads to engineering-out of the problems in later versions of the product. Moreover, when the buildup of spare parts reaches heavy proportions later, they will be of much higher quality. In this manner, Data General helped improve its product reliability at an annual compound rate of more than 10%.

The early-warning system may also call for upgrading and

streamlining diagnostic procedures. Diagnostic methods for a new product that work well in the lab often do not in the field. A process whereby field input is quickly assimilated into diagnostics can pay huge dividends over the service life cycle.

Another aspect of response to customer complaints is training of field maintenance staff. It is better to err on the upside with expenditures on training (as well as on the highest quality tools and documentation) since continued growth in the residual installed base should easily absorb any apparent lavishness.

Early customers of a new product always appreciate aggressive technical activity of this kind. It alleviates fears of getting a lemon and substantiates their belief that they made the right choice. Satisfied customers may talk to friends and other customers, thus helping the vendor carry out one of the most effective and cheapest marketing techniques known—word of mouth.

TRANSITION

During the interval between the time product shipments and service revenue have peaked, profit production from service is usually modest but growing. Whereas the theme of the first phase was "product growth at any cost," the theme of this stage is "controlling service resources." As revenues from the product decline and revenues from maintenance and service rise, management is faced with some critical issues.

One of them is whether to raise service prices. Usually these are not only justified—because the service buildup I described may make the service operation a money loser at this point—but also essential for continued effectiveness. A money-losing service operation is bound to get squeezed in the next budgeting session, which can lead to shortcuts in the initial stage of the next round of products. This, in turn, causes customer defections, which cause further budget cutbacks.

The solution lies in a fair price for service. A fair price often means annual price increases starting early in the transition phase and continuing through the service life cycle. The size of these increments should be tied to the product's failure rate and, to be fair, should seldom exceed the rate of inflation.

If failure rates are declining, it may be strategically smart to cut service prices for profitable products in the later stage of the service cycle. (Companies that don't offer service contracts—and therefore often don't differentiate service pricing by product—can still use the service cycle to set their spare parts pricing strategy.)

The acquisition of spare parts during this phase of the service cycle needs to be closely controlled. It's very easy to look down the road and extrapolate a promise of heavy material usage for a long time. But if the spare parts buildup continues after the growth rate of the service cycle starts to decelerate markedly, serious over-stocking of spare parts will be the unhappy result. This will spoil the service profit potential. Therefore, a good fix on the rate of decay is important.

In 1985, field service logistics management at Data General set a policy of restricting purchases of repair material for any product not in phase 1 or 2 of its service cycle. In the three years since, service inventories have been reduced by as much as $30 million.

After the product cycle has peaked, some manufacturers unfortunately fail to maintain the re-engineering activity they carried out in the period of fast sales growth. The service base is still growing, which presents opportunities to reduce product outages, material usage, or repair time. Phase 2 (and even phase 3) is not too late for installing engineering fixes that, though expensive to propagate in the field, still have many years of payback.

Data General has recently concentrated remedial reliability efforts on products no longer in the launch phase. In fiscal 1988 alone, this program is expected to save the service function upwards of $5 million.

Throughout this transition phase, the need for trained repair personnel continues to grow. Since by this time training should have become very efficient and effective, there is little point in being stingy with it now. Training more people than are currently needed may not be a bad idea so that enough maintenance experts will remain after attrition to handle the service requirements throughout the remainder of the product's service cycle.

MATURITY

As with good wine or cigars, this is the time for the company to reap the rewards of patience. This is harvest time, bringing strong revenue and profit growth. Since all repair asset acquisitions should have been made by now, it will also be a time of very strong cash flow. Moreover, it is a period of the greatest equipment density, with the repair force being at its most proficient.

Unless there is unusually heavy competitive activity, the programmed service price increases should continue. If a product is attracting service competition because its service price is too high, pressure will remain on the manufacturer to make the product more reliable in order to reduce the cost of providing the service. The early part of the maturity phase is a good time to introduce premium service options—car dealers, for example, have a great deal more success selling service contracts on older cars than on new ones—or value-adding options, like the "disaster recovery" services some computer vendors offer.

This is not a time for spare parts acquisition. In fact, every effort should be made to start disposing of material through sale of it, through refurbishing old equipment for sale, through its demanufacture for components, or through scrapping.

Some improvement programs can still be pursued for a product that has either a very high population or a very high failure rate. When these two circumstances occur together, the manufacturer still has an opportunity to recoup its investment in such an improvement effort.

END OF LIFE

While this term suggests that the product is ready for the glue factory, there is still plenty of life left for service revenue and profit generation. But since the item is no longer being manufactured, it may have vanished from headquarters' sight. Nevertheless, depending on the product cycle length and decay rate, as much as 50% of the equipment shipped may still be in use.

This remaining installed base not only yields a service profit annuity but also represents an opportunity for upgrading to newer products. If the manufacturer has prepared a migration path and has established a good service track record, customers may be quite ready to buy the next-generation product.

If service (or spare parts) price increases stopped in phase 3, a return of high failure rates at the end-of-life phase can justify a resumption, particularly for mechanical or electromechanical goods. (High failure rates at the front and back ends of the service cycle are often called the "bath-tub effect.") Contract or spare parts price hikes made to offset poor service productivity, balance a defecting customer base, or support unprofitable manufacturing will backfire. But price rises designed to restore a reasonable return to a well-run maintenance function delivering high-quality services are not gouging. Such value pricing is in the best interest of the customer as well as the vendor.

If these hikes encourage upgrading to the manufacturer's newer products, then the service revenue and profit sacrifices become only temporary. If, however, product development has not established a clear migration choice for replacing an end-of-life product, a service price hike is obviously not a good idea.

Continued attrition of replacement material is advisable through scrapping and salvage operations. The only technical programs of benefit at this stage are those that cut repair time without any appreciable engineering or training expense.

SPECIAL CHALLENGES

Each phase of the service cycle poses problems for the entire service operation, but each extends its most severe challenge to a different business segment. In particular:

Phase 1 (and before)—The technical services unit must work very hard to ensure a successful launch of the product and the rapid remedy of any technical glitches in it.

Phase 2—To avoid overstocking of inventory, logistics management must accurately call the turning point in spare parts demand.

Phase 3—While generating premium and value-adding services to boost total revenue, the service marketing function has to assess the advisability of continued service price increases.

Phase 4—Though the product may be passé in the minds of many at the company, field operations has to understand that it is not so in the eyes of customers. This function has to maintain a staff skilled with the product despite the attrition and relocation of personnel.

3
Good Product Support Is Smart Marketing

Milind M. Lele and Uday S. Karmarkar

When making purchases, customers often believe they are buying more than the physical item; they also have expectations about the level of postpurchase support the product carries with it. This support can range from simple replacement of a faulty item to complex arrangements designed to meet customer needs over the product's entire useful life. Our investigations show that defining these expectations of support and meeting them effectively can be critical to a successful marketing effort. Consider:

Caterpillar Tractor and John Deere, two companies whose marketing strategies are based on providing superior product support. Over the past quarter century both have concentrated on strengthening their dealers' service capabilities and on upgrading parts availability. They have backed these efforts with extensive service staffs and emergency parts ordering systems. They have directed equipment design to emphasize reliability and serviceability, and to minimize downtime. These two companies have made product support cornerstones of their organizations' corporate cultures and values.[1] This has remained true despite damaging strikes, recession, and acreage taken out of production.

The failure of Olivetti to establish itself in the United States, despite considerable investment during the past 15 years, primarily because of poor product support. The company has vacillated in its choice of distribution channels, thereby demoralizing its dealers. Parts and service training support have been inconsistent and usually poor. Initial buyer enthusiasm for new products has been repeatedly dampened by inadequate documentation and user training. As a result, despite excellent products at competitive prices, the company has failed to gain a strong foothold in the U.S. market.

Caterpillar and Deere illustrate the value of using support to improve marketing effectiveness. Product support, however, is an underutilized marketing resource in many companies. Developing and executing support strategies with marketing impact are difficult, and managers frequently do not know where to begin.

To maximize the marketing impact, managers need to have an accurate idea of customer support expectations and how to measure them. They can then use this information to segment existing markets in a new way or, in some cases, even to define new markets.

In developing a support strategy, it is necessary for managers to make trade-offs between effectiveness and cost. Our studies show that these trade-offs are often quite complicated and need to be evaluated carefully. Managers need to understand the nature of each trade-off and to develop a suitable framework for choosing among competing alternatives.

Why Support Fails

To many people, product support means parts, service, and warranty. In the early stages of market growth, customers concentrate more on technology and features and are concerned with only a few aspects of support, such as parts and service. As the market starts to mature, customer needs become more sophisticated. Product support encompasses everything that can help maximize the customer's after-sales satisfaction—parts, service, and warranty plus operator training, maintenance training, parts delivery, reliability engineering, serviceability engineering, and even product design.

In many companies, however, the earlier limited view still holds sway; as a result they separate product support from marketing strategy. In our experience, companies in which this is the case exhibit some or all of the following characteristics:

An explicit support strategy is lacking. The company views product support as a collection of individual tasks—enhanced product and/or service reliability, upgraded parts availability, improved training of service personnel, investment in additional service facilities—without an overall integrating theme. Improving support means "more of the same."

Responsibility for support is diffused. Many companies do not centralize responsibility for product support; individual departments such as reliability engineering, service administration, and customer relations carry out support tasks. As a result, management receives a disjointed picture of product support and its relation both to the customers' needs and expectations and to the company's overall product design and marketing strategy.

Support needs are considered late in the development cycle. Managers often fail to contemplate such needs until after the design is frozen and the marketing strategy decisions have been made. Individual departments adopt support strategies that may not be compatible with one another.

Management focuses on individual support attributes. Because of the diffusion of responsibility, management tends to focus on internal matters—engineering reliability, parts availability, warranty costs—rather than on customer-oriented measures such as downtime per failure.

Taken together, the foregoing characteristics lead to an often-observed cycle:

1. Top management becomes concerned about customer complaints relating to product support.
2. Individual departments demand more resources to improve customer satisfaction.
3. Lacking an overall strategy, investments in individual areas (e.g., reliability, parts inventories) rapidly reach a point of diminishing returns.
4. Customer complaints continue because basic problems have not been addressed.
5. The cycle repeats.

The net result is a waste of resources and potential or actual loss of market share to competitors with superior support strategies. To break the cycle, managers must first appreciate how customer expectations can affect support and marketing strategies and then learn how to use these expectations constructively.

Segmenting the Market

Customer expectations about product support add a crucial dimension to market segmentation. In most cases the package of support services that must be offered—implicitly or explicitly—changes significantly from one market segment to another. While many companies break down markets in terms of product features and performance, few segment markets on the basis of customers' support expectations. The result is that some support areas are overserviced while others are neglected.

Think of a word processor for a secretarial station. Potential buyers range from small one-secretary offices to large companies. There appear to be two market segments—one needing a basic model at a low price and the other a more comprehensive model at a higher price. Yet when customer expectations about support are analyzed, distinct differences emerge.

In the *one-machine office* the duration of downtime because of failure is crucial. Equipment failure means work virtually ceases, which can be extremely expensive. Disruption costs may be high because a small office cannot spare the people to search for replacements. The customer therefore expects both a low failure rate and minimum downtime per failure. Support costs or maintenance expenses are of secondary importance.

In the *multimachine office* downtime is important but not crucial; another functioning machine can be used to get important work out. Assuming that both the failure rate and downtime per failure are reasonably low, the customer is likely to be more interested in keeping maintenance and repair costs low over the life of the product.

These different expectations regarding support focus on varied attributes—failure frequency and downtime on the one hand, and maintenance and repair costs on the other—that form two distinct support segments. To meet customers' needs in each segment, management can choose a variety of strategies. For the word processor market, a company could (a) design for higher reliability (and charge a premium), (b) provide parts and service support as needed without a fixed-fee service contract, (c) develop a monthly service contract, or (d) use a spare machine on-site and incorporate its cost in the maintenance contract.

Each of these support strategies affects such major elements of marketing as product design and development, production and delivery, sales, and pricing. Choosing the right strategy involves a series of trade-offs such as product cost versus support effectiveness, product cost versus support cost, and support cost versus support effectiveness.

The importance of customer support expectations as an added dimension in market segmentation now becomes evident: different strategies are best for different segments. Ignoring these differences runs the risk of under- or overservicing segments, or under- or overpricing the product and the support services. The three steps involved in developing effective support strategies for a given product are:

1. Defining customer expectations regarding support.
2. Understanding the trade-offs implied in each support strategy.
3. Identifying the strategies that best fit management's objectives.

In planning a support program, however, managers need to be aware of the character of customer expectations, of the limitations of different support strategies, and of the interactions among strategies.

Defining Customer Needs

A major problem in segmenting the market on the basis of customer expectations lies in defining what these expectations are. Unlike product features or performance levels, customer support expectations focus on intangible attributes such as reliability, dependability, or availability. Without a suitable framework, the task of defining support segments is very difficult.

Because these intangible qualities can be viewed as proxies for underlying costs, the life-cycle cost concept used in equipment purchasing decisions can provide the basis for quantifying customer preferences regarding support. The life of a product after it is placed in service can be viewed as a sequence of uptimes and downtimes, terminated eventually by final failure, obsolescence, or sale and replacement. As the product goes through this cycle, customers can incur three types of costs:

1. Fixed costs on each failure occasion, independent of the length of downtime.
2. Variable costs that depend on the length of downtime and whose major component is the value of service lost (opportunity cost).
3. Maintenance costs of the product or service.

Because random events determine some of these costs, and since customers are likely to be risk averse, another factor must also be considered: uncertainty concerning the length and frequency of failure, the time needed for repair, and the magnitude of costs incurred.

To illustrate how underlying costs measure customer expectations, consider a washing machine used by a household and a large crawler tractor used by a builder. If the washing machine breaks, the homeowner incurs a repair bill (the fixed cost of failure). By and large, the homeowner is unwilling to pay a large premium to reduce the downtime (low variable costs of failure). Other things being equal, the purchaser of a domestic washing machine wants to keep repair costs low (high reliability).

On the other hand, if the crawler tractor breaks, the builder incurs significant fixed costs (of repair) and variable costs (wages paid to crews that sit idle until the tractor is back in action). Very often, the builder pays out more in wages for every hour the tractor is down than for repairs (the variable costs are far higher than the fixed costs). For this reason, the builder wants a tractor with both high reliability and low downtime per failure, and may even trade off reliability for less downtime.

In practice, customers incur fixed, variable, and maintenance costs. They are also risk averse and therefore concerned about uncertainty. Furthermore, as we have observed, in many cases customers do not clarify the relative importance of costs and risks. "I want a dependable product" often describes a wide variety of support needs. To define customer expectations accurately it is therefore necessary to find out which costs and risks customers are likely to be concerned about and then to develop suitable techniques for measuring them.

MEASURABLE ENTITIES

Once the costs and risks of concern to the customer have been identified, managers can single out attributes such as reliability, availability, and dependability, and measure these in such terms as failure frequency, mean time between failures, downtime per failure, and the like.

While conceptually straightforward, translation of expectations into measurable terms is complicated by the fact that many customer expectations regarding support are nonlinear, support effectiveness is measured by many different variables, and statistical averages are misleading.

NONLINEAR EXPECTATIONS. By and large, we are conditioned to think linearly: if one hour of downtime is bad, two hours are twice as bad. Unfortunately, customer expectations regarding support do not follow this simple logic. Instead, a threshold can be established for each expectation.

During the harvest season, for instance, farmers are extremely sensitive to the length of time a piece of farm equipment is out of commission because of a failure. Their reactions to downtimes lasting a half-day versus a day or more are vastly different. A downtime failure of a combine that can be repaired in four hours or less is tolerable; in fact, it often provides a welcome respite from harvesting. As the length of downtime increases past four to six hours, however, farmers become concerned, and by eight hours or so, they may be frantic. Beyond eight hours, the actual period of downtime is immaterial; farmers will go to almost any lengths to get up and running again—even if it means purchasing a new or used combine.

Farmers appear to have a similar threshold regarding the frequency with which a combine fails. Naturally, they hope it never fails; but, being realists, they're willing to accept an average of one or two failures per season. Farmers' tolerance of failure decreases very rapidly beyond this point, however, so that a combine design averaging three or four failures per season acquires a poor reputation. This attitude appears to be independent of the downtime duration at each failure; the number of failures is what the farmers remember, not how quickly the repairs were made.

Not all support expectations have clear thresholds. For instance, customers expect gradual improvements in the operational availability of a product or service (i.e., in its effective use during a given period). Since expected life-cycle costs—the purchase costs combined with discounted maintenance and repair costs less discounted salvage value, if any—vary in a smooth progression, expectations about these are predictable and linear. Customer reactions (to operational availability, life-cycle costs, and so on) are proportional to the value of the support variable.

SUPPORT EFFECTIVENESS. Only in the case of low-cost household appliances like toasters or alarm clocks does a single variable such as reliability adequately measure support effectiveness. The farmer measures the support provided to his combine or tractor in terms of at least two variables—failure frequency and downtime per failure. The sophisticated purchaser of electronic office equipment weighs the support packages available as well as the training and programming assistance provided.

Moreover, customer preferences are often noncompensatory. Customers rank-order their preferences and do not consider an excess of one type of support as a substitute for deficiencies in another. A contractor buying a bulldozer, for example, wants both high reliability and low downtime per failure. He will be dissatisfied with any equipment that causes excessive downtime per failure, no matter how infrequently the failure occurs. Similarly, the office equipment buyer wants rapid response, irrespective of how infrequently it may be needed. For both, the risks and requirements of downtime are too high.

STATISTICAL AVERAGES.   One customer may get a dreamboat; another a lemon or a succession of lemons. Parts can be obtained over the counter—right away or ten days later. To cope with random fluctuations, people tend to use the average or the mean: the average weekly sales, the average wage rate, the average time between failures, and so forth.

In our investigations, we found ample evidence that averages are not only misleading but potentially dangerous when measuring support effectiveness. An industrial equipment company, for example, prided itself on the apparently high reliability of its product. Engineering tests indicated that the mean time between failures for its major product line was 400 hours. Since the average annual usage was 600 hours, management felt satisfied; after all, the machine experienced between one and two failures per year.

On conducting a survey of users, however, the company received a rude shock. True enough, the average number of failures was 1.65 per year. But, more than 40% of the users reported more than two failures a year; and of those, 20% had four or more failures. As the sales vice president put it, "If that's true, over 40% of our customers are not happy with our performance!"

This situation is also true of other support measures such as downtime per failure. These measures tend to be distributed in a skewed fashion, with a significant proportion of them lying well above the mean. For this reason, the mean is an extremely misleading measure. A more appropriate measure is a percentile, such as 80th or 90th percentile of the variable in question. This measure would have shown the industrial equipment company that a large proportion of their users were in fact experiencing more than two failures a year. Similarly, the office equipment company that assured purchasers, "We can usually have a service person out to your location within four to six hours" would have found that response time in the 80th percentile was closer to two working days.

Choosing an Alternative

Having defined customer needs, the company can set about designing suitable support strategies. Normally, the manager can use one of several alternative support approaches. Each meets certain customer needs, such as greater reliability, shorter downtime per failure, or lower repair costs. At the same time, each affects the manufacturer's costs or revenues by creating higher product costs, increasing support costs, or lowering revenues. Choosing an alternative involves a trade-off between the effectiveness in meeting customer needs and impact on costs.

Such trade-offs are complex; neither effectiveness nor cost can be judged in terms of a single variable. Since support strategies meet diverse customer needs and affect the manufacturer's costs in various areas, trade-offs have to be made along several dimensions of effectiveness and cost.

Two additional factors further complicate the process of choosing a support strategy—the limitations of individual strategies and the interactions among strategies.

LIMITATIONS OF STRATEGIES

The building blocks of any support package are the individual strategies designed to improve reliability, make the design modular, provide equipment on loan, and add diagnostic capabilities. Exhibit I lists some typical strategies, together with suppliers' costs and customers' benefits. While the impact of each varies with the technology and the industry, we have observed that all strategies

Exhibit I.   Support Strategies: Costs and Benefits

Support strategy	Suppliers' costs	Customers' benefits
Improve product reliability	Design, engineering, and manufacturing	Lower rate of failure
Use modular designs, component exchange	Design, engineering, and inventory holding	Less downtime per failure, greater availability
Locate service facilities near markets	Site and facility; transportation and inventory	Faster access, less downtime, greater parts availability
Provide diagnostic equipment	Design, manufacturing, and service training	Faster diagnosis, less downtime, greater parts availability
Provide equipment on loan/standbys	Holding equipment for loan	Less downtime
Offer longer warranty periods and wider coverage	Warranty reserves and repair	Less uncertainty
Use mobile repair units	Transportation, inventory, and personnel	Faster response, improved service availability

exhibit diminishing returns to the customer, increasing costs to the supplier, and limited areas of impact.

DIMINISHING RETURNS.   Every support strategy produces diminishing returns with respect to customer benefits; beyond a certain point, further improvements are increasingly ineffective. For example, reliability improvements that extend the mean time between failures increase the availability of equipment to the customer, but the rate of increase slows down past a saturation point. Customers recognize this phenomenon, and once this point has been reached their focus shifts to other concerns, such as repair time.

INCREASING COSTS.   The initial improvements in any strategy are the simplest and therefore the cheapest. Succeeding improvements are progressively more expensive. It will cost the manufacturer more to raise the mean time between failures from 100 to 150 hours, for instance, than it did to raise it from 50 to 100 hours.

LIMITED IMPACT. Each of the strategies shown in Exhibit I affects only part of the failure and restoration cycle. Diagnostics reduce the time required to locate the failure but do not affect repair time. Providing equipment on loan lowers the variable costs of a failure but does not alter the fixed costs.

INTERACTIONS OF STRATEGIES

The foregoing limitations require the use of a suitable combination of individual strategies to meet customer needs. In synthesizing an overall strategy, a manager must know how individual strategies interact to ensure that the proposed combination achieves desired levels of customer benefits while keeping supplier costs as low as possible. Specifically, the manager needs to be aware of how strategy interactions can raise or lower overall costs to the supplier, complement benefits, and cause benefits substitution.

COST ADJUSTMENT. The way in which separate strategies interact affects the overall cost. For example, increasing reliability will lower the cost of supplying equipment on loan. It may, however, raise the cost of warranty repairs because it requires more expensive components.

BENEFITS COMPLEMENTARITY. Certain combinations tend to reinforce the benefits of individual strategies. For instance, diagnostics are more effective with modular designs, which, in turn, are more effective when used in conjunction with on-site repair.

BENEFITS SUBSTITUTION. One strategy may serve as a substitute for another in terms of customer benefits. For example, speed of repair is less important when equipment loans are made available; therefore, both diagnostics and to a lesser degree modular design are substitutes for equipment on loan. Modular design reduces the need for large field inventories of spare parts; thus, these two strategies are to a certain extent substitutes for each other.

Developing a Structured Process

The need to use several measures of cost and effectiveness and the limitations and interactions of individual strategies make a structured process for choosing support strategy essential. In its absence, a manager may not realize that existing strategies cost more and are less effective than alternatives, may yield to the pressures of individual departments and choose a suboptimal strategy, or may fail to make the decisions needed to stay competitive.

While situations vary, in general a manager should:

Define suitable measures of cost. Life-cycle costs are often appropriate; other measures can also be used.

Categorize all feasible support alternatives. Alternatives involving major design changes should not be excluded as they could be essential to improving support effectiveness.

Develop techniques to evaluate the cost and effectiveness of alternative strategies. Computer simulation, use of mathematical modeling, or field trials may be useful.

Measure the cost and effectiveness of each alternative. As measurements will be imprecise, it is necessary to show ranges and estimates of error.

Choose one measure of cost and another of effectiveness and plot the results. The most important or significant measures should be analyzed in this step; other measures will be checked later.

Identify key strategies. Some strategies will stand out as superior in cost and effectiveness.

Repeat trade-off analysis using other measures. Determining if different measures change key strategies is a valuable check.

This process can narrow the options to two or three major choices. The final decision will depend on external factors such as management's preferences, the competitive situation, or other marketing or product concerns.

What to Focus On

Support strategies are not static; a strategy that is effective today will, if unchangeable, become ineffective in meeting future customer needs. Generally, customer satisfaction increases with improvements in one area (e.g., reliability) up to a point. As diminishing returns to the customer set in and the manufacturer's costs increase, companies will need to switch to another, often radically different strategy, like lending equipment. And when customers demand higher levels of satisfaction than can be economically provided with loaners, the company has to switch to still another approach, like improving access to components that fail and thereby reducing repair time.

This pattern appears to be characteristic of product support systems in general. A different, dominant strategy provides the most customer satisfaction at successive stages, and the level of customer satisfaction increases progressively. Each rise in the level of satisfaction raises the manufacturer's costs and accentuates the need for choosing another, more efficient support strategy.

To ensure that their products remain competitive, managers must identify the various stages that exist for their products and market segments. Having chosen a support strategy, they must ascertain their company's and competitors' relative positions, anticipate when customer needs or competitive pressures will require the company to shift to the next stage, and plan for shifts in support strategy.

A manufacturer's relative market position often determines support strategy. If customers and competitors perceive the company as a leader in identifying and meeting support needs, management can set the pace at which support effectiveness is improved. On the other hand, a company that is perceived as an "also ran" has to follow and, if possible, anticipate changes in the strategies of any leaders or in customer expectations.

Since shifting to a new stage raises the level of effectiveness considerably, companies that are slow to react to changes in customer needs and/or the level of support provided by competitors risk being frozen out. Improvements in the level of support given in other industries, raising customers' expectations across the board; pressure on competitors to maintain or increase market share; and introduction of new support techniques—any or all of these could signal the need for a shift. Managers also need to plan for such shifts to ensure that existing support strategies don't box them in.

Designing Support: A Case Study

An industrial equipment manufacturer started to design a new series of industrial tractors to replace its current models in the

mid- to late 1980s. The company was aware of customer dissatisfaction regarding existing levels of support, which it had made
several efforts to improve. Realizing the value of designing support
and product strategies in parallel and recognizing that responsibility for support was fragmented, management appointed a study
team reporting to the president. The team's charter was to develop
strategies that would profitably deliver superior support for the
new series of industrial tractors.

Existing marketing data indicated a number of diverse customer
needs regarding product support. Although it identified individual
support elements such as greater parts availability, higher reliability, and more service training, the data gave little insight as to
how customers measured overall support effectiveness or made
purchase decisions.

To determine failure frequency, causes of failure, downtime per
failure, and the components of downtime, the study team mailed a
survey to the entire user population and received more than 3,000
responses. In addition, the team used a combination of focus groups
and in-field interviews to determine customer preferences and develop measures of support effectiveness.

The team's investigations showed that customers focused on two
key factors: the downtime caused by an individual tractor failure
and a combination of how often their tractors failed, how much
total downtime these failures caused, and the level of regular maintenance required.

The relative importance of these factors in purchase decisions
varied. For one customer group, downtime per failure made the
greatest impact on purchase decisions, while a second group
weighed other factors as well. This suggested the existence of two
separate support segments. The team decided to use the following
measures of support effectiveness for both segments: the 85th percentile of downtime per failure (i.e., no more than 15% of the
failures exceed this level of downtime), and the annual operational
availability or ratio of uptime to the sum of uptime, downtime, and
maintenance time.

The team felt that the operational availability ratio best captured
the effects of improvements in engineering reliability. It also
smoothed out random fluctuations in parts availability and showed
the impact of improvements in maintainability and serviceability.

When the team analyzed the causes of downtime, it found that
parts delay accounted for more than half the total downtime, with

Exhibit II. *Alternative Support Strategies for an Industrial Tractor*

Key	Strategy
A	Improve fill rate for parts from 91% to 95%
B	Improve mean time between failures from 350 to 450 hours
C	Develop and install microprocessor-based diagnostic capability in each tractor
D	Provide faster parts service using parts vans
E	Redesign tractor to permit faster modular exchange of electrical and hydraulic components
F	Provide users with tractors on loan during serious failures
G	Redesign tractor for modular exchange of electrical, hydraulic, and engine-driven train components
H	Redesign tractor as in strategy E and provide loaners
I	Redesign tractor as in strategy G and provide loaners
J	Redesign tractor as in strategy C; provide loaners and built-in diagnostics

repair time taking up a third, and travel time the rest. This fact suggested some alternative strategies: increased dealer-level parts inventories, improved service training, and the use of mobile repair vans. Where downtime was critical, equipment on loan would be furnished, if economical.

When the team analyzed the causes of failures, it discovered that a large number were breakdowns in electrical and hydraulic components. Individually, these failures were easy to repair; their cumulative effect was, however, large. Engine and power-train failures did not have the same impact because, while each failure caused considerable downtime, such failures occurred infrequently. These facts suggested some additional strategies: improved reliability (especially of electrical and hydraulic components) and tractor design to permit modular exchange of defective components in the field.

After identifying all feasible alternatives, summarized in Exhibit II, the team developed a computer-based simulator, which duplicated as far as possible the effect of using a given strategy or combination of strategies in terms of downtime and operational availability. Finally, the team calculated the costs of the various alternatives, using a life-cycle cost model.

KEY TRADE-OFFS

To identify the optimal choices, the team then plotted the costs and effectiveness of the various strategies. Exhibit III shows a typical plot. Overall, effectiveness improved substantially (for example, the 85th percentile of downtime was reduced from 45 hours to 10 hours or less. However, support costs increased at least fourfold too). In addition, the analysis showed that:

> While parts delay was a significant factor in total downtime, improving parts availability had little impact. This was because most repairs required several parts, and absence of even one part caused at least a one-day delay because of shipping time.
>
> Built-in diagnostics had little impact; in most cases, diagnostic time wasn't important.
>
> Equipment on loan was not economic until overall reliability had reached approximately 400 hours between failures.
>
> Equipment loans and modular exchange were complementary. Loaners reduced customer downtime while modular exchange reduced the number of loaners by allowing rapid in-field repairs.

As shown in Exhibit III, there were basically three stages—from 50 hours of downtime to 30 hours, from 30 hours to 20 hours, and from 20 hours to 10 hours. In each stage, the most efficient strategy was quite different. In Stage I, improving reliability was the best strategy. In Stage II, providing loaners was the most efficient, while in Stage III, a combination of modular exchange and loaners was most efficient.

MANAGEMENT'S CHOICES

After reviewing the team's analysis, management decided that under current market conditions, supplying loaners (Strategy F in Exhibit II) was the most cost-effective. However, loaners would not provide long-term advantages because competitors could easily do the same. Therefore, the company decided to make major changes

Exhibit III. Trade-Off Analysis Plot of Support Strategies

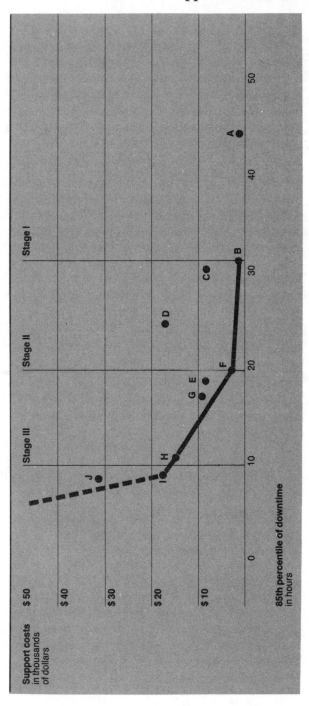

in its design philosophy and to aim for greater modularization of critical components. A combination of modular exchange and loaners would provide superior support at least cost, while the long lead times required for design changes would ensure long-term competitive advantage. Management therefore decided to proceed as follows:

1. Improve the reliability of its existing design to allow use of equipment on loan.
2. Introduce equipment on loan (Strategy F) in the mid-1980s, or earlier if competitive pressures demanded it.
3. Change its design approach to allow progressive modularization of key components.
4. Switch over to a combination of modular exchange and loans (Strategies H and I) in the late 1980s.

The industrial equipment manufacturer needed three to five years to change its design and to modularize its components. Had the company concentrated on improving reliability of its existing product, it would have found itself locked in and unable to change without incurring large engineering and tooling costs as well as a premature phase-out of its current designs.

Note

1. Thomas J. Peters and Robert H. Waterman, Jr., *In Search of Excellence: Lessons from America's Best-Run Companies* (New York: Harper & Row, 1982) and "How Deere Outclasses the Competition," *Forbes*, January 21, 1980, p. 79.

4
The Case of the Tech Service Tangle

Benson P. Shapiro

Linda Yu had reserved a window table at her favorite restaurant near the offices of the Pigments Division of Industrial Chemicals, Inc. The grand Friday lunch was an indulgence that Linda, the division vice president of marketing, had come to enjoy since the introduction three years ago of WP-88.

WP-88, a specialized white pigment and color enhancer used in a wide variety of differentiated, top-of-the-line products—including house paints, industrial coatings, textile dyes, and printing inks—was so superior to its predecessors and competitors that it now dominated the high-performance white pigment market in the United States. A patent granted in 1986 covered U.S. usage of the product as well as its production process. All in all, the pigment was one of the biggest success stories in the history of Industrial Chemicals. A division with annual sales of $30 million four years ago now generated $200 million in WP-88 revenues alone.

Linda, 37, was a rising star, and she enjoyed her status. She especially liked the opportunity to influence the direction Industrial Chemicals would take over the next several years. At the moment, she was seeking allies for a new approach to pigment marketing, and she had planned this lunch as a first recruiting effort and a trial run of her ideas.

Linda's lunch guest was Hugh Swann, 48, a chemical engineer and 17-year company veteran, who had toiled obscurely for most of his career in the division's research lab. But now Hugh was an even bigger star than Linda: he'd been chief chemist on the research team that had developed WP-88. He'd received a big raise, a bonus, and a long-coveted promotion to vice president for research and development.

"Hugh, let me make a suggestion," Linda said. "They have a veal in white-pepper cream sauce that will make you a happy man. Trust me."

"Fine with me," Hugh replied. "Anything white makes me a happy man these days." They both laughed.

"Well," Linda said, "that's why I asked you to lunch. I've been doing a lot of thinking about the future of WP-88, and frankly, I'm starting to get concerned. There's no question we'll be the industry leader for a long time; our product and process patents will see to that. But the glory days are over, Hugh. We're not going to see 50% to 60% growth rates any more; in fact, we're projecting growth this year of 20% at best. Within three years, sales could flatten out."

"Of course they could," Hugh conceded. "We've saturated the market."

"Well, not quite saturated, but I'm glad you agree with the forecast. The point is, it's time to stretch our thinking. We can't keep acting like WP-88 was the end of the rainbow. This division has lots more to offer—or at least it should have."

"I couldn't agree with you more," Hugh said.

Linda beamed. This was going to be easy. "Just follow my thinking for a minute. Our plant expansion last year means we can raise output 30% without any additional investment. So a big piece of incremental revenue falls straight to the bottom line. Given our margins, the extra earnings would be huge. The problem is, we've captured about all the current market we're going to capture. We've already got an 80% share in our segment of paints and dyes. We've still got some growth in specialty inks, but essentially our biggest customers are buying as much WP-88 as they're going to. Right?"

"Right."

"Wrong," Linda corrected. "The fact is, there are all kinds of applications our customers haven't thought of yet. Not to mention applications we haven't thought of yet. How hard have we really tried to expand the possibilities for WP-88? How hard have we tried to educate our customers? How aggressively have we promoted WP-88 as a brightener and enhancer? For heaven's sake, Hugh, the paint companies should be using it in almost all of their high-performance products. There must be hundreds of applications out there."

"But Linda, that's not our problem," Hugh protested. "Our customers have their own people to work on applications."

"But they don't know the chemistry the way we do. You're always saying WP-88 isn't just better, it's different—physically and chemically different from what we've sold before. You know Integrated Coatings? Well, they just bought a marine paints company out on the West Coast, and they're trying to use WP-88 with a new solvent. They've been having a lot of problems, Hugh, and they need our help."

Hugh said nothing, but he was still paying attention. So Linda continued. "What I'm suggesting is, we need to offer in-depth technical service. Hire field engineers who will work with customers to solve their problems and develop new uses for WP-88. The big paint companies have specialized labs around Detroit to work with the auto companies: we need technical people there to work with the paint companies. Our textile business is coming along, but if we had technical people in North Carolina to work on new dyes, who knows how much faster it would grow? Imagine if we work with one of the big paint companies on a new coating that Ford thinks is the greatest thing in ten years. Think how that builds our reputation. And think of the revenues!"

"And what if one of these new products lays an egg?" Hugh countered. "What if Ford buys a corrosion-resistant paint we helped develop and it doesn't do the job? What does that do to our reputation?"

"Hugh, I'm talking about making a name for ourselves as a top-drawer technical house. Creating new applications, modifying old ones, smoothing out processing problems. Transforming our business from a division that sells materials to a division that collaborates with its customers to make new products."

Hugh didn't like what he was hearing. It certainly wasn't what he had in mind for Pigments. He wanted to enlarge the division's research lab, and he was looking to hire three top-notch research chemists to round out his staff.

"Linda, just where do you think these field engineers are going to come from? I certainly hope you're not planning to raid R&D. I need *more* staff, not less. We hit a home run with WP-88, and we put this division in the big leagues. We need another home run, not a few sacrifice flies. Why do you think I'm borrowing lab space from Adhesives? I've got people working on two projects that might be the next WP-88. We can't dilute our efforts."

"Hugh, it's a question of vision. The whole chemical business is moving towards more technical collaboration, more aggressive work downstream. To be a credible supplier, to compete successfully when the next breakthrough comes along, we have to start setting the standard not only for innovative products but for innovative service. We're talking about the long-term future of this division."

"Let's talk about the short term for a minute," Hugh said. "The money for this has to come from somewhere. Tech service isn't cheap, you know. Formulation chemists and field engineers get big bucks. And they're not easy to find."

"I'm not talking about an army," Linda said. "Eight people or so. One tech service representative at each of our district sales offices, maybe two in places like Detroit or Chicago. It won't be cheap, but it's a solid investment."

Lunch arrived and was set before them with a flourish. Linda's appetite was not what it had been.

"Hugh, hear me out. I don't underestimate the value of new products. But a development like WP-88 happens once in a career. Who ever dreamed this product would generate these kinds of revenues? Most of the time, for most companies—and I mean for *this* company, *now*—developing 'new products' means finding new ways to use existing products. WP-88 is still in its infancy. We haven't begun to identify all the ways it can be used."

"Fine," Hugh said with some heat. "But you started off talking about growth rates of 60%. We can't sustain that, or anything like that, by mining new applications for WP-88. We've been soaring, and at some point we have to come to earth. But I want to soar again, and that means another big new product. And *that* means hard scientific work with imagination and insight. In other words, concentrated R&D. So don't even think about diverting our technical resources to tech service. We need them where they are. And don't lecture me about vision!"

"I think you're wrong, Hugh. Not about new products—of course they're critical. But the new revenues we can pick up from our old customers are bigger than you think. And what about all the smaller companies that lack technical expertise? Think about all those additional sales opportunities."

"Linda, even if you're right about incremental sales—and I'm not saying you are—have you really thought through all the problems? What kind of tech service are you talking about? Process engineering support, like with this solvent problem on the West Coast? That could mean tech service people in the factory once a week. Or are you talking about product formulation? Let's say we give out the formula and processing requirements for some of the standard paints and inks. That's not going to be of much use to our most sophisticated customers.

"And what about standard formulations that only work with certain ingredients, say, a paint that needs a particular latex resin vehicle? Do we want to be in the business of certifying other suppliers? Remember, every supplier's materials interact differently with every other supplier's materials. Do you want us to come up with prototype formulas for every combination of color, tone, solvent, and resin, every drying character and spreading character? That would take forever."

She raised her hands as if to fend him off. "Hugh, you're making this more complicated than it has to be."

He pressed on. "And what about confidentiality? You're talking about in-depth discussions between technical people. Two or three customers make up 70% of our market in most industries. Do you really think our technical people will *never* share one customer's proprietary information with another customer, not even by mistake? Can you picture the storm that would kick up?

"Or what if *we* make a significant discovery in the course of working with one customer? They'll think it's partly theirs, and maybe they'll be right. But to the extent it's ours, how can we defend not sharing it with other customers? Where does our contribution end and the customer's contribution begin?"

"Look, Hugh, I haven't thought through every last detail. But plenty of other companies have solved these problems. We wouldn't be the first company to build a tech service staff. And when you look around at other businesses—steel, computers, engineered plastics—the industry leaders in each case are the companies that do the most technical collaboration with their customers. The real question is not whether to offer tech service; it's when and how."

After a long, uncomfortable silence, the lunch check arrived. Linda decided to split it.

Back in her office, Linda reflected on the discussion. Maybe it had been a mistake to float the idea past Hugh first. After all, her most natural ally was Terry Lamb, the division's aggressive young vice president for sales. If WP-88's growth rate started to plateau, he and his people would feel the effects as directly as she would herself. Maybe she and Terry should have approached Hugh together as a team.

Linda picked up the phone. Four minutes later, Terry met her at his office door.

"Come on in, Linda," he said. "Always happy to make time for marketing."

"Listen, Terry, I'll come right to the point. I just had lunch with Hugh Swann. I've been thinking through an idea, a really important idea for the future of WP-88 and this division, but Hugh's so full of himself and his little R&D kingdom that he can't see it."

"Tell me about it."

Linda ran through the important points: the saturated market and plateauing growth, the increasing role of service, the new applications, the incremental sales, the new, smaller customers. Terry listened quietly and nodded from time to time, but when Linda reached the crux of her idea—a technical service team that would spend most of its time in the field with customers—he started walking around the office as she talked. At last he interrupted.

"But Linda, who's going to pay for all this? Our big customers are already rattling my cage about price. Just last week I got hell from High Gloss Paint about our 'monopoly' pricing. When our second biggest customer says it wants lower prices, not more service, we try to listen. That 5% increase last month rubbed a lot of people the wrong way. Just last week we were talking about scaling back volume discounts. Now this? We can only push so hard."

"But that's my point, Terry. I know we're getting pressure on price. But tech service will help take some of that pressure *off*. Customers will be getting that much more for their money. I don't want to soak them for tech service, just recover our costs. And we won't be just another supplier anymore. We'll be a partner."

"A partner?" Terry smiled. "Have you ever met any tech service types? Goldway Chemical had a field engineering operation when I was there. I used to cringe when those guys talked to my customers. I'd spend time developing personal relationships, finding out who really matters at a company, who makes the decisions, and then some guy with a pocket protector and a textbook comes into the mix, some guy who doesn't know the first thing about the business. And what does he bring back? Not a bunch of orders, just a bunch of problems. We've got a standout product here. Why mess with success?"

Linda didn't hide her surprise. "This is going to be good for your people," she insisted. "Tech service people will get all kinds of information that your salespeople couldn't get, that we wouldn't expect them to get, that they're not trained to get. Field chemists would get past the purchasing agents we deal with now right to the people in the plants, right to the customer's technical staff. They'll give us detailed technical feedback that we've never had. They'll see potential new applications early. They'll help educate your people and make them even more effective. And they'll report to your organization—I'm sure Hugh won't want to get within a mile of them."

Terry stopped pacing and sat down on the edge of the desk. "Look, Linda, we all know we're under pressure from corporate for more profits, so why aren't we talking about more profits? This tech service thing is just an added expense. If you really want to dip into profits to boost sales, why not just cut the price? Or better yet, hire more sales staff. The name of this game is *move product*, Linda, and the way to move product is with more salespeople. If I have a choice between adding a tech service person or a salesperson, I'll take the salesperson any day. They generate the orders. Look, if you want, we can give my people more technical training. But believe me, they can push more pigment out the door than a hundred field chemists."

He stood up and resumed his pacing. "Not to mention the problems with customer relations. Who do these service people report to in sales? Will they be under field sales managers? Or do they report to the salespeople who handle the individual accounts? Who sets their priorities? How do we avoid having the same tech rep call on competitors, or on customers whose customers compete? We could really get ourselves in the soup in concentrated businesses like auto paints.

"Anyway," Terry went on, "the way to keep the sales curve rising is to *sell*. We've hardly scratched the surface in Europe; in fact, I'm in London and Frankfurt next month. And we both know we haven't done a good enough job with the smaller, specialized companies over here. We're just hitting our stride in marine coatings."

Linda stood up. "Terry, we've had a five-year streak of record growth. But that streak is coming to an end. Sure, Europe is a big priority, and so are the smaller U.S. companies, but those are short-term fixes. The real future for this division is still here at home, and I think it's still with our biggest, oldest customers. I don't know how I'm going to convince you of that, but I'm sure going to try. Let's talk on Monday."

How Do You Sustain Growth?

Executives with experience in marketing and R&D analyze the future of WP-88.

DAVID L. SLINEY

Linda is jumping the gun with her plans to build additional volume through technical service. The division's sales have increased from $30 million to more than $200 million. Where has this fantastic growth come from? From the hides of other suppliers whose products are being replaced with WP-88. That means a competitor or competitors have lost at least $170 million in business over the past three years—business they are no doubt anxious to recapture. Linda's first priority should be to secure and protect the division's existing base, before adopting new policies to promote growth—especially if those policies may alienate current customers.

Indeed, the Pigments Division is more vulnerable than its upward-sloping sales curve suggests. A small number of customers comprise a large share of its business. The division has their business because of the superior performance of its product, not because of deep or enduring relationships forged through years of reliable delivery and service. Many of its current customers would probably prefer to be doing business with their old suppliers; they know them, like them, and trust them. So Linda has to tread carefully. She may be right that tech service is a way to build deeper customer relationships. But the decision must be evaluated from that perspective—not as a vehicle to gain new revenues.

Terry, meanwhile, is right to raise the issues of price and customer backlash. Under pressure for greater profitability, Linda's short-term instinct is to pop the price, first with an across-the-board hike and now with a possible reduction in volume discounts. She's mistaken if she thinks that technical assistance will mollify customers who feel they're being gouged.

What Linda (and her colleagues) really need is for the division's general manager to step in and objectively evaluate WP-88's current positioning. Thus far, the debate over tech service has suffered from a common problem—functional myopia—that creates stark and unnecessary either/or choices. Hugh, who runs research and development, genuinely believes that the division needs more research on new products. Terry, who manages sales, genuinely believes that the division needs (surprise!) more salespeople.

But why create trade-offs that don't need to exist? For example, I'm not convinced the division's customers need a comprehensive program of technical assistance—or, at least, need it badly enough to justify the enormous investment it requires. Linda seems to think of technical service as high-level competitor intelligence. In fact, it can be a bottomless pit. A serious tech service operation would require an enormous commitment of research time, scientific manpower, and laboratory capacity—a commitment that may overwhelm the division's resources.

That doesn't mean Linda should abandon the concept. She and Terry should identify one or two customers who are enthusiastic about technical service and initiate pilot projects to work with them. These projects would help the division estimate the organizational infrastructure required to support a more comprehensive tech service operation and gauge its actual (as opposed to assumed) value to existing customers.

I do agree with Linda on one important point: WP-88 is in its infancy. That means there is great opportunity to plan for the future with market research, dialogue with customers, and experimentation.

JOSEPH ALVARADO

Linda Yu is off to a poor start in selling the idea of technical service to her colleagues. And she shouldn't expect things to get any easier—even though her proposal for deep technical involvement with customers in research, development, and production could have a big impact on WP-88 sales over the long term.

In any company, tech service faces at least two critical obstacles. First, the costs of tech service are always more visible and quantifiable than the benefits. Let's say a field chemist works with a big customer to incorporate WP-88 into one of its new marine coatings—the first of many small contributions by tech service. The incremental impact on the division's total revenues will be relatively modest. And who gets "credit" for the additional revenues? Who's to say the customer would not have included WP-88 without technical input from the field chemist? Any program with difficult-to-quantify benefits and easy-to-quantify costs faces great odds. Linda's approach thus far hasn't improved those odds.

Second, all companies face pressures to shift resources away from projects with long-term potential payoffs towards projects with quick and certain rewards. This means that a tech service program, even if it is adopted, can quickly get biased toward day-to-day problem solving rather than working with customers on new products and applications, which is where the real potential is. I can just hear the argument inside the Pigments Division a year after Linda's program gets off the ground. "Our biggest ink customer has a problem right now with WP-88 in one of its specialty lines. Why is our best field chemist in that customer's research lab working on a new product that might never see the light of day, instead of in his factory solving the problem on the ink line?" Linda's answer—providing assistance with processing *and* new product development—solves the trade-off problem but makes even greater demands on resources.

On the other hand, Linda is quite right to argue that many companies, even those selling supposedly low-technology products, have provided extensive technical service for years. Inland Steel is one of those companies. So these technical and organizational obstacles can be surmounted. But Linda must address them directly if she hopes to launch a technical service program and keep it running.

Technical assistance in manufacturing processes has been a fixture in the steel industry for decades; it's a part of doing business. All of the integrated companies have teams of people who visit plants to help solve specific manufacturing problems (say, a customer's stamping line with an unusually high reject rate). But for the last five years, Inland has been collaborating with customers before the production process—in the design, development, and prototyping of automobiles, major appliances, and other big products. This brand of "tech service" is most relevant to Linda's proposal.

Unlike Linda's division, which has enjoyed skyrocketing sales, Inland made its strategic commitment to technical collaboration during a period of steadily decreasing demand for its products. Automobile companies, our largest market, were downsizing their cars, looking to replace steel with substitute materials such as plastics and aluminum, and shopping the world for the lowest cost steel supplies. Inland Steel developed an early involvement program to respond to these threats. We wanted to increase our customers' technical knowledge of steel and the wide variety of its potential uses and applications. We also wanted to become part of the new product design process early enough to develop "new" steels to meet performance needs our current products couldn't meet. Finally, we wanted to understand and influence our customers' entire approach to design and development and be considered a full-fledged partner.

Our program has been up and running since 1985 and we have a dozen or so technical people. Their target constituency is our customers' advanced engineering groups, not their manufacturing engineers. We have had many successes, but the challenges of getting this organization up and running were enormous. It took extensive cooperation between Inland's research department, the sales organization, and our traditional tech services arm—all for a program whose long-term impact we could not quantify. Many of those challenges remain.

If Linda is serious about establishing a tech service operation, she has to start from scratch to win the support of Hugh and Terry. And she shouldn't try to win their support by promising quick results. Tech service is, in part, a matter of faith, or as Linda says, of transforming the character of an organization. There will always be pressures to cut costs, shift technical resources where they can have the most immediate impact, and demonstrate quantifiable benefits to justify investments. Without an organizationwide commitment to technical service for the long haul, Linda's program, even if adopted, could be beaten down at any time.

ABRAHAM B. COHEN

I'm not surprised that Linda's proposal ran into stiff opposition. Organizations are set up to run today's businesses, not tomorrow's. On the other hand, much of Linda's proposal deserves opposition. I have serious reservations about its timing and scope, although for different reasons than Hugh and Terry.

Tech service is hardly a revolutionary idea; what really surprises me is that the Pigments Division has managed to maintain its market leadership without it. Indeed, Linda may be overestimating the effect of tech service on future revenues. Early in the life cycle of a product, technical support can have a real impact on growth and profitability. But later in the cycle, when the market is saturated and customers are more self-reliant technically, the payback is not nearly as great. In Du Pont's photo-imaging business, for example, our pigment vendors' tech service groups helped us develop many new and specialized niche markets. But when you compare pigment sales volumes in such niche markets to the huge volumes in mass markets like paints, inks, and textiles, it's hard to believe that specialized applications, even in the aggregate, can reverse an otherwise slowing growth rate.

Linda has also failed to adequately answer the one implicit question from her colleagues she should have most anticipated: What's in it for me? In companies like Du Pont, where tech service has long been an integral and effective part of the corporate culture, most managers already know the answer. It's understandable that Hugh and Terry, however shortsighted their reactions, still need to be convinced that tech service will help their own areas of the business.

Hugh must recognize that R&D cannot develop the right technology and products for future market needs in a vacuum. As an R&D manager, I invariably found my tech service colleagues to be a direct pipeline to leading-edge market opportunities. With their help, we found attractive markets for photo-imaging technology that were outside our conventional photographic businesses. This led to a basic shift in our research focus, and ultimately, to a series of new and profitable ventures in the color publication and microelectronics markets.

Tech service was also a major factor in our ability to rapidly penetrate international markets. If Terry is serious about increasing market share in Europe, he better ask how the division expects to compete with the fast-response customer service local suppliers can provide without a locally based tech service operation.

I'm not sure what Linda plans to say on Monday, but I have a few suggestions.

First, scale down the proposal. Why start immediately with one tech service representative for every sales district? Why not adopt a pilot program, say, two reps at a tech service lab that operates alongside Hugh's R&D facility? This will reduce start-up costs, address Terry's concerns about sales force management, persuade Hugh that tech service and R&D can work together, and teach the division how best to implement a larger program.

Second, accept Terry's offer to train his salespeople more extensively. Having the two tech service reps do the training would promote team spirit and an even more effective tech service presence.

Third, urge Hugh to assume responsibility for the program's technical direction and the tech service lab, at least during the trial period. This will allow for effective communication among scientists developing and supporting new applications and begin to chip away at Hugh's concerns about "raiding" his facility.

I'm a strong proponent of technical service. But it is not a cure-all, particularly for a company with a commanding share of a saturated market. A modest program makes more sense in this environment. After all, if the pilot program is a big success, it can always be expanded.

JAMES A. PRESTRIDGE

Anyone who has been involved with the type of expansion the Pigments Division has experienced appreciates the organizational and personal strains it creates. A growth rate of 50% to 60% means the division doubles in size every 15 months or so. If such growth continues for a few years, the challenges become almost unbearable. Management becomes completely submerged in day-to-day crisis control, while strategic planning gets put on the back burner. Meanwhile, as key managers experience what seems to be limitless success, their aspirations rise even more sharply than the growth curve. They start to believe that they (rather than the product) have created the company's prosperity and that they are invincible.

Eventually, though, people begin to recognize that such meteoric growth can't go on forever. The impact of this realization on the organization and senior management can be, and often is, devastating.

The Pigments Division is on the verge of this realization. Growth is slowing down, and the next big product is still in the lab. It has a strong technical franchise—but not an unassailable one. Its recent success is tied to one product protected by U.S. patents and sold to relatively few customers. The emergence of a substitute, the loss of an important customer, a patent challenge or infringement by a large competitor, shortages of a key ingredient, or a multitude of other threats could quickly burst the division's bubble.

Linda's real contribution is in raising the red flag. Her proposal has many weaknesses, but even her analysis, which is quite sound, is greeted with an utter lack of enthusiasm. That's no surprise. Everyone has a lot to lose—or gain—from a change in the status quo.

It's interesting that neither Hugh nor Terry disputes the problem Linda has identified; their objections (and alternatives) to the tech service proposal are along straight functional lines. If Linda consulted the division's vice president of operations, I'm sure he or she would add another alternative. After all, with 30% excess capacity and a projected annual growth rate of 20%, the division is perilously close to running out of capacity. The world truly hates a monopolist that runs out of manufacturing capacity for a raw material.

So where is the division manager while all this is going on? Probably struggling to cope with the crisis of the moment: a personnel problem, headquarters' pressure for more profits, environmental regulations. But it's time for the division manager to intervene. This situation will not yield to strictly rational analysis among equals. An "acceptable" plan executed precisely and vigorously would be better than an "ideal" plan pursued in the face of internal dissension. Who could argue against "hitting another home run"? But in the businesses I know, home runs are few and far between—and more often the result of a lucky swing than long-term planning.

Linda's program has three flaws that the division manager must remedy. First, she has not defined the division's problems in a way everyone agrees with. Second, she has proposed a solution (and a fairly radical one at that) without cataloging and evaluating all significant options. Finally, a highly charged subject is framed in qualitative rather than quantitative terms. This combination is guaranteed to drive everyone up the wall with frustration. It's up to the division manager to address these weaknesses and persuade the team to work together enthusiastically with shared purpose.

This is not a case about tech service. Leadership is the real issue.

Note

At the time of this article's publication David L. Sliney was marketing vice president of Monsanto Chemical Company in St. Louis, Missouri. Joseph Alvarado was general manager, bar and structural sales for Inland Bar and Structural Company, a division of Chicago-based Inland Steel. Abraham B. Cohen had recently retired as a research director at E.I. du Pont de Nemours, and was a consultant on new venture management. James A. Prestridge was vice president of Teradyne, Inc.'s Component Test Group in Agoura Hills, California.

PART

V

Turn Sows' Ears into Silk Purses

Introduction

Every company has service and product failures. Superior companies plan for these events and use the experience to improve business processes or build customer satisfaction through artful recovery. The typical firm has no consistent strategy for dealing with these "fall-downs," tending to treat each one on an ad hoc basis. The worst companies choose to ignore these events entirely, arguing that complaining customers are not worth keeping.

One reason that many firms have difficulty handling problem events is that the production or service process is designed to flow one way, from the supplier to the customer. There is often no systematic approach to accommodate complaints or suggestions *from* the customer, which means that when a customer is most angry and frustrated, he or she often gets the worst service.

The first article in this section, "The Case of the Complaining Customer," by Dan Finkelman and Tony Goland, presents the familiar situation in which a customer, whose dry cleaning order has been lost, becomes increasingly frustrated and demanding when the cleaner fails to respond to his complaints quickly and graciously. Four customer service authorities offer their views on how the cleaner should handle the situation. All of the experts agree that the manager's response is symptomatic of larger problems in the company's operations. As in many companies, the manager's propensity is to deny responsibility for the problem, justify the company's processes, blame the customer for ill feelings, and suggest that his or her business is not valued. This manager clearly does not see the company's practices from the customer's point of view, and refuses to recognize that underlying problems could be addressed systematically to prevent a similar occurrence in the future.

Relationships between supplier and customer develop over a long period of time, but are established through a series of specific events. A particularly negative experience can shatter a long-standing relationship and undermine the years of effort that went into building it. On the other hand, a well-handled crisis can change a customer's indifference into fierce loyalty.

"The Profitable Art of Service Recovery," by Christopher Hart, James Heskett, and W. Earl Sasser, shows how to turn potentially damaging service problems into recoveries that build customer satisfaction. The authors maintain that "the battle for market share is won not by analyzing demographic trends, ratings points, and other global measures but rather by pleasing customers one at a time." Effective recovery programs begin with conscious management of product and service problems, i.e., measuring the costs of failure. Companies must encourage two-way communication with their customers, assuring them that complaints and suggestions will be taken seriously. In order to respond quickly to complaints as well as anticipate errors before they occur, the service provider must empower all employees with the skills, motivation, and authority to make service recovery an integral part of operations. A dynamic service recovery program allows the front line to take initiative and improvise.

The profit implications for good recovery are striking. At Club Med, for example, "one lost customer costs the company at least $2,400; a loyal guest visits the resort an average of four times after the initial visit and spends roughly $1,000 each time." Furthermore, an unhappy customer is likely to take his or her business elsewhere and convince others to do the same, while a happy customer is likely to share a positive experience with several acquaintances. Many companies do not take these dynamics into account. Instead they "concentrate on attracting new customers that may actually represent unprofitable business and neglect to take steps to retain more valuable existing customers."

If they are anticipated and well managed, mistakes are valuable opportunities to uncover information about the quality of business processes, enhance a culture of commitment to the customer, and build customer loyalty. A well-handled mistake may actually work to a company's advantage; most customers do expect problems, but do not expect an artful recovery.

Although the two articles in this section focus on service recovery, their recommendations are applicable for product suppliers as well. As products and relationships with customers become more complex, the service component is increasingly vital in influencing the consumer's overall perceptions. Commitment to effective recovery is an important agenda item for all managers. It "shifts the emphasis from the *cost* of pleasing a customer to the *value* of doing so."

1

The Case of the Complaining Customer

Dan Finkelman and Tony Goland

In an effort to improve service, Presto Cleaner installed a new computer system, designed to cut the customers' waiting time and simplify the drop-off and pickup processes. But the system was only a few months old when Mr. J.W. Sewickley, the company president, received an angry letter from Mr. George Shelton, whose laundry had been lost by the new system. Mr. Shelton's letter described his experience with Presto Cleaner's complaint-handling operations and demanded compensation and an apology. To respond to the complaint, Mr. Sewickley sent the letter to his customer complaint office, asking for more information. The answer came back from Paul Hoffner. He explained that there were extenuating circumstances and suggested that some customers may not be worth keeping. Is the customer always right? Where should a company draw the line on compensation and service? What is the best way to handle cases of complaining customers?

Mr. J.W. Sewickley
President
Presto Cleaner

Dear Mr. Sewickley: October 14, 1989

My wife and I are angry, frustrated, and disappointed ex-customers. We weren't always that way. In fact, for a year prior to the recent set of events, we were exceptionally pleased with your service. When you opened your store at the intersection of Adams and Broadway, we were delighted. Even though you're not exactly the least expensive dry cleaner in the area, my wife and I felt that the convenience of the location, the extra early and late hours of operation, and the helpfulness of the staff more than made up for the cost.

That was before you installed your computerized system. The following set of facts will tell you why we are not doing business with Presto Cleaner and what you need to do to get us back as satisfied customers.

July 28: I dropped off some laundry at the store, and the counterperson introduced me to the new computer system. I filled out a "preference card" (light starch for my shirts, folded in a box, and so on) that was entered into the computer. I selected an identification code number (my phone number) and bought a special bag customized with my identification number. The bag was only $3, no big deal. Ideally, the next time I had laundry, all I would have to do was put my laundry in the bag and drop it off. No waiting in line, no waiting for a receipt, the computer knew what I wanted done. When it came time to pick it up, I would just pay, get the laundry, and go. Easy, convenient, time saving. *Supposedly*.

August 4: My wife stopped in to pick up the July 28 order and dropped off the bag with the new laundry (4 of my shirts, 2 blouses, 1 suit, 1 skirt). The counterperson had her fill out her own preference card and entered that information into the computer.

August 10: On the way home from work, I stopped in to make a drop-off and a pickup. Guess what, Mr. Sewickley? I needed to buy a second special bag if I wanted to use the new system every time. I had to stand in line and wait my turn and finally give my order to the person behind the counter. It took forever. The great new system required the counterperson to enter every item, its color or other distinguishing feature, and also what operation I wanted done (clean, press, and so on). It took more than ten minutes. The old system was actually faster.

Then when I finished with the drop-off, I told the counterperson I also had an order to pick up. She asked me for the receipt. I explained that I had used the new computerized system with the bags, so I didn't have a receipt. She asked for my identification number. When she punched it into the computer, it said that my wife had picked up the order earlier in the day.

When I got home, I asked my wife if she had picked up the order. She said she had because she had a business meeting the next day and needed a suit that was at the cleaners. I asked about the bag, and after looking everywhere, including the backseat of the car, we finally determined that she had picked up a previous order and definitely not the order with the special bag. Missing were 4 shirts, 2 blouses, 1 suit, and 1 skirt.

August 11: I called the store from work and explained the problem. The counterperson was very courteous, apologized, and said that the store would be searched for the missing items.

August 14: I went to the store to pick up the last order. I stood in line, waiting for roughly 15 minutes for the two people in front of me to struggle through the computer system. I finally got my order and asked about the lost clothing. After a lot of asking around, the counterperson finally determined that the clothes had not turned up at the store. We next tried to locate the order in the computer, only to discover that when my wife and I had chosen identification numbers, she had used our home phone number and I had used my business number. After searching the computer using both numbers, we still turned up nothing. The counterperson said he would put a tracer on the order back at the plant.

August 15: My wife left work early to take our next laundry order to one of your competitors that has a store near our house. It's open only until 5:30, but there's less nonsense.

August 19: I picked up the order from the nearby Kwik N' Klean on my way to my favorite men's store to buy four new shirts. I didn't have enough shirts to make it through two weeks of work because of the four that were still missing. I am enclosing the sales slip for the four new shirts. I fully expect you to reimburse me for these shirts.

August 22: I called the store to see if my clothes had been found. There was still no word from the plant.

August 25: I called the store again. It had heard from the plant, and the plant did not have the clothing.

Why, Mr. Sewickley, did they not call me? I asked how to pursue a claim for lost items and learned that I should call a Mr. Paul Hoffner at the office.

I immediately called Mr. Hoffner and was told that he was not available. I left a message for him to call back as soon as possible.

August 26: I called back again. Mr. Hoffner was not available. I left the same message.

August 27: I called back again. Mr. Hoffner was not available. I asked if there was anyone else who could handle a claim for lost items and was told that only Mr. Hoffner could do that.

August 31: Mr. Hoffner called. I told him that I wanted to put in a claim. He was totally unaware of the situation, so I had to explain it to him. He suggested that he call the store and the plant to find out if there was any progress. I got the distinct impression that he didn't believe me and that he felt he needed to check with the store to make sure that I really was a customer and that there really was missing laundry. I assured Mr. Hoffner that I was a real customer. In fact, for more than a year, my wife and I have averaged between $20 and $30 worth of dry cleaning every week. Despite my assurances, Mr. Hoffner insisted that he had to check before anything could happen. When I pushed to find out what the process was, Mr. Hoffner said that if the clothing really was lost, I could fill out a claim form and apply for compensation.

September 7: A week had passed with no word from Mr. Hoffner. I called. He wasn't available. I left a message.

September 11: Still no word from Mr. Hoffner. I called and miracle of miracles, he answered the phone. After all that time, the only thing he could tell me was that neither the store nor the plant could find the clothes. I asked him to send the claim form.

September 18: No claim form had yet arrived in the mail, so I called Mr. Hoffner again. I got him and asked about the form. He said he had delayed sending it because he was sure that the clothes would be found. I insisted that he send the form immediately.

September 21: The claim form arrived, and I discovered

that it required that I attach both the original purchase receipt for the clothes and the counter receipt for the laundry order. Mr. Sewickley, do you keep your year-old receipts for clothing? And with the new computer system, there are no counter receipts!

It took two more calls to get through to Mr. Hoffner to complain about these requirements. He said that they were necessary to guard the company against fraud. He did acknowledge that since your own system no longer produced counter receipts, I couldn't be expected to send them in. But as far as the receipts for the clothes were concerned, he suggested that I go back through our charge card records to come up with the proof of purchase. I flatly refused. I told Mr. Hoffner that we have done more than $1,000 worth of business with Presto Cleaner over the past year and that we were not in the business of extorting money from dry cleaners. Further, I told him that if my word wasn't good enough for him, he could kiss our business good-bye, along with that of our friends and colleagues at work, who would soon hear all about the Presto Cleaner way of doing business.

September 22: Having had a terribly busy week, we forgot that my wife needed a dress cleaned for a business function Saturday night. Since it was Friday morning when we discovered this, our only real option was for my wife to drop off the dress at Presto Cleaner in the morning.

September 23: I went in to pick up the dress. The woman behind the counter recognized me and told me that the store had found our lost clothes. Apparently, they had been mysteriously included in another customer's order and only just now returned. She had no clue how this could have happened with the new system. She was, as usual, cheerful, apologetic, and polite about the mix-up. I paid for the order, picked up the dress, and went home.

September 25: Since there was no way to call your office over the weekend, I waited until Monday to try to reach Mr. Hoffner. He was again unavailable, so I left him the last message he will ever get from me: the clothes were found, but I would still like to talk to him.

Mr. Sewickley, that was more than two weeks ago, and I

still haven't heard from Mr. Hoffner. I am outraged by this entire episode, by the way your company treats customers, by Mr. Hoffner's conduct, by the lack of communication, and by the ridiculous system you introduced. I am particularly incensed at having to pay for clothes that were delivered almost two months late and by having to purchase new clothes to cover your company's mistake.

I expect the following: a full refund for the order that was lost; full payment for the four shirts that I had to buy to make up for the lost order; and a full apology from Mr. Hoffner. If all of those are forthcoming, I might consider giving your company another chance at my business. Otherwise, my wife and I will never patronize your company again.

Sincerely,

George Shelton

Memo
To: JWS   Oct. 29, 1989
From: Paul Hoffner
Re: Customer Complaint

This is in response to your memo requesting background information to respond to the customer complaint of Mr. George Shelton. I have reviewed his letter as well as our own file concerning this matter. I am convinced that we did make a good-faith effort to do right by Mr. Shelton, although he may not recognize it as such. Nevertheless, should you wish to mollify the customer, I would be perfectly happy to play the role of fall guy if it would help. As far as extending compensation to the customer is concerned, his demands seem to me far in excess of any real liability: he did get his clothes back, he will keep the four new shirts and use them, as well. I would certainly extend an apology to him—if he would like it from me, fine; I assume that it would be even more satisfactory coming from you, along with an offer to clean his next order free of charge.

Having said this, there are some mitigating circumstances that you should be aware of. I would not share these with the customer, but present them to you so that you will understand more accurately and fully what really happened, rather than what this one customer says happened. Again, that does not mean that a mistake was not made; there was a mistake, and we should take responsibility for that. But we acted in a way consistent with company policy and operations. Let me describe what really happened:

1.) The customer dropped off his clothing on literally the first day of operation of the new computerized system—a system that everyone at headquarters agrees is the key to our future success. Everyone also agrees that there will be problems, including, unfortunately, some lost customers. Mr. Shelton may be one such example. As you remember, because of delays with the system vendor and the software, we had only one week to train our people on the new system. Also, as I'm sure you're aware, not all of our store personnel are great at using this technology. It has taken more time than expected to get them to understand all of the steps they have to take to prevent mistakes.

2.) As I suspected all along, the real problem in this case was that the clothing was picked up by another customer. This is not that unusual. When it happens, we must rely on the goodwill of our customers to return what is not theirs. This time, because the customer was an infrequent user of our service, it took him more than four weeks to bring the clothes back in. Also, he dropped the clothes off at a different store. Unfortunately, we have more than one case of lost clothes at a time (please note all the letters of complaint that you don't have, proof that the system works most of the time), so we cannot call every customer and ask him or her to come in and identify the clothes. Our policy, therefore, is simply to wait for customers to come in and then offer them a chance to identify the clothes.

3.) Much of Mr. Shelton's gripe concerns the early period (approximately August 12 through August 25) during which time he felt he was kept in the dark. But as you know, our process is designed to get the stores and the plant to figure out problems. My written record shows that the plant did two thorough searches before reporting the lack of results to the store. It's hard to fault it for thoroughness. Apparently, the store also delayed referring the customer to me, probably thinking that the clothes would turn up and, perhaps, not wishing to have to report bad news concerning our new computer system. The process also may have taken this much time because of our standing company policy that requires all reports between stores, the plant, and the office to be in writing.

4.) After I spoke with the customer, I spent the next ten days or so checking with the store and the plant in an attempt to determine what exactly had happened and to locate and identify the clothes. By the end of the first week, I felt sure that the clothes had mistakenly gone to another customer. But there was no way to retrieve them, other than to wait for them to turn up. I did not tell the customer this, of course; after years of experience, I have found that customers only get more upset at the idea that a stranger has their clothes.

5.) Unbeknownst to me, the missing clothes were returned to the Adams and Broadway location on September 14. The customer who had mistakenly received the clothes dropped them off at one of our suburban locations, which then forwarded them to the plant. The plant used our standard identification process, sent them to the Adams and Broadway store, and then wrote me a memo, which I received on September 23. Before I could call the customer and inform him, he had picked up his clothes. I did get one more very angry message from the customer, which I decided not to return, since further communication would unlikely be of any benefit.

6.) Mr. Shelton's letter has several misstatements of fact. While there is no point in disputing these points with him, you should know the following:

(a) I did not delay in sending him a claim form. I sent the form after he requested it and do not know why it was not received. When he called back on September 18, I sent another form. I did not tell him that I had delayed in sending the form. I told him we were trying to locate and identify his clothes.

(b) When I spoke to the customer regarding the standard claim form, I did not tell him to produce proof of purchase. I told him it would be helpful to us if he could get a good estimate of the value of the items.

7.) As you can tell from the tone of Mr. Shelton's letter, he is a very demanding, persistent individual. What his letter does not tell you, however, is that he inundated us with the sheer volume of his calls. Given the number and frequency of his calls, there was no way for me to demonstrate progress on his problem before he called again. When he writes that he "left a message," you should know that his "messages" were usually cryptic. He often did not leave a phone number and, on more than one occasion, even refused to leave his name. For example, he would say, "You know who this is." My secretary found all of this quite distressing. Moreover, I've never run into a customer so anxious to be compensated.

This brings up several interesting questions: How do we make up for the mistake we made without being browbeaten into excess compensation? For example, his four shirts would cost us more than $200; refunding his order would add another $35; if I had swiftly processed his original claim, it would have come to over $600.

In other words, despite Mr. Shelton's threats, I think our system worked. Although we did misplace his clothes, he got everything back, and we avoided a major expense. Now some restitution, such as one free order and a written apology, should be enough. If that is not good enough for Mr. Shelton, it seems to me we should ask, "Aren't there some customers we are better off losing?" Maybe this is a customer that Kwik N' Klean deserves!

How Should Presto Cleaner Respond?

Four authorities on customer service consider Presto Cleaner's customer complaint.

LEONARD A. SCHLESINGER

Mr. Sewickley should replace Paul Hoffner. His response—and consequently Presto Cleaner's—to the situation appears to be oriented toward driving customers away, not toward building a business.

First, look at the situation. Presto Cleaner should be commended for implementing computer-based systems that increase the speed of service and eliminate paper pushing. However, the decision to introduce the system with limited employee training and no advance customer preparation or education created a nightmare. This could have been avoided. Each operating unit could have invested resources to set up a separate line or section of the store to indoctrinate customers in the new system without disrupting the normal flow of business. Hoffner resorts to identifying the rushed implementation of the system as an acceptable excuse for the customer problem. This clearly is not the case.

Certainly, mistakes will happen—all organizations make them. But mistakes provide organizations like Presto Cleaner the opportunity to recover in ways that actually build customer loyalty rather than lose business. This fact seems to escape Paul Hoffner. He appears to have adopted an internally focused and strictly rational approach to search for the missing clothing. He therefore ignores the customer's emotions. Unreturned phone calls and unsent forms serve only to turn a small mistake into a big one. The assumption that Presto Cleaner must actively guard against the potential of customers' fraudulent claims pervades all aspects of his relationship with Mr. Shelton. It is an attitude that other customers and the Presto Cleaner staff must notice as well. If you regard your customers as a band of potential cheats and believe that you must protect yourself from them, how can you possibly deliver to them the kind of service they deserve?

Having blown several opportunities to impress Mr. Shelton with Presto Cleaner's desire to solve his problem, Mr. Sewickley now faces the question of restitution for the situation. Mr. Shelton is clearly angry, and his request is undoubtedly greater than it would have been a few weeks earlier had Presto Cleaner handled the situation more ably. Paul Hoffner believes the request is absurd and actively encourages Mr. Sewickley to consider losing the Sheltons as customers. But we know from consumer research that for every complaint such as Mr. Shelton's, there are 20 or more customers who leave quietly and unnoticed and thereby provide the organization with no opportunity to learn from its mistakes. Mr. Hoffner is about to ensure that no learning occurs even when the customer complains. Purely in economic terms, the loss could be enormous. Assume that Presto Cleaner manages to lose one customer a day (not an unreasonable assumption given the company's behavior in this situation). Based on Mr. Shelton's estimates of his laundry expenditures, the annual revenue loss from such an unnoticed customer defection would reach almost $500,000.

In that context, Mr. Shelton's request is not at all unreasonable. If I were Mr. Sewickley, I would use the opportunity presented by the complaint letter to make one last attempt at service recovery. I would immediately reimburse Mr. Shelton's $235. But rather than write a simple apology letter, I would deliver the check myself and stress the following points:

What happened was unacceptable; there are no excuses for it.

Presto Cleaner will reimburse all out-of-pocket losses.

Presto Cleaner does not want to lose Mr. Shelton and will do *whatever* it takes to get him back.

My assumption is that this dramatic gesture will bring Mr. Shelton back to Presto Cleaner.

Lastly, Mr. Sewickley should use this complaint and the company's response as a learning opportunity for the company. The organization must establish a clear model of customer relations and service standards at the top. The Shelton complaint provides an opportunity for a broad discussion of customer problem resolution. In a competitive business environment, the risks of not capitalizing on this opportunity could be catastrophic.

DINAH NEMEROFF

Presto Cleaner has a dual challenge: to regain Mr. Shelton's business and ensure consistent customer-satisfying service to all customers. Both issues underscore why this is really "A Case *for* Problem-Free Service." While responsive service after the sale is a prerequisite for organizations today, their primary goal should be problem-free service. Every business should aim to close its customer complaint department! Problem prevention, not problem resolution, is a superordinate service-quality objective.

Unfortunately, Shelton already is knee-deep in problems, and these have grown geometrically, as is often the case. Presto Cleaner's Mr. Hoffner, his interactions with Shelton, and his lack of follow-through have made a bad situation worse. To remedy the situation, Presto Cleaner's president, Mr. Sewickley, should take some immediate first steps. First, he should send a letter of apology to Shelton with two enclosures: a $235 check, to cover the $35 charge for the delayed order and the $200 cost of four new shirts, and a $50 certificate for future Presto Cleaner service. He should act on the principle that, having made service mistakes, Presto Cleaner should bear all the customer's out-of-pocket costs. In addition, to demonstrate that anything short of highly satisfying service is not Presto Cleaner's way, Sewickley should enclose the $50 certificate.

This solution is based on the four-rung customer satisfaction ladder we're working to implement at Citibank. The system works like this: rung 1, customers say, "This company doesn't work"; rung 2, customers' basic service requirements are met; rung 3, customers get service personalized to their needs; and rung 4, customers say, "The service wows me!"

Ironically, Presto Cleaner's new computer system was geared to take the company's second rung, basically satisfying service, to a higher level of personalized service—rung 3. However, the total service failure moved Shelton down to rung 1. Therefore, a rung 4, "Presto Cleaner wows me!" action is called for. Sewickley's restorative actions most likely will regain Shelton's business. It should also enhance Presto Cleaner's reputation in the long term.

The larger issue on Sewickley's agenda must be to modernize Presto Cleaner's quality performance, just as he's working to update his technology. Both service and infrastructure should be state-of-the-art. Shelton's experience suggests there is much to do. For example, Presto Cleaner's policies to deal with customer problems require a thorough review. How can the stores and plant respond more quickly to customer difficulties? How can quality be designed into new procedures *before* they're introduced? Such policy reviews, interdepartmental teamwork, and quality-assurance issues are classical service-quality priorities. Sewickley should establish and communicate profitability-based customer satisfaction as a primary company goal and implement a diversified service-quality program.

Two imperatives are key to Presto Cleaner:

Strive for problem-free service. Presto Cleaner needs to "do it right the first time." As Shelton's experience illustrates, customer problems are costly to resolve, lead directly to lost business, and erode customer goodwill.

Even with first-rate customer service, customers do not "fully recover" from service problems. Citibank research shows that customers who've had problems resolved *to their satisfaction* are, nevertheless, on average 20% less satisfied than problem-free customers. Also, Presto Cleaner's management should not make the common mistake of viewing customer complaints as a comprehensive report card of the company's service. Complaints are a small subset of customer problems, registered by the vocal few; the majority of troubled customers silently desert to competitors. Presto Cleaner executives should understand the type, frequency, and severity of customer problems to implement a problem-free service plan. Such experiences must be seen from the customer's perspective. In large-scale organizations—or when employees rarely interact with customers—systematic customer feedback must be used to gather this crucial data.

Improve customer service. Because it's a rare business that can close its customer complaint department, this service function must be efficient and responsive.

Presto Cleaner's customer service problems begin with the customer-unfriendly computer system and Paul Hoffner, but they do not end there. A Presto Cleaner customer with a problem is in a limbo of missing laundry, knowing neither what to expect nor how to get help.

I recommend three strategies we've found valuable at Citibank:

Trust the customer. Service policies that assume customers are honest, and it's only the occasional crook who must be caught, are the appropriate ethical standard.

First-request service. A customer should only have to contact a business once to have his or her problem solved or question answered—ideally, this can be done immediately. If this isn't possible, the business takes on the follow-up burden.

Manage customers' expectations. When follow-up is necessary, telling the customer what to expect can significantly increase his or her satisfaction. When the service investigations department in one Citibank business instituted this particular procedure, specifying time frames for next steps, customers' satisfaction increased by 40%.

Such service improvements are neither easily nor quickly made, in Presto Cleaner or any organization. In fact, they can be expensive to implement, since up-front investment is frequently required. Nevertheless, the long-term payback is rewarding. A business *can* significantly decrease its cost of quality—foremost by preventing problems, not just fixing them. And when a company consistently provides customer-satisfying service, that business can keep and grow its customer base and earn more of each customer's business.

RON ZEMKE

There are three rules of thumb for creating an effective customer service focus in an organization: understand and respond to customers' expectations, do whatever it takes to be perceived as "easy to do business with," and be good at problem solving. Presto Cleaner has done an excellent job of ignoring all three.

In our studies, good recovery—fixing things that have gone wrong for the customer—accounts for 38.7% of the differences between companies perceived as very good or very bad at serving customers. This has proven to be an especially important distinguisher in retail operations like Presto Cleaner.

For the long term, Mr. Sewickley is going to have to do four things to ensure that the level of problem solving at Presto Cleaner is at least competitive. First, he'll have to make it clear that customer-contact employees, like Paul Hoffner, are expected to go out of their way to solve customer problems. Second, he'll have to set standards for both response time and appropriateness of redress. Third, he must see that customer-contact people are henceforth trained to deal with customers who have been, or believe that they have been, wronged by the company. And finally, he is going to have to scrap his marvelous new system or get help redesigning it from a customer-use point of view. As it stands, the new system threatens to make Presto Cleaner about as customer friendly as a state department of motor vehicles.

Right now, however, Mr. Sewickley must take over as Presto Cleaner's chief problem solver. It is especially important that he not follow Mr. Hoffner's advice and write off the Sheltons. Through word-of-mouth, the Sheltons can do a great deal of damage to the business. A simple "You won't believe how the dry cleaner messed us around!" tale, told often enough, can cost Presto Cleaner as much as 2% of annual revenues. Beyond that, Hoffner's assumption that the Sheltons are a lost cause is probably incorrect. The fact that they bothered to write to the company—something less than 10% of unhappy customers will do—suggests that they want to be coaxed back into the Presto Cleaner fold.

Here's what Mr. Sewickley should do to make it easy for the Sheltons to continue being Presto Cleaner customers. Call George Shelton and apologize—profusely, if necessary. The goal is to make sure that the customer knows that Sewickley doesn't condone lackadaisical treatment of customers or consider problems such as the one the Sheltons experienced as par for the course. And he should be prepared to listen more than he talks. Mr. Shelton probably has a large amount of pent-up frustration that he wants to dump on someone. So let him dump it. It won't cost a dime to hear him out, and frequently the sum and substance of what an upset customer wants is to be heard. Sewickley should try to enlist Mr. Shelton both in solving the problem his family encountered and in suggesting ways that the new system can be made more user friendly. Until now, Shelton has been denied any sense of control over the situation. Give him back some control. Enlisting upset customers to create acceptable solutions also works to bring them from an upset and irrational mind-set to a thinking and reasonable one.

If necessary, Mr. Sewickley should be prepared to "buy the problem"—spend the $235, the cost of the new shirts and the dry cleaning order. The odds are, however, that Mr. Shelton will drop his demands that Presto Cleaner pay for his replacement shirts once he is talking to the president.

Remember: Sewickley is trying to install a new system. If too many customers are walking around saying bad things about the new way of doing business with Presto Cleaner, there will be no business to do.

And he should follow up with some form of symbolic atonement. He definitely has to send a personalized follow-up letter that refers to their conversation and what will happen as a result of it. But at this point, an additional gesture is necessary. A certificate for free work is OK, flowers would be better.

In the last analysis, Mr. Sewickley is both arbiter and role model for customer relations and customer treatment at Presto Cleaner.

If he "blows off" a customer who is initially unreasonable or uses bad language or is simply unpleasant, Mr. Hoffner and every counter clerk in every store will do the same. If Mr. Sewickley shows patience and understanding and evidences a sincere desire to do what it takes to keep Presto Cleaner customers happy and coming back, everyone in his employ will follow suit.

CLAUS MØLLER

Presto Cleaner's poor service on the front lines reflects the unresponsive and irresponsible employee attitudes of upper and middle management. Mr. Hoffner is not the villain in this case but the victim of a service-management culture that has not built a support system that encourages employees to demonstrate a positive attitude toward the customer.

Customers who take the time and energy to complain are doing companies a favor. They help companies stay in business. Mr. Hoffner must change his attitude; Presto Cleaner should too. When customers complain to Presto Cleaner, employees should say thank you. This company should train its employees to listen to customers and change fundamental attitudes so that customers' complaints are viewed as opportunities for positive change, not as reasons to be defensive.

Quality management involves changing attitudes at every level of the company. It is not just for managers. Nor is it just a question of implementing technology and systems. The problem in this instance lies not in the details of what happened but in the flawed values embedded in the procedure.

Mr. Shelton's disappointment stems from bad customer service rather than bad technology. Customer dissatisfaction is often based on emotions, but when asked to explain why they are dissatisfied, customers give rational explanations—even when they are not the real cause. Let me illustrate. When I worked with SAS years ago to improve the company's service, we asked flight attendants to distribute forms asking customers to rate the service. I observed that the process itself was flawed: attendants did not make eye contact, and when customers asked, the attendants would not explain the reason for the forms.

Not surprisingly, customers responded negatively. And when they did, they commented on what I call hard service quality:

material aspects such as the space between the seats, waiting time, punctuality of flights, even the fact that champagne was served in plastic glasses.

I then trained attendants to interact better with customers— letting them know why the forms were being distributed or why planes were not on time. After that, the customers responded to the forms by saying they were satisfied. And they named all the same hard qualities as the reasons for their satisfaction! When people are not aware of the "soft" qualities for their dissatisfaction, they invent a lot of socially "reasonable" explanations as justification.

Likewise, the problem here is not the specific incidents that took place but the attitude Mr. Shelton encountered. Had Mr. Hoffner demonstrated a genuine interest in Mr. Shelton's problem and given less attention to defending himself, I doubt that the customer would have been dissatisfied. Instead of showing interest in Mr. Shelton's problems, Mr. Hoffner refused to admit to either his customer or his boss that he might be wrong. He is more interested in making the customer wrong than in admitting his own error. He treats the customer as an irritant.

The actions of Mr. Hoffner signal a deeper flaw in the company— which clearly has no defined service policy. Companies should design systems so that employees relate to customers—not technology. Presto Cleaner has flip-flopped its priorities by implementing a computer system that seems to have been designed more for the shop and company than the clients! At least that is the signal sent to its customers. Presto Cleaner also needs to use its time better. If this company spent the same amount of money and time on motivating its staff that it does on writing notes and memos, it would be much better off.

Clearly the company must improve the attitudes of its staff by creating an environment that promotes the best in people. I distinguish between "internal service"—how employees are treated within a company—and "external service"—how employees treat customers. The external service-quality will never exceed internal service-quality. Companies must create responsive attitudes through internal service. Companies must give employees responsibility to make decisions and be prepared for them to make mistakes. They must treat employees as they expect employees to treat customers. One goal to motivate people is to suggest that they treat their customers as they would treat guests in their homes.

I recommend that the company give Mr. Shelton what he requests—along with something extra, such as a complimentary dinner for him and his wife. I also suggest that Mr. Hoffner work on the front line for a while to see how the new system is working and to stay in touch with customers.

Note

At the time of this article's publication Leonard A. Schlesinger was associate professor of business administration at the Harvard Business School. Dinah Nemeroff was corporate director of customer affairs at Citicorp/Citibank. Ron Zemke was president of Performance Research Associates in Minneapolis. Claus Møller was president of Time Management International, a management development company in Denmark.

 *Logistics*

5717 Arapahoe Ave, Unit 1, Boulder, CO 80303

standard	

Qty	Location / Title
1	**N1-F10 - 03 - 035 - 43336**
	Keeping Customers (The Harvard Business Review Book)

Seller ID: 058-1695267-5216356
Order ID: 124001
Email: brouzan@nl.edu
Order Date: 6/3/2004 11:43:33 AM

Thanks for your order! If you have any questions please contact us at *info@blogistics.com.*

TO REORDER YOUR UPS
DIRECT THERMAL LABELS:

1. Access our supply ordering web site at **UPS.com**
   or Contact UPS at 800-877-8652.
2. Please refer to Label #0277400801 when ordering.

2

The Profitable Art of Service Recovery

Christopher W. L. Hart, James L. Heskett, and W. Earl Sasser, Jr.

Mistakes are a critical part of every service. Hard as they try, even the best service companies can't prevent the occasional late flight, burned steak, or missed delivery. The fact is, in services, often performed in the customer's presence, errors are inevitable.

But dissatisfied customers are not. While companies may not be able to prevent all problems, they can learn to recover from them. A good recovery can turn angry, frustrated customers into loyal ones. It can, in fact, create more goodwill than if things had gone smoothly in the first place. Consider how Club Med-Cancun, part of the Paris-based Club Méditerranée, recovered from a service nightmare and won the loyalty of one group of vacationers.

The vacationers had nothing but trouble getting from New York to their Mexican destination. The flight took off 6 hours late, made 2 unexpected stops, and circled for 30 minutes before it could land. Because of all the delays and mishaps, the plane was en route for 10 hours more than planned and ran out of food and drinks. It finally arrived at 2 o'clock in the morning, with a landing so rough that oxygen masks and luggage dropped from overhead. By the time the plane pulled up to the gate, the soured passengers were faint with hunger and convinced that their vacation was ruined before it had even started. One lawyer on board was already collecting names and addresses for a class-action lawsuit.

Silvio de Bortoli, the general manager of the Cancun resort and a legend throughout the organization for his ability to satisfy customers, got word of the horrendous flight and immediately created an antidote. He took half the staff to the airport, where they laid out a table of snacks and drinks and set up a stereo system to play lively music. As the guests filed through the gate, they received personal greetings, help with their bags, a sympathetic ear, and a chauffeured ride to the resort. Waiting for them at Club Med was a lavish banquet, complete with mariachi band and champagne. Moreover, the staff had rallied other guests to wait up and greet the newcomers, and the partying continued until sunrise. Many guests said it was the most fun they'd had since college.

In the end, the vacationers had a better experience than if their flight from New York had gone like clockwork. Although the company probably couldn't measure it, Club Méditerranée won market share that night. After all, the battle for market share is won not by analyzing demographic trends, ratings points, and other global measures but rather by pleasing customers one at a time.

Opportunities for service recovery abound. Any problem that employees who are close to the customer can discover and resolve is a chance to go beyond the call of duty and win a customer for life. We're not talking about gas leaks in Bhopal or Tylenol poisonings, which threaten large-scale damage and demand top management's attention. We're talking about mistaken billings and late deliveries, the seemingly small issues that can ignite a person's temper. The stuff angry letters to the chief executive are made of.

It's tempting to dismiss the occasional problem as petty and complaining customers as cranks, but managers should resist those easy outs. No business can afford to lose customers, if only because it costs much more to replace a customer than it does to retain one—five times more, most industry experts agree. Companies that alienate and frustrate their customers will soon have none left to bother them. Those that go out of their way to please customers will soon have many more.

Good recoveries from service problems do happen, but usually because some exceptional individual like de Bortoli takes the initiative to solve a customer's problem. Companies should not depend on such rare instances of resourcefulness. They should take steps to ensure that everyone in the organization has the skill, motivation, and authority to make service recovery an integral part of operations.

The Road to Service Recovery

Service companies must become gymnasts, able to regain their balance instantly after a slipup and continue their routines. Such grace is earned by focusing on the goal of customer satisfaction, adopting a customer-focused attitude, and cultivating the special skills necessary to recovery.

Ironically, recovery skills come especially hard to companies that joined the quality-control movement and have spent the past decade making their service-delivery systems streamlined and efficient. Accepting admonishments to "do the right thing" and adopting manufacturing's philosophy of "zero defects," they developed rigid systems to achieve it. They introduced sophisticated technologies and enacted strict policies to control employee behavior. The idea was to ensure that even uneducated, unmotivated workers could consistently deliver high-quality service. By the 1980s, many such systems had been developed—to improve service in everything from scheduling airline departures and posting banking transactions to maintaining hotel rooms. All of these systems were modeled after assembly-line production systems.

These production-oriented service-delivery systems have gone a long way toward achieving consistently high service standards. But they're not bulletproof. The fact is that in services, no matter how rigorous the procedures and employee training or how advanced the technology, zero defects is an unattainable goal. Unlike manufacturers that can adjust the inputs and machinery until products are uniformly perfect, service companies cannot escape variation. Factors like the weather and the customers themselves are beyond a company's control. The best airline reservation system can't prevent the airport from fogging over. A restaurant that creates the most artistic food presentations can't prevent a customer from disliking the taste.

When the inevitable problems arise, customers are almost always disappointed. The typical service delivery system is completely unprepared to deal with exceptions. Studies we've done show that more than half of all efforts to respond to customer complaints actually *reinforce* negative reactions to a service.

The surest way to recover from service mishaps is for workers on the front line to identify and solve the customer's problem. Doing so requires decision making and rule breaking—exactly what employees have been conditioned against. Workers have been taught that it's not their job to alter the routine. Even if they'd like to help the customer, they are frustrated by the fact that they are not allowed to do it. Worse yet, they don't know how. We have all heard the typical responses: "It's not my fault." "It's not in the computer." "I'll have to ask my supervisor." Meanwhile, airline passengers stew over the meetings they've missed; restaurant patrons return home hungry and annoyed.

Companies shouldn't abandon their production-oriented systems, but they should complement them with an equal facility for service recovery. They should be as comfortable with the exceptions as they are with the rules. Developing the perspective to recognize service-recovery opportunities and the skills to act on them is clearly an effort, but one well worth making.

Mistreating customers can have a devastating effect on the business, as this example shows. John Barrier, a 30-year customer of a bank in Spokane, Washington, parked his car in a lot owned by the bank while he did business across the street. An attendant told him he could get the parking validated if he did business at the bank, which was not his usual branch. Barrier cashed a check, but afterward was refused the validation because he had not made a deposit. He patiently explained to the receptionist that he was a long-time customer and that he had millions of dollars in the bank's checking, investment, and trust accounts. She was unmoved. He less patiently explained the situation to the branch manager, to no avail.

The customer paid for the parking, but he was so steamed that he drove 40 blocks to his home branch and explained the incident to his usual banker. He said if he didn't receive a phone call by the end of the day, he would close all his accounts. The call never came, he made his first withdrawal of $1 million, and Americans across the country heard the story when it hit the evening news. Needless to say, the bank executives were embarrassed and worked hard to persuade the customer to give the bank another chance.

Companies that want to build the capability of recovering from service problems should do these things: measure the costs of effective service recovery, break customer silence and listen closely for complaints, anticipate needs for recovery, act fast, train employees, empower the front line, and close the customer feedback loop.

Measure the Costs

Measurement precedes management. This is especially true for service recovery—managers often underestimate the profits lost when a customer departs unhappy, and therefore they undermanage ways of avoiding such losses. They concentrate on attracting new customers that may actually represent unprofitable business and neglect to take steps to retain more valuable existing customers. Measurement often is the only way of getting top management's attention. What gets measured is truly what gets managed here.

Errors have certain costs associated with them. Some take the form of money-back guarantees, warranty work, or replacements, which fall on the company. But dissatisfied customers almost always get stuck with certain costs—the money they spend for phone calls, the time they spend making their cases, and the aggravation they must endure throughout. The customer left stranded on the highway because her car was not repaired properly might miss an important meeting, have to pay for a tow truck, and spend time waiting for the repair to be made. Many service companies conveniently overlook these hidden costs, but the customer surely won't. Companies known for excellent service will go the extra yard to cover all the costs a failure incurs or, if the inconvenience is so great that the company cannot completely compensate the customer, the tone of the response must signal the company's regret.

A study done for the U.S. Office of Consumer Affairs found that in households with service problems with potential costs of more than $100, 54% would maintain brand loyalty if their problems were satisfactorily resolved. Only 19% would repeat their purchase if they were unhappy with the problem resolution. For less expensive problems ($1 to $5), 70% would maintain brand loyalty if their problems were resolved satisfactorily; only 46% would repurchase if the problem wasn't fixed.[1]

Considering how much it costs to lose a customer, few recovery efforts are too extreme. At Club Med, one lost customer costs the company at least $2,400: a loyal guest visits the resorts an average of four times after the initial visit and spends roughly $1,000 each time. The contribution margin is 60%. So when a Club Med customer doesn't return, the company loses 60% of $4,000, or $2,400. It also has to replace that customer through expensive marketing efforts.

Break the Silence

Every customer's problem is an opportunity for the company to prove its commitment to service—even if the company is not to blame. The theatergoer who forgets his ticket will long be grateful if the usher slips him in. The service experiences customers rave about most are those in which they were at fault but the company responded anyway.

Of course, you can't solve a customer's problem until you know what it is, so all good recoveries start with identifying the sore spots. Service company executives know very well that some customers make a point of being heard. They write letters, make phone calls, ask to speak to the manager—and the manager's manager. Listening to these customers is important.

But companies shouldn't attend to just the squeaky wheels. They must also be active problem finders. Complainers are the exception; most unhappy people don't speak up. They may think the situation is hopeless, or they don't want to create a scene. Or they can't be bothered to write a letter or make a phone call—it's one more hassle in what may have been a string of many. There are many ways service businesses can encourage this "silent majority" of dissatisfied customers to identify themselves so the company can win them back.

The simplest way is to make it easy for customers to complain. Many businesses have established "800" numbers so customers can report problems easily and at the company's expense. American Express has installed such lines and estimates that it achieves responses more quickly and at 10% to 20% of the cost of handling correspondence. Marriott Corporation has a 24-hour "hot line" in its hotels, which makes it easy for guests to complain on the spot. It's worth adding that hot lines should be staffed sufficiently to prevent a common shortcoming of centralized telephone systems— too few incoming lines. Repeated busy signals do nothing to improve customers' attitudes.

A more direct way to solicit complaints is to ask a simple question like, "How was everything?" Many customers who can't be bothered filling out forms or making calls will volunteer their impressions of the service they received when asked to. And even if the customer has nothing to say, the company has sent the signal that it cares. That's why British Airways has installed what it calls Video Point booths at Heathrow Airport in London so that travelers can tape their reactions upon arrival. Customer service representatives view the tapes and respond. Maine Savings Bank in Portland offers its patrons $1 for every letter they write suggesting ways to improve service. The bank averages more than 500 letters a year from customers who might have kept their ideas to themselves; it extended its lobby hours after many customers made that suggestion.

An even more aggressive approach to unearthing problems is to look for trouble in the making—to listen carefully for offhand comments customers make and to tune into and anticipate their needs. An alert employee of a Marriott hotel that caters to businesspeople overheard a guest fretting about the lack of privacy in the concierge lounge where he wanted to hold an impromptu meeting with a few colleagues. The hotel worker called the front desk and arranged for a vacant suite so the guest could hold his meeting without distractions.

A participant in a service-recovery workshop shared this striking example of a company that recognized a problem it didn't create but nonetheless was prepared to solve:

"A while back, there was a very bad fire in my house. The next day I was raking through my possessions, my family sitting on the front stoop, when a Domino's Pizza truck pulled up. The driver got out and approached us with two pizzas. I told him I didn't order any pizza and explained that our house had just burned. 'I know,' he replied. 'I saw you when I drove by half an hour ago. I figured you must be really hungry, so my store manager and I decided to make a couple of pizzas for you. We put everything on them. If that's not how you like them, I'll take them back and get them made the way you like—on the house.'"

"I couldn't believe it," the participant concluded. "Do you think I'd ever buy pizza from anyone else?"

More formal "listening devices" like questionnaires and customer suggestion boxes are effective only if someone monitors them continually and acts on complaints and suggestions in a timely fashion.

Stew Leonard's, a retail dairy store in Norwalk, Connecticut, renowned for its service, has a suggestion box, which pays off handsomely. One evening at about 6 P.M., Stew Leonard, Jr. found a crisply worded complaint written by a customer just a half-hour earlier. "I made a special stop on my way home from work to buy chicken breasts for dinner, but you're sold out. Now I'll have to eat a TV dinner instead." As Leonard was reading the complaint, a Perdue chicken truck happened to pull up to the store's loading dock. Within minutes, someone was heading off to the frustrated customer's house with a complimentary two-pound package of fresh chicken breasts.

Anticipate Needs for Recovery

Companies can narrow the search for problems (read "opportunities") by monitoring certain areas of the organization and addressing them in their service-recovery strategies. Complex scheduling that involves coordinating the movement of people or equipment, for instance, tends to be problem-prone. There, one error can trigger a devastating chain reaction, as in airline flight cancellations.

We were among a group of professors studying service excellence that recently felt the brunt of a failure to anticipate the need for recovery. En route from Boston to Columbus, Ohio, with a stop at Washington National Airport, the group was not warned that, because of a take-off curfew at Washington National, a late departure from Boston might mean the flight would not be allowed to continue to Ohio. In fact, the US Air plane was held overnight in Washington, making it impossible for the group to make it to its meeting the next morning. Worse, the harried late-night staff at US Air counters was shorthanded, so already disgruntled passengers had to stand in line for an hour for assistance. If ever there was a problem waiting to happen, this was it. Because the company failed to anticipate it, both US Air's frontline employees and its customers suffered.

New services and products also tend to create confusion and spawn unexpected requests. When Dallas–Fort Worth International Airport first opened, it proved very confusing to passengers. Not only was the airport of unusual design and size but it also included one of the first rail systems to shuttle passengers between terminals. It took the airport months to change the layout and reposition signs to make the airport more "user friendly"—months of confusion and frustration for those who used it.

Areas where turnover is high and workers are therefore inexperienced are also worth watching. The first person most air travelers encounter is the operator of the security gate. Of all airline employees travelers meet during a trip, this person is probably the lowest paid and the least experienced in handling people—yet he or she has the job of creating a positive first impression. Security is therefore a leading candidate for preparation for airline service recovery.

Fixing customers' problems as they crop up is good and is necessary. But service companies should put those isolated incidents to use by tracking problems to see where they occur most often and which ones tend to recur. They can then prepare the organization. When the CEO of an insurance company locked the keys in the trunk of his rental car at a Sheraton Hotel in Boca Raton, Florida, the staff rose to the occasion. The bellman informed the CEO that a locksmith under contract with the hotel would replace the keys within 15 minutes. Meanwhile, other staff members used a rolling auto-jack stored nearby to jack up the car and push it out of the driveway where it was blocking check-in traffic. Obviously, it wasn't the first time someone had lost a set of car keys.

Act Fast

Identifying a problem quickly—even before it registers with the customer—is fruitful only if the company responds fast. Our most recent research suggests that customers who have bad experiences tell approximately 11 people about it; those with good experiences tell just 6.

Service problems quickly escalate, so the opportunity to prove one's commitment to the customer is fleeting, especially if the company is at fault. In general, the company's first priority should be to complete the service promptly. The customer whose car breaks down because it was serviced improperly wants her car fixed. The bank customer whose account is in error wants it properly credited.

Paul Hawken, CEO of Smith & Hawken, a garden supply mail-order company based in Mill Valley, California, found a simple way to speed response time: by using the phone instead of mail. Early in the company's history, customers with routine inquiries and problems received form letters in reply. Management found that approach to be cost-effective, but the savings came at the customer's expense. In one instance, an old and valuable customer placed an order on an American Express card, which the company mistakenly thought was invalid. It sent the usual form letter. The customer wrote back. The company sent another form letter. The customer wrote back. When a manager finally realized that the order had been held up two months because of crossed correspondence, he was horrified. The company prided itself on customer service, yet it had managed to anger and frustrate one of its best clients.

The person who made the discovery immediately sent the woman her order and swallowed the $90 charge. And the company learned a lesson: from that moment on, Smith & Hawken stopped using the mail to handle questions or problems: now someone picks up the phone and resolves them in minutes instead of months. And the cost of the phone call is offset by the elimination of paperwork.[2]

The urgent resumption of service and an apology are often sufficient to make amends. But not always. Some situations call for a gesture that clearly says, "We realize there's been a mistake, and we want to make it up to you." Many restaurants will automatically give patrons a glass of wine or a free dessert if the wait for a table is too long. First Union National Bank in Charlotte, North Carolina, sends a dozen roses to customers who have been badly inconvenienced. In some cases, branch managers or bank executives personally deliver the flowers. Such extraordinary efforts require extraordinary preparation at every organizational level.

Train Employees

The organization must train the people who interact directly with customers, and then it must empower them. That is, it must give them the authority, responsibility, and incentives to recognize, care about, and attend to customer needs. Empowering the bottom of the organizational pyramid can be threatening, especially to middle-level managers, who may read it as an erosion of their own authority and worth. But it is absolutely essential to good service recovery. Employees close to the customer are the first to know about problems and are in the best position to determine what can be done to satisfy the customer.

Training can go a long way in developing the communications skills and creative thinking needed to deal with irate customers. Recovery training should focus on teaching employees how to make decisions on their feet and on developing an awareness of customers' concerns.

The most effective way to develop recovery skills is through simulated real-life situations and role playing. Agents for the U.S. Secret Service, who are among the world's most highly trained recovery specialists, go through a comprehensive assortment of recovery drills before they work in the field. Agents spend hours thinking about what might happen and discussing and planning for all the possible contingencies. Each agent—no matter how senior—goes through follow-up training sessions once a year.

Sonesta Hotels uses games as part of its orientation program for new employees. Trainees are divided into two teams, each of which in turn receives a description of a problem and is asked to come up with a solution. The opposing team has five possible answers to compare the response with. Points are awarded depending on how well the responses fit the general criteria of keen observation, responsiveness, care and concern, and compensation for true loss.

The American Association of Homes for the Aging distributes a board game, "The Game of Aging Concerns," which retirement homes use to give workers practice in dealing with tough issues. The game consists of a board, six playing pieces, a die, and 40 cards, each describing a real problem or role-playing situation. One card reads: "Mr. Talbot, 78, complains, 'Your facility is too cold and makes me ill.' He demands that you turn on the heat. Other residents want the air-conditioning left on. The heating/air-conditioning system is centrally controlled." Another reads, "A 72-year-old man who is intoxicated walks into the dining room and acts disruptive."

As players draw cards, they read them aloud, describe how they feel, and say what they would do. The idea is to expose players to a variety of concepts, give them feedback and reinforcement, and allow them to internalize a set of criteria for evaluating real-life problems. And the spirit of the game paves the way for an ongoing dialogue among workers.

To help develop recovery skills, training should also give people a sense of the whole organization. Extreme specialization of tasks gives operators tunnel vision, which makes it hard to see problems in the making. A worker who understands the entire service delivery process is more likely to understand the interconnectedness of the system and find a quick solution. The most direct way to develop this perspective is by rotating workers through different jobs and departments.

Managers know how to solve customers' problems, but people don't want to wait for their concerns to travel through the organizational hierarchy or to bounce from one department to another. Nor can managers answer every phone, stand behind every counter, process every piece of paper. So service recovery ultimately rests on the shoulders of employees on the front line. This implies a very different role for employees who have direct customer contact.

In addition to following rules, sticking to a routine, and treating every situation alike no matter what, front-line workers must be able to do the opposite: bend the rules, take initiative, and improvise. Building a staff that can do both requires rigorous and conscious effort and is at the heart of a company's ability to recover from service mishaps.

Empower the Front Line

Training can give employees the perspective that service recovery requires, but the company must empower them to act. It must give employees the authority, responsibility, and incentives to follow through with customers.

The authority to act refers to the set of resources the employee has access to and the decisions they are permitted to make. In most service companies, only managers can spend money or otherwise make things happen. Organizations that empower workers make it clear that they are permitted to use their judgment to make phone calls, credit accounts, or send flowers. For example, Montgomery Ward chairman Bernard F. Brennan has authorized its 7,700 salesclerks to approve checks and handle merchandise-return problems, functions that once were reserved for store managers.

Responsibility goes one step further. It says that employees are *supposed* to recognize and attend to customers' needs. Managers can instill that sense of purpose in many ways—through training and reminders in newsletters and by developing an overall environment that puts customers first.

Responsibility means the obligation to act, not just to accept blame. One couple was visiting a resort on the coast of Mexico in the middle of August when the water main from the town broke. The heat and humidity were ferocious, and the hotel was without air-conditioning and water for most of four days. Repair attempts were feeble. The water would run for just a few hours before things would fail again. Each time the system broke, the general manager gathered the guests in the lounge and prattled on about how he took "full responsibility" for everything. When he said *responsibility* he meant blame. What customers wanted, of course, was action.

Good service companies rely on "standard operating procedures" for problems that come up from time to time. At McDonald's, for instance, employees know that when a customer complains that his burger is cold, they should automatically give him a fresh one, no questions asked. For other situations, management can only establish guidelines. Many of the problems at the Minneapolis Marriott City Center are one-of-a-kinds, so management has authorized employees to spend $10 at their discretion to satisfy guests. Once when a guest complained mildly about not being able to find a particular book in the hotel gift shop, the cashier, at the end of her shift, walked to a local bookstore, purchased the book with her $10, and delivered it to the guest's room. The guest was, of course, astonished.

The Minneapolis Marriott also put together a "Sweet Dreams" package consisting of a cordial, a small bud vase with a carnation, and homemade cookies. Hotel staff members are encouraged to give it to customers who are having difficulties the hotel can't otherwise fix. When one guest mentioned that her flight was four hours late and that she was exhausted, the staff person at the front desk sent a "Sweet Dreams" package to her room. Another associate noticed a guest with a hacking cough; she included a box of cough drops with the package.

A company's reward structure must give employees positive reinforcement for solving problems and pleasing customers—not just for reducing the number of complaints. Good recoveries should be publicized and held up as examples to inspire others. Federal Express created the "Golden Falcon" and "Bravo Zulu" awards to recognize service and recovery excellence. Winners get a gold pin, recognition in the company newsletter, and a phone call from the chief operating officer as well as ten shares of company stock.

As the nature of jobs with high customer contact changes, companies may find it necessary to change their hiring requirements or reassign workers. Embracing the notion of empowerment, the Marriott Desert Springs Resort revised the job description for its front-desk clerk/cashiers, room controllers, and front-desk supervisors: the major—indeed the *only*—goal of these positions is to ensure that "our guests experience excellent service and hospitality while staying at our resort." The resort charges the people in those positions with learning the correct technical procedures, using their authority to do anything to keep guests happy, using their power to satisfy guests on the spot without hassle, assisting in finding the ultimate cause for guests' problems, and informing managers of ways to improve the overall hotel, working conditions, or guests' comfort.

If this seems logical, why don't more services do it? Many are afraid that empowered employees will "give away the store." They overlook the fact that tying employees' hands effectively guarantees that some customers won't return. The cost of keeping those customers is small compared with what it takes to replace them.

Close the Loop

If a customer's complaint leads to corrective measures, the company should tell the customer about the improvement. Closing the loop makes customers feel as if they're part of an extended quality-control team. If it's something that can't be fixed, the company should simply explain why.

In our service-management classes, we ask each student to send one letter of commendation and one letter of criticism to service companies where they had memorable experiences. All contain suggestions for service improvements. The responses to these hundreds of letters from the real world are revealing. Only about two-thirds of the companies that receive thoughtful, constructive, but critical letters bother to respond. A smaller proportion of the companies receiving praise write back. Worse yet, more than half of all responses to letters of criticism either reinforce or fail to counter the senders' original negative perceptions.

Effective ways of closing the loop include making timely telephone responses, asking the customer for even more feedback, and letting the customer know how his or her suggestions might be implemented. These efforts tend to give customers a more positive impression than various forms of remuneration.

Brilliant Recoveries

Recovery is a different management philosophy, one that embraces customer satisfaction as a primary goal of business. This mind-set can change the rules of the game for service companies. It shifts the emphasis from the *cost* of pleasing a customer to the *value* of doing so, and it entrusts frontline employees with using their judgment.

While many organizations pay lip service to the notion of serving customers, few are wholly committed to it. Even those that see the connection between 100% customer satisfaction and the ultimate success of the business are often ill-equipped to retain dissatisfied patrons.

But recovery is fundamental to service excellence and should therefore be regarded as an integral part of a service company's strategy. When a worker at a San Antonio hotel accidentally broke the glass vase a guest had carried from Mexico, the resident manager drove 150 miles to replace it. Customers remember such experiences. In service businesses, the old adage must be revised: To err is human; to recover, divine.

Notes

1. U.S. Office of Consumer Affairs, *Consumer Complaint Handling in America: An Update Study, Part II* (Washington, D.C.: Technical Assistance Research Programs Institute, April 1, 1986), p. 50.
2. From Paul Hawken, *Growing a Business* (New York: Simon & Schuster, 1988).

PART
VI

Convert Customer
Satisfaction into Profits

Introduction

Many companies equate volume with profitability, or recognizing the distinction, have no comprehensive programs for identifying and managing the most profitable customers. An essential component of profitability is the cost to serve customers, which, as we have seen throughout this book, varies by customer, by product, and over time. Managing these costs—in addition to production, development, and presale costs—is becoming increasingly important as customers push more and more responsibilities and demands onto their suppliers. Just-in-time production systems, small-lot deliveries, and fast-cycle-time supply are among the new business practices that are putting pressure on suppliers. Sometimes these efforts reduce costs for both parties by enabling systemic improvements such as inventory reduction, for example. In other cases, instituting these practices increases the cost to serve, satisfying customers while profits suffer. Profitable customer management requires regular review of supplier costs, prices, and customer value.

The first article, "Manage Customers for Profits (Not Just Sales)," by Benson Shapiro, V. Kasturi Rangan, Rowland Moriarty, and Elliot Ross, presents a methodology for analyzing the cost to serve relative to net realized price. By designing a matrix with net price and cost to serve as variables, suppliers can classify customers into four groups: (1) carriage trade (expensive to serve but willing to pay top dollar), (2) passive (less costly to serve but willing to accept high prices), (3) bargain basement (inexpensive to serve but sensitive to price), and (4) aggressive (demanding the highest product quality, the best service, and low prices).

Knowledge of this customer dispersion invigorates decisions on price, service offerings, and account selection. At the same time, effective customer management requires attention to variables such as customer's situation (economics, buying power, decision-making dynamics, and relationship to seller) and migration patterns (changes in organizational buying behavior over time), which are the primary determinants of a customer's position in the price/cost matrix. Managers tend to assume that net realized price correlates with cost to serve. The authors found, however, that this assumption is often false. Some customers who pay a lower price may demand high-quality service (aggressive customers), while those who pay a high price may be relatively inexpensive to serve when the full range of presale, production, distribution, and postsale costs are considered.

Likewise, the value created for a customer may have little relationship to the cost of providing a product and its support services. For example, a simple action, such as calling ahead with status information when a delivery is delayed, has low supplier cost, but high value to the customer. Consequently, management must view both the costs to serve and the value to the customer independently of net realized price: "The best managed companies know their costs well and set prices on the basis of product value to customers rather than cost to serve." Further complicating the process is the tendency of customers to move from one quadrant of the matrix into another, over time, as they become more familiar with the product and develop new service demands.

The authors stress that in analyzing costs, prices, and profit dispersion, companies should focus their selling strategies by concentrating on the matrix quadrants where customer behavior is consistent with company strengths. In this way, suppliers can balance costs, prices, and account selection to achieve the most profitable order mix.

The next article, "Suppliers—Manage Your Customers," by Randy Myer, documents how aggressive, fast-growing companies are often the least profitable accounts. As noted above, sophisticated customers demand high-quality support and low prices, often eroding profits. Powerful retailers, for example, are currently extracting concessions and dictating terms, while suppliers are swallowing the costs. This article illustrates how suppliers can win back control of sales by suggesting innovative and flexible options that help keep costs down while pleasing customers.

The authors advocate a three-step program for analyzing customer profitability and allocating resources to capture profits effectively. The first step is to understand the "customer return on assets," the CRA. Unlike the traditional return on assets statement, which measures product performance, the CRA measures customer performance by accounting for marketing, sales, product development, delivery, and service costs. The next step is to establish multifunctional teams qualified to deal with each customer's strategies and service requirements. Team alignments should reflect segmentation of customers by service needs, rather than simply by geography or size. The third step is to make teams accountable. Customer performance, rather than revenue or gross margin, should be used as the basis for assessing team performance. With these internal mechanisms in place, suppliers can manage customer profitability more consistently and creatively. One firm, for example, which discovered that its large orders were subsidizing smaller ones, "set up a staggered price schedule that reflected the cost differentials [between large and small orders]. With no change in revenue, average order quantity increased by 33%, producing big savings in selling and distribution costs."

The last article in this section, "Zero Defections: Quality Comes to Services," by Frederick Reichheld and W. Earl Sasser, might be considered the linchpin of the entire collection. The data presented in this article illustrate how customer longevity (i.e., keeping customers) has a measurable and significant impact on profits. For example, the first year a credit card customer is on the books, she or he costs the company $51 in marketing and startup costs; by the fifth year, the same customer returns $55 in profit. By viewing customers as relationships rather than discrete transactions, managers can calculate the customer's net worth over time. Customer longevity results in increased sales from referrals, reduced operating costs (e.g., no need to remarket to an existing customer), ability to raise prices, and the opportunity to improve business practices gradually, as customers' needs evolve. Conversely, defecting customers can have a greater negative influence on profits than "scale, market share, unit costs, and many other factors usually associated with competitive advantage."

In this light, many costs that are erroneously viewed as expenses should be seen as investments in long-term profitability. For example, customer complaint handling is not an annoyance to be minimized, but a strategic investment in customer relationships (see Part V for a more detailed discussion of service recovery). Understanding why customers defect to a competitor can help a company decide which service-quality investments will be profitable and whether certain customers are worth keeping.

The articles in this section suggest that customer satisfaction is not an end in itself. Suppliers must constantly weigh the costs of satisfying customers against the short- and long-run returns of keeping those customers satisfied. A culture that emphasizes customer management as well as product and service management will help translate customer satisfaction into supplier profits.

1
Manage Customers for Profits (Not Just Sales)

Benson P. Shapiro, V. Kasturi Rangan, Rowland T. Moriarty, and Elliot B. Ross

High sales volume does not necessarily mean high income, as many companies have found to their sorrow. In fact, profits (as a percentage of sales) are often much higher on some orders than on others, for reasons managers sometimes do not well understand. If prices are appropriate, why is there such striking variation? Let's look at two examples of selling and pricing anomalies:

A plumbing fixtures manufacturer raised prices to discourage the "worthless" small custom orders that were disrupting the factory. But a series of price hikes failed to reduce unit sales volume. A study of operations two years later revealed that the most profitable orders were these custom orders. The new high prices more than compensated for costs; customers weren't changing suppliers because of high switching expenses; and competitors had shied from short runs because of the conventional wisdom in the industry.

A prominent producer of capital equipment, realizing it was losing big sales potential in its largest accounts, started a national account program. It included heavy sales support with experienced account managers; participation by high-level executives; special support like applications engineering, custom design services, unusual maintenance work, and expedited delivery; and a national purchase agreement with a hefty graduated volume discount.

Customers, however, viewed the program as merely a dog-and-pony show, having no substance. To convince the skeptics, top executives personally offered greater sales and service support and even more generous discounts.

Sales finally turned upward, and this "success" justified even higher levels of support. But profit margins soon began to erode; the big national accounts, the company discovered, were generating losses that were large enough to offset the rise in volume and the profitability of smaller, allegedly less attractive accounts.

Clearly these two companies discovered that it costs more to fill some orders than others. The plumbing fixtures executives raised prices precisely because they knew it was costing them more to fill small custom orders. The capital equipment company willingly took on extra costs in the hope of winning more sales. Management in both companies recognized that their price tags would vary, the first from boosted prices on custom orders, the other because of volume discounts. But executives in both companies failed to see that the cost and price variations would cause profound differences in the profitability of individual accounts and orders.

Many companies make this mistake. Managers pay little attention to account profitability, selection, and management. They seldom consider the magnitude, origins, and managerial implications of profit dispersion. In this article, we examine three central aspects of this important factor: costs to suppliers, customer behavior, and management of customers.

Costs to Suppliers

Profit, of course, is the difference between the net price and the actual cost to serve. In terms of individual accounts and orders, there can be dramatic differences in both price and cost.

Despite legal constraints that encourage uniformity in pricing, notably the Robinson-Patman Act, customers usually pay quite different prices in practice. Some buyers can negotiate or take advantage of differential discounts because of their size or the functions they can perform themselves, like in-house maintenance or technical support. And some customers exploit deals and promotions more than others. Moreover, the costs of serving customers and filling orders can vary significantly.

Presale costs vary greatly from order to order and account to account. Geography matters: some customers and prospects are located far from the salesperson's home base or normal route. Some customers require seemingly endless sales calls, while others place their orders over the telephone. Some must be courted with top-level executives backed up by sophisticated account management techniques, while others need little special effort. Such variations in cost reflect differences in customers' buying processes or the nature of their buying teams. (Some teams are large and geographically and functionally dispersed; others are small and concentrated by location and/or function.) Finally, some customers demand intensive presale service, like applications engineering and custom design support, while others accept standard designs.

Production costs also vary by customer and by order. Order size influences cost, as do setup time, scrap rate, custom designs, special features and functions, unusual packaging, and even order timing. Off-peak orders cost less than those made when demand is heavy. Fast delivery costs more. Some orders call on more resources than others. A company that inventories products in anticipation of orders, however, will have difficulty tracing production costs to particular orders and customers. Accounting policies and conventions, furthermore, often cloud the distinctions in product costs.

Distribution costs naturally vary with the customer's location. It also costs more to ship via a preferred transportation mode, to drop ship to a separate receiving location, to find no back-haul opportunity, or to extend special logistics support like a field inventory.

Postsale service costs also differ. Sometimes customer training, installation, technical support, and repair and maintenance are profit-making operations, but businesses often bundle such services into the product price and the buyer pays "nothing extra" for them. For some items, including capital equipment, postsale costs are heavy.

Thus there are variations among customers in each of the four components of cost: before-the-sale expenses, production, distribution, and after-the-sale service. Moreover, if prices and costs do not correlate, the distribution of gross income will have a dispersion that is the sum of the individual price and cost dispersions, and thus much greater than either. Of course, prices and costs are often viewed as correlated, but our research suggests that they usually aren't—which produces a broad dispersion of account profitability.

With real cost-plus pricing, profitability could be uniform across customers despite wide variations in both costs and prices. But there is evidence that prices seldom reflect the actual costs in serving customers (though they may be somewhat related to production costs). In many businesses, the difference between the highest and lowest prices realized in similar transactions for the same product is as much as 30%, not including quantity discounts.[1] Look, for example, at the relationship between prices and total costs in one month's orders for a manufacturer of pipe resin (see Exhibit I). The diagonal line indicates a price level equal to costs. If gross margin were the same on all orders, the orders would all lie along a line parallel to the diagonal line. Instead, they are widely dispersed. Nearly 13% of sales volume resulted in losses of about a nickel a pound, while about 4% of volume generated an eight-cent profit. The rest fell somewhere between.

This pattern is not unusual. In a wide variety of situations, we have consistently observed a lack of correlation between price and the cost to serve. Some orders and customers generate losses, and in general the dispersion of profitability is wide.

Customer Behavior

It is useful to think of customers in terms of two dimensions: net price realized and cost to serve. To show graphically the dynamics of the interplay between seller and buyer, we have devised a simple matrix (see Exhibit II). The vertical axis is net price, low to high, and the horizontal axis is cost to serve, low to high. This categorization is useful for any marketer. The *carriage trade* costs a great deal to serve but is willing to pay top dollar. (This category would include the customers of our introductory example, who placed small orders for high-cost custom plumbing fixtures.) At the opposite extreme are *bargain basement* customers—sensitive to price and relatively insensitive to service and quality. They can be served more cheaply than the carriage trade.

Serving *passive* customers costs less too, but they are willing to accept high prices. These accounts generate highly profitable orders. There are various reasons for their attitude. In some cases the product is too insignificant to warrant a tough negotiating stance over price. Other customers are insensitive to price because the product is crucial to their operation. Still others stay with their current supplier, more or less regardless of price, because of the

Exhibit I. Wide Gross Margin Dispersion for a Pipe Resin
Manufacturer for One Month

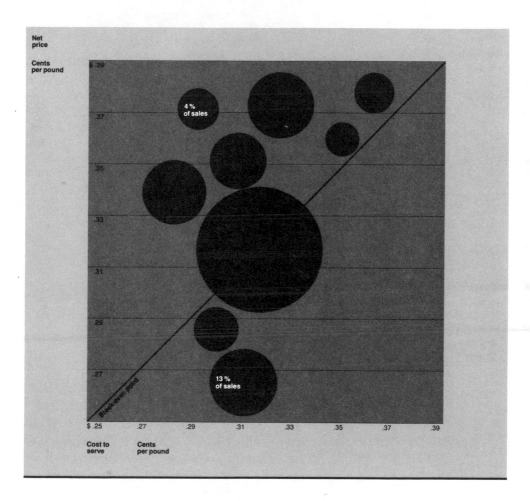

prohibitive cost of switching. As an example from another industry, many major aircraft components cannot be changed without recertifying the entire aircraft. And in some cases vendor capability is so well matched to buyer needs that cost to serve is low though the customer is receiving (and paying for) fine service and quality.

Aggressive customers, on the other hand, demand (and often receive) the highest product quality, the best service, and low prices. Procter & Gamble, boasting an efficient procurement func-

Exhibit II.   Customer Classification Matrix

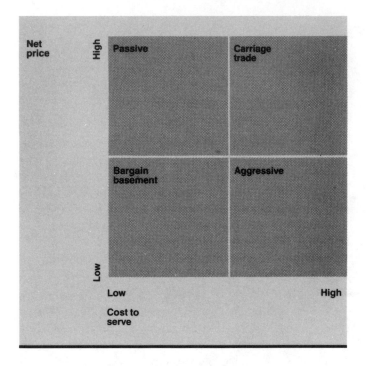

tion, has a reputation among its suppliers for paying the least and getting the most. Aggressive buyers are usually powerful; their practice of buying in large quantities gives them leverage with suppliers in seeking price deals and more service. The national accounts described in the second example at the beginning of this article drove hard bargains with the capital equipment supplier.

Marketing managers often assume a strong correlation between net price and cost to serve; they reason that price-sensitive customers will accept lower quality and service and demanding customers will pay more for better quality and service. Thinking in terms of service and quality demands unfortunately deflects attention from the critical issue of cost to serve. In addition, weak cost accounting practices that average costs over products, orders, and customers often support the high-cost, high-price myth. But as we have seen, costs and prices are not closely correlated.

A supplier of industrial packaging materials recently analyzed the profitability of its large national accounts. For each one it

Exhibit III.   **Customer Matrix of an Industrial Packaging Materials Supplier**

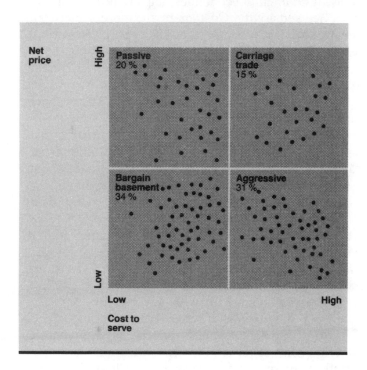

calculated approximate indicators of net price and cost to serve, based on averages of the aggregate values of a year's transactions. Top officers expected to find most of its customers in the carriage trade quadrant and the rest in the bargain basement. They were shocked when the results put about half of the 164 large customers in the passive and aggressive quadrants (see Exhibit III).

We believe this pattern is more common than is generally recognized. Among the various factors influencing buying behavior, the most important are the customer's situation and migration patterns.

CUSTOMER'S SITUATION

Four aspects of the customer's nature and position affect profitability: customer economics, power, the nature of the decision-making unit, and the institutional relationship between the buyer and seller.

As we all know, fundamental economics helps determine a buyer's price and service sensitivity. Customers are more sensitive to price when the product is a big part of their purchases, more sensitive to service when it has a big impact on their operations. Independent of economics, buying power, of course, is a major determinant of the buyer's ability to extract price concessions and service support from vendors. The power of big customers shows in their ability to handle many aspects of service support in-house—like breaking bulk—for which they demand price adjustments. Sometimes small customers also wield considerable power. A technological innovator that influences industry standards commands the eyes and ears of suppliers. Thus the relationship of cost to serve and customer size in this industry is not clear without careful measurement.

In respect to the decision-making unit, the purchase staff is generally sensitive to price, while engineering and production personnel are sensitive to service. These roles will affect decisions, depending on who most influences vendor choice and management. Naturally, this element is bound up with any relationships that have built up between the buyer and seller. Long-standing friendships, long histories of satisfactory performance, and appreciation for any special help or favors all tend to make customers reluctant to pressure suppliers for price and service concessions. Procter & Gamble rotates the responsibilities of its purchasing department members to discourage the development of strong personal relationships with vendors.

MIGRATION PATTERNS

Changes in organizational buying behavior and competitive activity can produce predictable patterns of change in customer profitability. Often a relationship begins in the carriage trade category. Customers need extensive sales and service support, insist on high product quality, and do not worry much about price if the product is new to them. They need the functionality and will pay for it.

Over time, however, as the customers gain experience with the product, they grow confident in dealing with the vendor and operating with less sales and service support or even without any.

The cost of serving them is likely to decline, and they are likely to become more price sensitive. In addition, the buying influence of the customer's procurement department often grows, while the role of engineering and operating personnel diminishes. This shift of course reinforces the tendency toward price sensitivity and away from service concerns. Finally, through rival product offerings (often at lower prices), customers gain knowledge that improves their competence with the product and thus their ability to demand price concessions and lessen their dependence on the vendor's support efforts.

If the customer perceives the product as trivial (as in the case of office supplies) and therefore does not seek it avidly, price sensitivity will not necessarily increase as service needs abate. In terms of the matrix of which Exhibit II is an example, migration will be toward the passive and bargain basement areas. If the buyer values the product and it is complex or service sensitive (like CAD/CAM equipment), the buyer may pressure the supplier for price reductions even while service requirements remain high. The migration tends to be downward from the carriage trade toward the aggressive quadrant, as in the case of electrical generation equipment for utilities. In commodities like pipe resin, a combination of customer experience, expanding influence of the purchasing staff, and increasing competitive imitation often leads customers into the bargain basement category.

Management of Customers

The shifts toward the bargain basement and aggressive quadrants are part of the general tendency of products to evolve from high-margin specialties to low-margin commodities. The dispersion of customer profitability we have observed can be managed. We suggest a five-step action program: pinpoint your costs, know your profitability dispersion, focus your strategy, provide support systems, and analyze repeatedly.

Pinpoint your costs. Manufacturers can usually measure their factory costs better than costs incurred by the sales, applications engineering, logistics, and service functions. For instance, few companies have a sense of the cost of unscheduled executive effort to handle the demands of aggressive customers. So it seems likely that customer profitability varies more widely in businesses where a large percentage of the total expenditure is incurred outside the factory. This would be the case in many high-tech companies that have low manufacturing costs but spend a great deal on sales, design engineering, applications engineering, and systems integration.

Because many specialty products are custom designed and manufactured and carry heavy nonfactory costs, the cost dispersion for these products is greater than for commodities. But as we pointed out in our pipe resin example, profit dispersion can be high even in a commodity product.

Costs incurred at different times in the order cycle have different effects on the true cost to serve the customer or order. In major sales with long order cycles and long lead times, the presale effort may begin several years ahead, and service under warranty may extend several years after installation and billing. If the cost of capital is 15%, a dollar spent two years before the billing of the customer is worth $1.32, and a dollar spent three years after billing is worth only 61 cents at the time of delivery. Companies with long lead times and order cycles, such as sellers of power generation equipment and commercial airliners, with long-term, substantial service liabilities, evidently have cost dispersions much larger than average, except where progress payments balance out cost flows. These companies need particularly good control systems and management judgment to measure costs and act accordingly.

Companies with poor cost accounting systems have no way to determine order, customer, product, or market segment profitability. Consequently, their cost control and management systems will be weak, and the result is likely to be above-average dispersion of costs. The sales manager of a large office equipment supplier who lacked adequate cost information described his situation thus: "It's management by anecdote. Salespeople regularly make passionate pleas for price relief on specific orders. When I press them for reasons, they say 'threat of competitive entry.' When I ask them if a cutback in service would be acceptable to make up for the price decrease, they give me a resounding no! What choice do you have in the absence of cost data, except to go by your judgment of the salesperson's credibility? I've wrongly accepted as many bad price relief requests as I've rejected."

An effective cost accounting system records data by product, order, and account, and records costs beyond the factory, including selling, transportation, applications or design engineering, and even unusual, unprogrammed activities like investments of blocks of corporate management time. Presale, production, distribution, and postsale service costs should all be recorded, analyzed, and related to orders and accounts.

Of course, there are enormous difficulties in creating and maintaining such a system. But even a system that estimates such costs only approximately can help a great deal. Twice a year, for example, one industrial company calculates the cost of serving three sizes of customers (large, medium, and small) and two sizes of orders (truckload and less-than-truckload) for a representative sample of accounts and orders. During the following six months, sales managers use these numbers to guide their decisions on price-relief requests.

Know your profitability dispersion. Once costs are known, the company can plot them against realized prices to show the dispersion of account profitability, as in Exhibit II. Clearly the framework must be adapted to the characteristics of the business. Similarly, the price axis should be defined in a meaningful way. Since list prices are often misleading, use some sort of net price. However, discounts should not be double-counted under costs as well. The ultimate objective is a measure of net profit by customer and order. Tracking cost and price data by order is an essential first step in building an account profitability matrix.

Companies that know their costs and use cost-plus pricing schemes will find most of their accounts in the bargain basement or carriage trade quadrants of the matrix. Though this pattern is perfectly reasonable, sales management should try to develop accounts in the passive quadrant. Many such customers will accept higher prices because they like the product so much. The cost to them of negotiating a lower price (or better service) outweighs the extra benefits they would get. The passive quadrant represents a region of maximum value for both the seller and the buyer.

A dispersion of profits is no bad thing; only not knowing it exists is. The best managed companies know their costs well and set prices on the basis of product value to customers rather than cost to serve. So they have some accounts in the passive categories. In fact, their profit dispersion will be greater than that of companies pricing on a cost-plus basis. The worst managed companies, ignorant of their costs and setting prices mainly in response to customer demands, are likely to have a large number of accounts in the aggressive category, with, obviously, pessimistic implications for profitability.

Focus your strategy. The next step is to use your knowledge of cost, price, and profit dispersion to define a strategy for managing your accounts. Here the company defines its personality. The low-cost, low-service, low-price provider would be in the lower left of a profitability matrix, while the company that offers differentiated and augmented products, intensive service, and customization—and, therefore, more value added—is in the upper right quadrant. Because any company's capability is necessarily limited, it cannot span the entire dimension. If it tries to, the poor focus will leave the company vulnerable to competition. This will allow rivals to jump into the aggressive quadrant with high service and low prices, drawing customers away from both the bargain basement and carriage trade quadrants. The result for the stretched-out company is reduced profitability.

The company has two strategy decisions to make. One is to locate the center of gravity or core of the company's business along the axis. The other is to define the range along the axis it will cover.

The fundamental choice to be made is the selection of customers, for companies that reside in a given quadrant will *generally* produce orders in that quadrant. Customers in each quadrant of the profitability matrix behave in a distinctive manner. The supplier has to decide which behavior is most consistent with its strengths. For instance, in an industry with high transport costs, like cement or sand, a customer located at the maximum practical distance from your plant is likely to be in one of the right-hand quadrants—for you. For a competitor whose plant is located near the customer, that account will probably be in a left-hand quadrant. Unless you can form a carriage trade relationship with that customer—realizing high prices because of the value of your services—you would do better to concede the account to your competitor.

Provide support systems. Unless it wants to follow a policy of cost-plus pricing, the company needs to develop processes and systems that will help it manage the profitability dispersion. The company's information system should produce reports based on order, customer, and segment profitability, not just on sales. Management must be oriented toward lateral cooperation among functions. A procedure that simply rewards salespeople for high unit sales and manufacturing personnel for low-cost production is unlikely to lead to the most profitable order mix.

Price setting rates special attention. Companies that operate in the bargain basement and aggressive quadrants of the profitability matrix must often set up centralized offices to price large orders and screen customers' demands for services. A "special bids" group is often the only way to give the quick replies and careful analyses such orders require. Such a group can best balance financial implications, production and operating capacity, and customer needs without giving away the store. Since carriage trade customers value the supplier's extra services, a cost-plus pricing policy may be appropriate for them. Finally, pricing for the trade in the passive quadrant has to be based on the value the customer places on the product.

The analysis, strategy, and customer negotiation functions must be kept separate. A men's and boys' coat manufacturer we know of is a good example of what happens when this rule is ignored. The owner's three sons headed divisions serving the department store, discount store, and export markets, while the owner himself managed the private-label business. He called on the three big general merchandise chains (Sears, Ward, and Penney), one of which gave him almost all of his business. The sons' divisions were very profitable, but the private-label unit was a big money loser.

Why was this so? Before a son went out to negotiate an order, the owner stressed the need to get high prices, keep costs reasonable, and secure orders that fit the company's abilities. The father analyzed large orders for profitability. But when the father went to talk to his biggest customer, no one pressured him to keep profits up. He consistently caved in to demands for lower prices, higher service, and better quality. His sons felt powerless to analyze his orders for profitability. The lesson: the same person should not set profit goals and negotiate with customers.

The more services a company provides, the more coordination is necessary among the engineers, field-service staff, and other functionaries in delivering the product and service. Likewise, the more a company increases its cost to serve, the more important interfunctional coordination becomes. Low-cost, low-price, low-service bargain basement operators don't need and can't afford elaborate logistics, field service, and other coordinating mechanisms. Carriage trade customers can't operate without them.

Deciding what strategic choices to make requires maintaining market research, pricing analysis, and cost-accounting functions. While these are high-leverage operations in which small investments can yield high returns, in hard times companies often view them as nonessential overhead expenses. This short-sighted attitude can be very damaging.

Repeat analysis regularly. A one-shot profit dispersion and strategy analysis is of little use. Buying behavior and migration patterns, like markets and competitors, are dynamic. Migration patterns gradually dilute a company's account selection and management policies.

Cumberland Metals (a disguised name) made pollution control components for the Big Three auto companies in the mid-1970s. Margins were very good, reflecting the high value the auto companies placed on the product, their lack of experience with pollution control, and the absence of competition. The entry of competitors in the early 1980s and, on the customers' part, a shift in influence from engineering to procurement staff signaled a fundamental migration in their buying behavior, but Cumberland management ignored the warning signs. This inattention caused long-standing customer relations problems and a prolonged earnings slump.

Cumberland Metals is unusual because it had only three large accounts. The loss of accounts and orders from the carriage trade quadrant is normally a matter of erosion.

How often a company should analyze profit dispersion and strategy depends on the rate of change in the market and in technology. In many cases, a once-a-year analysis integrated with the annual marketing plan makes sense. In high technology or other rapidly changing industries, a more frequent review may be better. In any case, the main difficulty lies in setting up good systems to track costs, prices, and profits; once the supporting information is available, the analysis is not difficult to perform.

Manage the Dispersion

A custom fabricator of industrial equipment, though operating at capacity, was losing money. The obvious problem was low price levels for the industry. Investigation, however, pointed to a mixture of poor pricing, poor cost estimating, and a lack of knowledge of profitability dispersion. Some bids were too aggressively priced: after winning contracts, the company then lost money on them. Executives had structured other bids to "make good money," basing them on inflated cost estimates. Astute competitors costed these bids better, handled the price negotiations more skillfully, and won the contracts. So the fabricator was winning only unprofitable bids.

The electrical products division of a large corporation, on the other hand, understood the importance of profitability analysis. It carefully analyzed its costs, developed a proactive pricing approach, and meticulously selected orders, products, and customers that fit its production competence and capacity. After a thorough before-and-after review, the financial analysis department at headquarters declared that the division had gone from a 5% loss to a 10% profit on sales in a glutted, static commodity market.

When meticulous analysis, a sensible strategy, and effective implementation are combined, a company can manage its profitability dispersion to generate profits, not just sales.

Note

1. See Elliot B. Ross, "Making Money with Proactive Pricing," *Harvard Business Review*, November–December 1984, p. 145.

2
Suppliers—Manage Your Customers

Randy Myer

Early in 1984, the top executives of an East Coast hardware chain made a momentous decision. Without consulting the company's suppliers, they decided to phase out its fleet of trucks and its network of warehouses. Maintaining this distribution system was costing the company about 5% of annual sales, and the executives believed the company was a large enough customer to expect suppliers to deliver directly to its outlets. According to the plan, if a supplier refused, the chain would buy its products through a wholesaler.

In a matter of months, the executives were hailing the move as a big success. As anticipated, individual stores now had to spend resources in processing numerous small "just-in-time" deliveries. But the realized savings in warehousing and transportation expenses far outweighed these processing costs.

What of the impact on suppliers, many of which considered the hardware chain a key account? Their perspective, of course, was quite different. Where suppliers had once made a single large shipment every two weeks to the chain's warehouses, some were now forced to make as many as 100 small shipments. Their order-handling and transportation costs took a big leap. Customer service levels had to improve. Shipments could not be assembled as carefully as in the past, and many were incomplete; scheduled into narrow one-hour time slots, shipments also arrived late. The order-handling and delivery snarls raised levels of out-of-stocks in the stores and created lost sales for those suppliers that did not raise their service performance standards.

This scenario typifies the trend toward domination of many consumer goods markets by fast-growing retailers like Wal-Mart Stores and Toys "R" Us. At the same time, mergers in department stores, auto parts, office supply, and other fields have led to the formation of new mega-channels. Fragmented markets are consolidating, and, increasingly, a handful of large, powerful retailers are ruling them.

In looking for new sources of profits, this new breed of sophisticated retailer is adopting new management systems, tighter controls, and better operating techniques, including point-of-sale orders, computerized order processing, and JIT deliveries. The result is lower costs and reduced inventory—often at the expense of the supplier.

This trend is only one aspect of a significant shift in the balance of power, which, for retailers, cannot come soon enough. In the United States, retailers as a group average a net return of about 1% on sales, whereas suppliers average 4%. In the United Kingdom, on the other hand, food retailers—regarded as a sophisticated trade class—yield an average net profit of about 4% against suppliers' 1%. While it is unlikely that we will soon reach the U.K. model, U.S. retailers can expect to take a bigger piece of the profit pie.

The issue, however, is not merely a simple shift of costs between players in a supply chain; it also involves the creation of unnecessary costs. Field data indicate that in the food industry, this trend has produced an increase in supply-chain costs of 25% to 30%. The bulk of these costs originate in transportation, warehousing, and inventory carrying (on the distribution side); unnecessary person-to-person communication (on the sales side); and ineffective promotion and advertising (on the marketing side). Excessive supply-chain costs in other principal consumer goods fields, like hardware and hard goods, probably run somewhat lower but are still in the 10% to 20% range.

Research shows that many suppliers are absorbing the bulk of that cost penalty, although few are aware of it. These penalties are manifested in many ways. Individually, these manifestations seem harmless enough; collectively, they can cause problems. They may include these demands on or actions affecting suppliers.

Shelf-stocking help from the supplier's sales force.

Unnecessary "emergency" shipment requests.

Unusually high claims of damaged goods in lines that are selling slowly.

Unauthorized product diversion and gray marketing.

Abuse of performance-related advertising allowances.

Delayed payment and extended dating.

Back-order and late-delivery penalty fees.

Why do such problems arise? For the oldest of business reasons: the new leaders in retailing and wholesaling are acting in their own interests. Wal-Mart, The Limited, Toys "R" Us, and others like them have unilaterally redefined relationships with their suppliers. By all accounts, they are not particularly interested in preferred supplier arrangements or supply-chain concepts. Instead, by extracting concessions and dictating terms, they determine how their suppliers will service them.

They have learned to restrict their inventory investment and at the same time to insist on high service levels, the lowest possible net purchase price, all allowable discounts, and the most lenient financing terms—usually without any reciprocal benefit to their suppliers. In short, these customers have found ways to get their suppliers to contribute directly to their own bottom lines. (There are limits, of course, to what a customer can demand. Revco and Dart Drug Stores so abused their suppliers that when they hit hard times for other reasons, suppliers cut them off with alacrity.)

This is not to suggest that Wal-Mart Stores (for example) is some rogue corporation, playing outside the rules of the game. No, its merchandising strategy is similar to successful competitors', past and present. Wal-Mart is only more relentless and thoroughgoing in execution of that strategy and in the operating side of its business. As a result, the suppliers of Wal-Mart and other leading retailers are forced to ask themselves basic questions: What services do we provide? What are customers costing us? Is this business worth the cost?

Market realities suggest it's the supplier that must take responsibility for remedies. Its customers are behaving rationally, reacting to competitive pressures for profit improvement and in conformity with the way most suppliers extend services.

Why should a customer buy a standard product at list price when sizable discounts and free services are available from the supplier's competitors? And if a supplier charges no more for short lead times or rapid delivery, why shouldn't the customer demand just-in-time delivery? If a supplier fails to adopt or enforce a late-payment penalty, why should the customer remit promptly? And if a supplier is willing to fork over promotion money early, why not take it? In today's retailing world, many suppliers are being pushed to the limits of their customers' imaginations. What alternative do suppliers have—to say no to demands and risk losing the business?

If suppliers hope to regain a measure of control over their destiny, they must assert themselves and take responsibility for managing their customers. In doing this, suppliers face challenges in two realms: reallocating resources in the company and redesigning programs to better serve outside customers.

Internal Moves

First let's look at resource reallocation, a process that can be summarized this way: improved measurement systems, team building, and organizational accountability.

MEASURING CUSTOMER ROA.   In many supplier companies, senior executives don't know which of their customers cost them most to serve or how high the added costs are. The reason: their information systems do not capture the relevant data. Suppliers tend to focus on product performance, but they should pay equal attention to customer performance.

Marketers use elaborate accounting systems to track product performance. Suppliers can track many elements by brand, including price sensitivity, advertising and promotion campaign effectiveness, and cost trends. Market research tracks product progress by region, channel, and competitor. And factories set manufacturing strategies that are focused by product group.

Customer management gets far less attention. When they track it at all, suppliers most often measure customer performance in terms of sales volume or gross margin with no allocation of direct SG&A costs or assets. Moreover, responsibility for this activity is often vested in the supplier's sales organization. Since salespeople are generally compensated in terms of revenue goals, not profitability, they are likely to endorse any customer-originated program that enhances or protects revenue, regardless of its impact on profitability.

Therefore, the sales function has little reason to worry about the profit or asset implications of trying to provide, for example, "100% service." Salespeople would like to see their company's plants and warehouses perpetually flush with inventory so the organization can avoid the revenue "losses" associated with back orders. When inventory problems arise, they expect the company to invest whatever is necessary—in overtime, air freight, or capacity—to fill its orders. The marginal return on that final dollar of investment may be paltry, but since no one above the sales level is monitoring customer performance, no one examines significant trade-offs and ROA from higher levels of service.

Like the customer, the sales force is merely acting in recognition of its own economics. Few companies possess accounting systems that track asset investments or profit contribution below the gross margin line by customer. To be sure, many companies measure revenue, cost of goods, price discounts deducted from the invoice, and product returns.

They track less frequently, however, the marketing, selling, product development, and delivery costs and the asset investment in receivables and inventory directly attributable to a particular customer. And rarely do they examine customer-service performance by customer: order fill rates, delivery time, sales-call frequency, quality problems, and postsale service history. In short, most suppliers simply have no idea who their most and least profitable customers are—knowledge essential to effective supply-chain management.

There is a practical way to measure customer performance, dubbed customer return on assets (CRA). (See Exhibit I.) Unlike traditional ROA measures, CRA excludes certain cost and asset categories; only direct customer costs for sales, marketing, postsale service, and distribution are deducted from gross margin. While the calculation includes direct customer assets for accounts receivable and inventory, it excludes noncustomer costs and assets like R&D, legal expenses, and plant and equipment investments not managed by account and therefore not attributable to customer profits on assets.

One consumer goods producer that applied the CRA measure to its customers found that while the average return was almost 30%, the range of performance was wide, from 5% to 55%. Headquarters looked more deeply into the cost elements and found that in almost every cost category, there was a sizable difference in the cost of serving each customer. The widest spread was in promotion expenses. (See Exhibit II.) The differences had less to do with customers' size than with their decision to participate in programs, which was a question of whether to buy only when products were discounted and discounts were large.

Sales cost was another category with a sizable spread; though

Exhibit I.

CRA: A Way to Measure Customer Performance

Revenue less:

Cost of goods sold
Reserves for damaged and returned merchandise
Discounts and allowances

= Gross margin less:

Sales cost
Promotion cost (excluding media advertising)
Product development cost
Direct warehousing cost
Customer freight cost
Postsale service cost

= Customer contribution to overhead divided by:

Direct asset costs
    Accounts receivable
    Inventory (finished goods)

= Customer return on assets

the average was about 4% of sales, the cost varied from 3% to 12%. It turned out that while account size was key, call frequency, the number of buying locations, and the need to cover individual stores were the main reasons for variations in sales cost for accounts of similar size.

Accounts receivable represented another category with widely different results. The terms of payment were 1% discount in 20 days and net 30 days. Yet the performance spread ranged from those who paid on average in 12 days to some who averaged more than 40 days. To compound the problem, most customers were taking the discount regardless of when they paid their bills.

Imagine headquarters' reaction if *product* performance had

ranged from 5% to 50% ROA. A fresh awareness of customer performance differences inspired top management to change its accounting system. The function now produces monthly customer reports and regularly highlights the least profitable customer accounts.

Suppliers that do not measure CRA build into their business patterns an array of assumptions, half-truths, and even myths about customer profitability. Prevalent is the notion, for example, that it is more profitable to serve large customers than small ones. But research suggests that, generally, size and profitability are not closely related. More often, customer profitability correlates *inversely* with customer growth rates, as one East Coast packaged-goods company recently discovered. Actually, the company's higher growth accounts were the least profitable. (See Exhibit III.) Giants like Wal-Mart headed this list of low performers, but fast-growing, medium-sized chains, including Food Lion and Drug Emporium, also placed high on the list.

These high-growth customers were able and willing to take full advantage of their suppliers. For example, they cherry-picked the product line, buying certain goods only when the deepest discounts were offered (like Crest toothpaste this month, Colgate next month) and dropping or limiting those items on reimposition of the regular price schedules. This practice enables the customer to offer a variety of products at very low prices—a foundation for growth in this business. Obviously, though, cherry-picking does not benefit the supplier whose products are available only when its margins are lowest.

A supplier that does not measure CRA by account is likely to find its profitability eroding. Had the East Coast supplier not awakened to its situation, its profits would have dwindled, as its more opportunistic customers flourished in comparison with its profitable-to-serve customers.

CUSTOMER TEAMS. The supplier's next move is to orient its organization—structurally as well as philosophically—toward customer management.

This means new reporting relationships, not just new responsibilities. Suppliers sometimes "layer" new customer responsibilities onto the existing product-driven system, complicating the old approaches and undercutting the new ones. Several major food companies, for example, have assigned certain customers to product

Exhibit II.

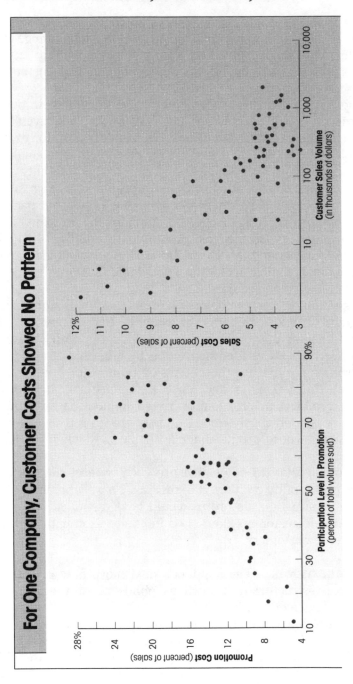

For One Company, Customer Costs Showed No Pattern

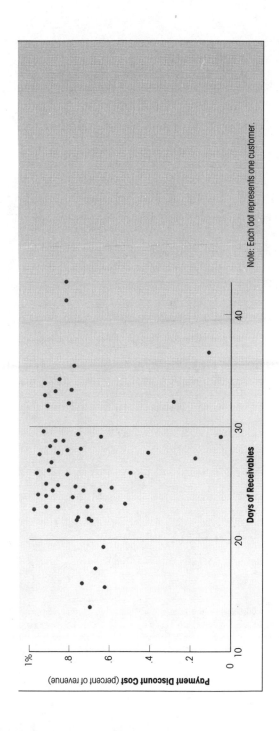

Payment Discount Cost (percent of revenue)

Days of Receivables

Note: Each dot represents one customer.

Exhibit III.

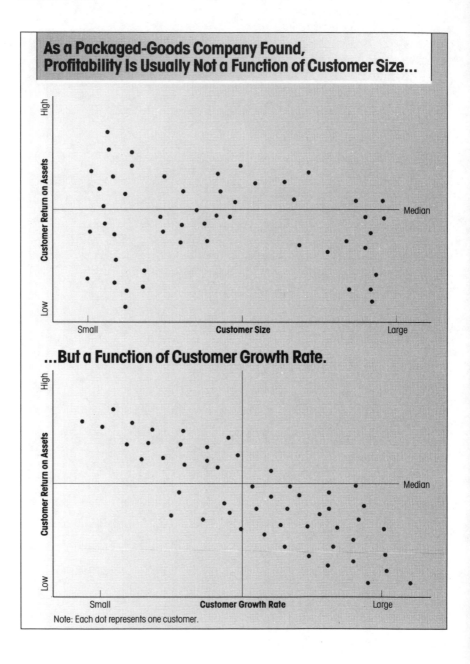

As a Packaged-Goods Company Found, Profitability Is Usually Not a Function of Customer Size...

...But a Function of Customer Growth Rate.

Note: Each dot represents one customer.

managers or distribution executives, encouraging them to "build a better knowledge of customer *X*'s needs" or "develop personal relationships beyond the sales force." Such measures are inadequate. A more effective approach is to assemble teams of functional experts to manage key accounts or groups of accounts.

The first challenge is to define the most effective grouping of customers. This is not as straightforward as it may sound. Campbell Soup, for example, groups customers regionally. Though a step in the right direction, this approach (primarily oriented to regional consumer preferences) fails to distinguish well among the very different retailers that operate in a given territory.

More appropriate is the approach taken by another big producer of packaged foods. It put together a team consisting of a marketing person, a distribution person, a sales manager, and a finance expert—all at senior levels—and ran what the company called the "Chicago Test." Conceived along the regional-consumer lines of the Campbell program, the test soon switched direction. The team realized that four types of customers in the same area (low-priced "warehouse" stores, broad-line and midsize supermarkets, upscale supermarkets, and convenience stores) demand very different kinds of service. It refocused the program to serve national accounts organized by type of chain, not by region.

Encouraged, the company rolled out the program nationally, assigning marketing people and organizing customer and support services by customer category. Two years later, the company has rung up a 5% to 10% improvement in customer profitability, which it attributes to the program.

Stores with common market strategy and service requirements, not common geography, should drive the supplier's team structure. The features to look for include the breadth and depth of product offerings, their pricing and promotion strategy, the product availability in the store, and available services (home delivery, salespeople with product knowledge, and so on). In consumer electronics, for example, Sears Roebuck, Montgomery Ward, and a few other major players have traditionally offered limited product selection and frequent sales promotions on selected items (although Sears recently installed an "everyday low prices" policy). Highland Superstores and Silo offer a broad product selection with everyday low prices across brands. Finally, local dealers offer modest brand selection but more service. In this market, a supplier should organize its resources around three reasonably distinct customer groupings.

The key is to refocus your resources—people, systems, and services—around the customer's needs and strategy. The most effective organization structures are teams in which responsibility for like customers are shared among sales, marketing, distribution, logistics, and financial staff. Charged with servicing their customers, teams have full responsibility for customer performance as well as the decision-making authority and the resources to implement their decisions.

What happens when such a team is faced with a customer "innovation" that creates friction costs? Say a customer demands store delivery or begins deducting inventory-carrying costs from its payments for shipments that arrive early. The team with responsibility for that customer reviews the standing policy and the proposed exception, assesses the CRA implications for the supplier, and makes a decision.

It may even decide to end the relationship; this has happened. One consumer electronics company was beset by excessive service demands from one of the top five retailers in the country. The retailer clearly was not committed to the product category (electric razors) and did not come close to generating the volume necessary to justify the services it was demanding. The supplier called a summit conference with the retailer, and when the retailer declined to change its trade practices, the supplier dropped the account. An unusual step, but sometimes a necessary one.

MAKING TEAMS ACCOUNTABLE. The last and most straightforward of the three internal considerations is accountability. Simply creating and empowering teams for customer management is not enough. The head office's tougher task is to assess team performance and reward good performers on the basis of gains made in CRA performance, not on revenue or gross margin.

Look at a company that supplies candy to supermarkets and convenience stores. The supermarket trade generates the bulk of its business and income, but over the long term, the supplier should be emphasizing convenience stores. The team servicing the supermarkets needs (and deserves) a different CRA target than the team servicing the convenience stores, because the profitability of the supermarkets is 5 to 10 percentage points higher in CRA than that of the convenience stores. The reason is that supermarkets sell more bulk candy, which has higher margins, they handle goods directly through their warehouses rather than use jobbers, and their volume per item is higher, which creates economies of scale for both the stores and their suppliers.

The different structure and strategy of the two channels create differing performance expectations. So CRA benchmarks must differ too. These allow the candy supplier's management to examine team performance in light of those targets.

Without accountability, internal and external supplier innovations lie dead in the water. A Midwestern personal-care products company assigned its marketing people to sets of customers with the terse mandate to "manage the accounts." The mandate amounted to more work with no clear accountability. Within a year, the program had expired. Why? Because the supplier had stopped short of measuring marketing effectiveness or investment by customer and had failed to reward its "relationship managers" for improvements along these dimensions. The message from management was clear, and clearly wrongheaded: Get to know your customers better—but remember that the road to the top is still based on market share.

You Get What You Pay For

Once suppliers begin to measure effectively and discover how their customers create friction costs, the natural temptation is to punish their least profitable customers by tightening policy enforcement, eliminating deviations, and otherwise "bringing the customer into line." This, of course, is not a productive way to respond. Ask your sales force how your most important customers would respond to a series of ultimatums that amount to this: "Do it our way or else!"

Customer management is a positive step toward building better relationships, and that's how it should be communicated. Once a supplier has decided to measure customer performance and manage by customer need, it should think about how to get a customer in sync with its own policies without risking the loss of its business. The following steps give the supplier the control it seeks and the customer the flexibility it wants:

1. Define certain customer deviations as acceptable, but know where and when to draw the line.
2. Create a menu of options for the customer.

3. Emphasize that every service has its price.
4. Establish prices that create appropriate incentives without alienating the customer.

Since each customer has its own merchandising strategy, the supplier should formulate performance and CRA targets for each strategic category of customer. For example, it makes no sense to identify customers in low-margin segments as wayward just because they are less profitable to serve than customers in high-margin segments. It should always be the supplier's prerogative to do business in low-margin segments in the hope that its customers there will enjoy high volume and high growth rates.

By the same token, customers who cherry-pick, buying only when discounts are at their deepest, should be seen for what they are—mercenaries that cannot be cultivated to the company's advantage. In short, the supplier needs to consider deviations from the norm, make policy exceptions on a case-by-case basis, and give some consideration to the long-term viability of each customer group.

Creating a menu of options is particularly important for those suppliers whose customers have an extensive range of strategies and requirements. (See Exhibit IV, which suggests the range of options a creative supplier can offer its customers.)

Payment terms are a good example. Most suppliers state a payment due date and offer a discount for early payment, like 2% off for payment in 10 days, with full payment due in 30 days. Though this is a time-honored system, it makes little sense from a financial or customer-management perspective. The supplier is trying to make the point that the float has a value. But why stop at two choices? A more flexible solution would be to pass on to the customer the cost of capital, expressed as a rate per day, with a stated maximum payment period. The customer could calculate (and the supplier verify) the discount applicable to payment in 10, 15, or 20 days. The goal is flexibility, with the customer getting a range of payment options.

So far, innovations in this area have tended to come up in trade categories where the relationships are closer to partnerships or where circumstances force the issue. An Argentinean leather supplier, for example, presented just such a payment schedule to a major U.S. handbag manufacturer, which accepted it. The Argentinean company, of course, had a severe inflation problem at home

Exhibit IV.

Expanding the Expected to Create a Menu of Options	
Traditional	**Nontraditional**
Regular sales call	Telemarketing sales call Electronic data interchange ordering and invoicing
Fixed promotion calendar	Flexible promotion dates Option packages for advertising and promotion support
Delivered product	Customer pickup at supplier's warehouses
Warehouse delivery	Direct plant delivery to customer
Normal terms	Extended payment terms at daily interest rate
Supplier-planned inventory	Joint inventory planning

that fueled the effort. Even absent this problem, however, the underlying customer-management principle was sound.

On the no-free-lunch principle, every service to a customer has its price. If a supplier offers not only traditional sales, marketing, distribution, and financial services but also more flexible options, it must assign the costs—which may be heavy—appropriately. Systems and programs for telemarketing, electronic data interchange (EDI), or direct plant shipment, for example, require an investment of assets and add to operating costs. With rare exceptions, the customers that use these service options should pay for them.

Unfortunately, suppliers often bundle their costs of sales, distribution, and financing into the product cost. The customer generally pays a price that reflects the average cost of sales calls, delivery, and order entry; any special services come free to that customer. Sophisticated customers can beat the system, since the supplier and its other customers bear the costs of their special requests or deviations from set policy.

To illustrate, when a midsize cosmetics company began to measure customer profitability, it discovered it was not recovering the high costs of serving small orders. Since it offered no quantity discounts for large orders—in other words, large accounts were subsidizing smaller ones—some chains were ordering in small quantities and demanding store delivery. To its dismay, the company found the cost difference between the small and large orders to be a full 8% of revenue. So over several years, the company set up a staggered price schedule that reflected the cost differentials. With no change in revenue, average order quantity increased by 33%, producing big savings in selling and distribution costs.

While some of the company's customers resisted the new program, most did not, probably because it was "sold" in terms of a discount schedule and not as a system of surcharges. Even Wal-Mart Stores came around, albeit more slowly; the supplier had to send back two payments before Wal-Mart forwarded the full amount due under the new pricing schedule.

Ideally, service-based pricing gives customers appropriate incentives without driving them away. But in practice, the potential for alienation is real because the supplier wants customers either to change their behavior or to pay a premium for services once provided free. It is not enough simply to design equitable programs; the supplier must sell them to customers. Two means to this end are:

> Structuring prices as discounts from a full-service standard price.
>
> Phasing in the program over an extended period, offering modest allowances initially and raising them over time.

In option one, a supplier can either ask customers to pay a higher price for extra service or offer them discounts in exchange for accepting a less expensive service. The economics are the same in either case, but discounts obviously have greater psychological appeal than price add-ons. A shrewd approach is to present a product list price that reflects the highest possible service level, including weekly store delivery, weekly sales calls, extended financing terms, and guaranteed order fulfillment. The supplier then offers the more efficient service alternatives at a discount from that standard. The customer selects a mix of services that fits its needs and gets a discount (not a surcharge!) for doing so.

Price incentives are likely to be more palatable if the supplier introduces them slowly. For salespeople as well as customers, service-based pricing is a more complex proposition than the typical product-based system. In product categories like computer mainframes or commercial aircraft, buyers are accustomed to complex pricing options. But in less sophisticated product categories, like soup or shoes, the learning takes time, so a phased program is the best way to go. By initially offering a compressed pricing schedule (instead of huge differences between high- and low-service options), suppliers give their customers a chance to get used to the menu-pricing approach.

When a customer recognizes the economics of a situation, rationality tends to prevail. If the most economical way to distribute a product is, say, through retail warehouse delivery from the plant, and if the pricing system reflects that fact, customers will gradually convert to that kind of delivery. Customers that insist on less efficient store delivery will have to pay an increasing premium for it. In the end, the behavior of individual customers and suppliers becomes consistent with the economics of the supply chain as a whole.

What to Tell the Troops

These structural and philosophical changes demand a great deal of work, especially when they conflict with the interests of entrenched constituencies—like a sales force accustomed to maximizing revenue instead of boosting ROA. You may have to sell your organization on the concept of customer management.

So how do you convert your organization? Begin by pointing out that for many consumer product categories, the costs of selling, buying, trade marketing, delivering, and paying for the product represent between 20% and 40% of the consumer price. Industries and individual relationships vary widely, but it appears that 25% to 50% of those relationship costs are unnecessary. This is clearly an unacceptable penalty on suppliers, especially in industries where profit margins are not robust.

Explain that friction costs are particularly high for companies in complex supply chains. In these relationships, customers have learned the importance of getting all they can out of their suppliers, especially those that offer a variety of free services. (If it is relevant, stress too that customers are likely to take advantage of suppliers that lack the leverage of strong brand names.) Customers cannot be expected to refrain from acting in their own financial interests. Responsibility for reducing friction costs therefore lies with the supplier.

Make it clear that your organization has to recognize and measure the scope of its problems. The first step is to establish a CRA reporting system. Next, assemble multidisciplinary teams to handle customer relationships and organize the teams by strategic segments, not by region. For each team, establish new performance and reward criteria tailored to your expectations of each customer group's performance. Clearly define accountability in your organization.

Emphasize the four basic principles of customer management: defining when certain customer deviations are acceptable, creating a menu of options, pricing all services, and designing the price structure as an array of incentives to be implemented over several years.

Establish objective benchmarks against which to measure the progress of your efforts. For example: Have we retained and increased our market share with key accounts? Have we enhanced ROA for these accounts? Are we winning their cooperation and participation? Has the entire supply chain benefited, and do our customers recognize those benefits?

Finally, an organizational commitment to customer management will not guarantee success. But the absence of such a commitment, starting at the top, will certainly doom the effort. Since managing your customers means a big shift in outlook, policy, and organization, you'll prosper from commitment at all levels.

3
Zero Defections: Quality Comes to Services

Frederick F. Reichheld and W. Earl Sasser, Jr.

The *real* quality revolution is just now coming to services. In recent years, despite their good intentions, few service company executives have been able to follow through on their commitment to satisfy customers. But service companies are beginning to understand what their manufacturing counterparts learned in the 1980s—that quality doesn't improve unless you measure it. When manufacturers began to unravel the costs and implications of scrap heaps, rework, and jammed machinery, they realized that "quality" was not just an invigorating slogan but the most profitable way to run a business. They made "zero defects" their guiding light, and the quality movement took off.

Service companies have their own kind of scrap heap: customers who will not come back. That scrap heap too has a cost. As service businesses start to measure it, they will see the urgent need to reduce it. They will strive for "zero defections"—keeping every customer the company can profitably serve—and they will mobilize the organization to achieve it.

Customer defections have a surprisingly powerful impact on the bottom line. They can have more to do with a service company's profits than scale, market share, unit costs, and many other factors usually associated with competitive advantage. As a customer's relationship with the company lengthens, profits rise. And not just a little. Companies can boost profits by almost 100% by retaining just 5% more of their customers.

While defection rates are an accurate leading indicator of profit swings, they do more than passively indicate where profits are headed. They also direct managers' attention to the specific things that are causing customers to leave. Since companies do not hold customers captive, the only way they can prevent defections is to outperform the competition continually. By soliciting feedback from defecting customers, companies can ferret out the weaknesses that really matter and strengthen them before profits start to dwindle. Defection analysis is therefore a guide that helps companies manage continuous improvement.

Charles Cawley, president of MBNA America, a Delaware-based credit card company, knows well how customer defections can focus a company's attention on exactly the things customers value. One morning in 1982, frustrated by letters from unhappy customers, he assembled all 300 MBNA employees and announced his determination that the company satisfy and keep each and every customer. The company started gathering feedback from defecting customers. And it acted on the information, adjusting products and processes regularly.

As quality improved, fewer customers had reason to leave. Eight years later, MBNA's defection rate is one of the lowest in its industry. Some 5% of its customers leave each year—half the average rate for the rest of the industry. That may seem like a small difference, but it translates into huge earnings. Without making any acquisitions, MBNA's industry ranking went from 38 to 4, and profits have increased sixteenfold.

The Cost of Losing a Customer

If companies knew how much it really costs to lose a customer, they would be able to make accurate evaluations of investments designed to retain customers. Unfortunately, today's accounting systems do not capture the value of a loyal customer. Most systems focus on current period costs and revenues and ignore expected cash flows over a customer's lifetime. Served correctly, customers generate increasingly more profits each year they stay with a company. Across a wide range of businesses, the pattern is the same: the longer a company keeps a customer, the more money it stands to make. (See Exhibit I.) For one auto-service company, the expected profit from a fourth-year customer is more than triple the profit that same customer generates in the first year. When customers defect, they take all that profit-making potential with them.

It may be obvious that acquiring a new customer entails certain one-time costs for advertising, promotions, and the like. In credit cards, for example, companies spend an average of $51 to recruit a customer and set up the new account. But there are many more pieces to the profitability puzzle.

To continue with the credit card example, the newly acquired customers use the card slowly at first and generate a base profit. But if the customers stay a second year, the economics greatly improve. As they become accustomed to using the credit card and are satisfied with the service it provides, customers use it more and balances grow. In the second year—and the years thereafter—they purchase even more, which turns profits up sharply. We found this trend in each of the more than 100 companies in two dozen industries we have analyzed. For one industrial distributor, net sales per account continue to rise into the nineteenth year of the relationship.

As purchases rise, operating costs decline. Checking customers' credit histories and adding them to the corporate data base is expensive, but those things need be done only once. Also, as the company gains experience with its customers, it can serve them more efficiently. One small financial consulting business that depends on personal relationships with clients has found that costs drop by two-thirds from the first year to the second because customers know what to expect from the consultant and have fewer questions or problems. In addition, the consultants are more efficient because they are familiar with the customer's financial situation and investment preferences.

Also, companies with long-time customers can often charge more for their products or services. Many people will pay more to stay in a hotel they know or to go to a doctor they trust than to take a chance on a less expensive competitor. The company that has developed such a loyal following can charge a premium for the customer's confidence in the business.

Yet another economic boon from long-time customers is the free advertising they provide. Loyal customers do a lot of talking over the years and drum up a lot of business. One of the leading home builders in the United States, for example, has found that more than 60% of its sales are the result of referrals.

These cost savings and additional revenues combine to produce a steadily increasing stream of profits over the course of the customer's relationship with the company. (See Exhibit II.) While the

Exhibit I.

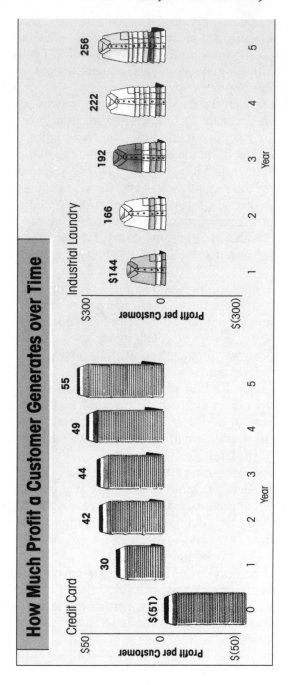

How Much Profit a Customer Generates over Time

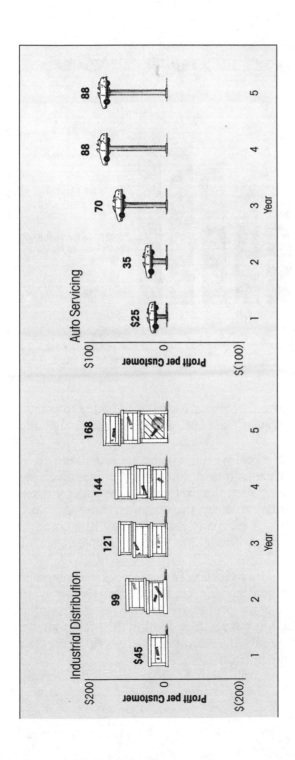

Exhibit II.

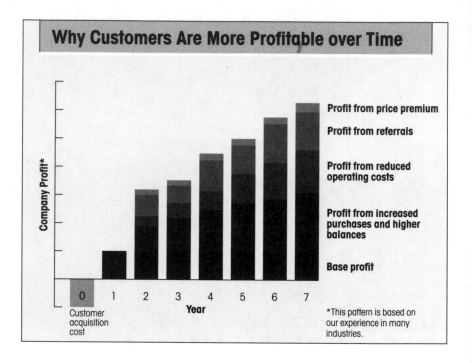

relative importance of these effects varies from industry to industry, the end result is that longer term customers generate increasing profits.

To calculate a customer's real worth, a company must take all of these projected profit streams into account. If, for instance, the credit card customer leaves after the first year, the company takes a $21 loss. If the company can keep the customer for four more years, his or her value to the company rises sharply. It is equal to the net present value of the profit streams in the first five years, or about $100.

When a company lowers its defection rate, the average customer relationship lasts longer and profits climb steeply. One way to appreciate just how responsive profits are to changes in defection rates is to draw a defection curve. (See Exhibit III.) This shows clearly how small movements in a company's defection rate can produce very large swings in profits.

The curve shows, for example, that as the credit card company

Exhibit III.

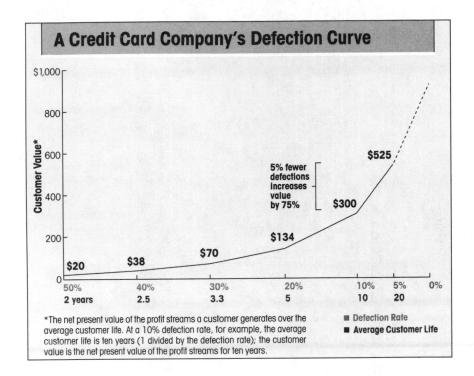

A Credit Card Company's Defection Curve

5% fewer defections increases value by 75%

$525

$300

$134

$70

$38

$20

50%	40%	30%	20%	10%	5%	0%
2 years	2.5	3.3	5	10	20	

Customer Value*

*The net present value of the profit streams a customer generates over the average customer life. At a 10% defection rate, for example, the average customer life is ten years (1 divided by the defection rate); the customer value is the net present value of the profit streams for ten years.

■ Defection Rate
■ Average Customer Life

cuts its defection rate from 20% to 10%, the average life span of its relationship with a customer doubles from five years to ten and the value of that customer more than doubles—jumping from $134 to $300. As the defection rate drops another 5%, the average life span of a customer relationship doubles again and profits rise 75%—from $300 to $525.

The credit card business is not unique. Although the shape of defection curves vary across industries, in general, profits rise as defection rates fall. Reducing defections by just 5% generated 85% more profits in one bank's branch system, 50% more in an insurance brokerage, and 30% more in an auto-service chain. (See Exhibit IV.) MBNA America has found that a 5% improvement in defection rates increases its average customer value by more than 125%.

Understanding the economics of defections is useful to managers in several ways. For one thing, it shows that continuous improvement in service quality is not a cost but an investment in a customer

Exhibit IV.

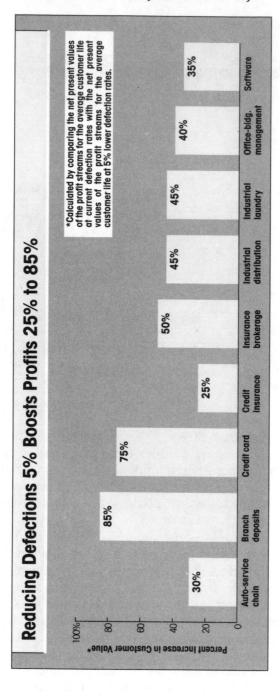

Reducing Defections 5% Boosts Profits 25% to 85%

Percent Increase in Customer Value*

Auto-service chain	30%
Branch deposits	85%
Credit card	75%
Credit insurance	25%
Insurance brokerage	50%
Industrial distribution	45%
Industrial laundry	45%
Office-bldg. management	40%
Software	35%

*Calculated by comparing the net present values of the profit streams for the average customer life at current defection rates with the net present values of the profit streams for the average customer life at 5% lower defection rates.

who generates more profit than the margin on a one-time sale. Executives can therefore justify giving priority to investments in service quality versus things like cost reduction, for which the objectives have been more tangible.

Knowing that defections are closely linked to profits also helps explain why some companies that have relatively high unit costs can still be quite profitable. Companies with loyal, long-time customers can financially outperform competitors with lower unit costs and high market share but high customer churn. For instance, in the credit card business, a 10% reduction in unit costs is financially equivalent to a 2% decrease in defection rate. Low-defection strategies can overwhelm low-cost strategies.

And understanding the link between defections and profits provides a guide to lucrative growth. It is common for a business to lose 15% to 20% of its customers each year. Simply cutting defections in half will more than double the average company's growth rate. Companies with high retention rates that want to expand through acquisition can create value by acquiring low retention competitors and reducing their defections.

Defections Management

Although service companies probably can't—and shouldn't try to—eliminate all defections, they can and must reduce them. But even to approach zero defections, companies must pursue that goal in a coordinated way. The organization should be prepared to spot customers who leave and then to analyze and act on the information they provide.

Watch the door. Managing for zero defections requires mechanisms to find customers who have ended their relationship with the company—or are about to end it. While compiling this kind of customer data almost always involves the use of information technology of some kind, major investments in new systems are unnecessary.

The more critical issue is whether the business regularly gathers information about customers. Some companies already do. Credit card companies, magazine publishers, direct mailers, life insurers, cellular phone companies, and banks, for example, all collect reams of data as a matter of course. They have at their disposal the names and addresses, purchasing histories, and telephone numbers of all their customers. For these businesses, exposing defections is relatively easy. It's just a matter of organizing the data.

Sometimes, defining a "defection" takes some work. In the railroad business, for instance, few customers stop using your service completely, but a customer that shifts 80% of its shipments to trucks should not be considered "retained." The key is to identify the customer behaviors that both drive your economics and gauge customer loyalty.

For some businesses, the task of spotting defectors is challenging even if they are well defined, because customers tend to be faceless and nameless to management. Businesses like retailing will have to find creative ways to "know" their customers. Consider the example of Staples, the Boston-based office products discounter. It has done a superb job of gathering information usually lost at the cashier or sales clerk. From its opening, it had a data base to store and analyze customer information. Whenever a customer goes through the checkout line, the cashier offers him or her a membership card. The card entitles the holder to special promotions and certain discounts. The only requirement for the card is that the person fill out an application form, which asks for things like name, job title, and address. All subsequent purchases are automatically logged against the card number. This way, Staples can accumulate detailed information about buying habits, frequency of visits, average dollar value spent, and particular items purchased.

Even restaurants can collect data. A crab house in Maryland, for instance, started entering into its PC information from the reservation list. Managers can now find out how often particular customers return and can contact those who seem to be losing interest in the restaurant.

What are defectors telling you? One reason to find customers who are leaving is to try to win them back. MBNA America has a customer-defection "swat" team staffed by some of the company's best telemarketers. When customers cancel their credit cards, the swat team tries to convince them to stay. It is successful half of the time.

But the more important motive for finding defectors is for the insight they provide. Customers who leave can provide a view of the business that is unavailable to those on the inside. And whatever caused one individual to defect may cause many others to follow. The idea is to use defections as an early warning signal—to learn from defectors why they left the company and to use that information to improve the business.

Unlike conventional market research, feedback from defecting customers tends to be concrete and specific. It doesn't attempt to measure things like attitudes or satisfaction, which are changeable and subjective, and it doesn't raise hypothetical questions, which may be irrelevant to the respondents. Defections analysis involves specific, relevant questions about why a customer has defected. Customers are usually able to articulate their reasons, and some skillful probing can get at the root cause.

This information is useful in a variety of ways, as the Staples example shows. Staples constantly tracks defections, so when customers stop doing business there or don't buy certain products, the store notices it immediately and calls to get feedback. It may be a clue that the competition is underpricing Staples on certain goods—a competitive factor management can explore further. If it finds sufficient evidence, Staples may cut prices on those items. This information is highly valued because it pinpoints the uncompetitive products and saves the chain from launching expensive broad-brush promotions pitching everything to everybody.

Staples's telemarketers try to discern which merchandise its customers want and don't want and why. The company uses that information to change its buying stock and to target its catalogs and coupons more precisely. Instead of running coupons in the newspaper, for instance, it can insert them in the catalogs it sends to particular customers or industries that have proved responsive to coupons.

Defections analysis can also help companies decide which service-quality investments will be profitable. Should you invest in computerized cash registers or a new phone system? Which of the two will address the most frequent causes of defection? One bank made a large investment to improve the accuracy of monthly account statements. But when the bank began to study defectors, it learned that less than 1% of its customers were leaving because of inaccurate statements.

A company that is losing customers because of long lines can estimate what percentage of defectors it would save by buying new cash registers, and it can use its defection curve to find the dollar value of saving them. Then, using standard investment-analysis techniques, it can compare the cost of the new equipment with the benefit of keeping customers.

Achieving service quality doesn't mean slavishly keeping all customers at any cost. There are some customers the company should not try to serve. If particular types of customers don't stay and become profitable, companies should not invest in attracting them. When a health insurance company realized that certain companies purchase only on the basis of price and switch health insurers every year, for example, it decided not to waste its efforts seeking their business. It told its brokers not to write policies for companies that have switched carriers more than twice in the past five years.

Conversely, much of the information used to find defectors can point to common traits among customers who stay longer. The company can use defection rates to clarify the characteristics of the market it wants to pursue and target its advertising and promotions accordingly.

The Zero Defections Culture

Many business leaders have been frustrated by their inability to follow through on their public commitment to service quality. Since defection rates are measurable, they are manageable. Managers can establish meaningful targets and monitor progress. But like any important change, managing for zero defections must have supporters at all organizational levels. Management must develop that support by training the work force and using defections as a primary performance measure.

Everyone in the organization must understand that zero defections is the goal. Mastercare, the auto-service subsidiary of Bridgestone/Firestone, emphasizes the importance of keeping customers by stating it clearly in its mission statement. The statement says, in part, that the company's goal is "to provide the service-buying public with a superior buying experience that will encourage them to return willingly and to share their experience with others." MBNA America sends its paychecks in envelopes labeled "Brought to you by the customer." It also has a customer advocate who sits in on all major decision-making sessions to make sure customers' interests are represented.

It is important to make all employees understand the lifetime value of a customer. Phil Bressler, the co-owner of five Domino's Pizza stores in Montgomery County, Maryland, calculated that regular customers were worth more than $5,000 over the life of a ten-year franchise contract. He made sure that every order taker, delivery person, and store manager knew that number. For him, telling workers that customers were valuable was not nearly as potent as stating the dollar amount: "It's so much more than they think that it really hits home."

Mastercare has redesigned its employee training to emphasize the importance of keeping customers. For example, many customers who stopped doing business with Mastercare mentioned that they didn't like being pressured into repairs they had not planned on. So Mastercare now trains store managers to identify and solve the customer's problem rather than to maximize sales. Videos and role-playing dramatize these different definitions of good service.

Mastercare's message to employees includes a candid admission that previous, well-intentioned incentives had inadvertently caused employees to run the business the wrong way; now it is asking them to change. And it builds credibility among employees by sharing its strategic goals and customer outreach plans. In the two target markets where this approach has been used, results are good. Employees have responded enthusiastically, and 25% more customers say they intend to return.

Senior executives at MBNA America learn from defecting customers. Each one spends four hours a month in a special "listening room" monitoring routine customer service calls as well as calls from customers who are canceling their credit cards.

Beyond conveying a sense of urgency, training should teach employees the specifics of defections analysis, like how to gather the information, whom to pass it on to, and what actions to take in response. In one company's branch banking system, retention data are sent monthly to the regional vice presidents and branch managers for review. They allow the regional vice presidents to identify and focus on branches that most need to improve service quality, and they give branch managers quick feedback on performance.

Employees will be more motivated if incentives are tied to defection rates. MBNA, for example, has determined for each department the one or two things that have the biggest impact on keeping customers. Each department is measured daily on how well performance targets are met. Every morning, the previous day's performance is posted in several places throughout the building. Each day that the company hits 95% of these performance targets, MBNA contributes money to a bonus pool. Managers use the pool to pay yearly bonuses of up to 20% of a person's salary. The president visits departments that fall short of their targets to find out where the problem lies.

Great-West Life Assurance Company of Englewood, Colorado, also uses incentives effectively. It pays a 50% premium to group-health-insurance brokers that hit customer-retention targets. This system gives brokers the incentive to look for customers who will stay with the company for a long time.

Having everyone in the company work toward keeping customers and basing rewards on how well they do creates a positive company atmosphere. Encouraging employees to solve customer problems and eliminate the source of complaints allows them to be "nice," and customers treat them better in return. The overall exchange is more rewarding, and people enjoy their work more. Not just customers but also employees will want to continue their relationship with the business. MBNA is besieged by applicants for job openings, while a competitor a few miles away is moving some of its operations out of the state because it can't find enough employees.

The success of MBNA shows that it is possible to achieve big improvements in both service quality and profits in a reasonably short time. But it also shows that focusing on keeping customers instead of simply having lots of them takes effort. A company can leverage business performance and profits through customer defections only when the notion permeates corporate life and when all organizational levels understand the concept of zero defections and know how to act on it.

Trying to retain all of your profitable customers is elementary. Managing toward zero defections is revolutionary. It requires careful definition of defection, information systems that can measure results over time in comparison with competitors, and a clear understanding of the microeconomics of defection.

Ultimately, defections should be a key performance measure for senior management and a fundamental component of incentive systems. Managers should know the company's defection rate, what happens to profits when the rate moves up or down, and why defections occur. They should make sure the entire organization understands the importance of keeping customers and encourage employees to pursue zero defections by tying incentives, planning, and budgeting to defection targets. Most important, managers should use defections as a vehicle for continuously improving the quality and value of the services they provide to customers.

Just as the quality revolution in manufacturing had a profound impact on the competitiveness of companies, the quality revolution in services will create a new set of winners and losers. The winners will be those who lead the way in managing toward zero defections.

PART

VII

Measure What Matters

Introduction

The three main themes of this collection—customer satisfaction, profitability, and analysis—all rely on measurement in order to be accomplished. However, the measurement systems in most firms do not accurately track customer satisfaction, customer retention, or customer profitability. In addition, these systems generally neglect a company's standing relative to its competition. Most measures are based primarily on inward-looking goals such as return on investment. Fundamentally, these measures focus on past performance rather than on potential performance.

Investors and managers should place more emphasis on externally derived measures of perceived quality, customer satisfaction, and customer loyalty because the strength of the company's relationships and reputation in the marketplace, relative to competitors, is at least as important as previous performance in predicting the likely future value of a firm. Statutory regulations for financial reporting force a narrow, asset-based, historical view of measurement. Effective managers take the initiative to construct more vibrant and accurate measurements of company health. The three articles in this section provide specific methods to augment and reshape existing measurements systems. These new systems create a more dynamic framework for setting goals and making profitable management decisions.

"How to Measure Yourself Against the Best," by Frances Gaither Tucker, Seymour Zivan, and Robert Camp, gives a brief, but compelling, example of noncompetitive benchmarking. Through this technique, companies look outside their own industry to compare business operations in order to identify the most efficient practices. In this case, Xerox was able to improve its warehouse operations by comparing them to L.L. Bean's. Other "best practices" revealed

327

through benchmarking include electronic data interchange systems used by drug wholesalers and bar-code weighing by electrical components manufacturers. The creativity and initiative inspired by these out-of-industry analyses lets companies set high standards and provides the basis for aggressive business redesign that yields greater customer satisfaction and higher profits.

The second article, "Measure Costs Right: Make the Right Decisions," by Robin Cooper and Robert Kaplan, argues convincingly that most of today's management control systems are based on a mass-production industrial paradigm that is fundamentally flawed in an environment of multiple product lines and marketing channels. These antiquated schemes allocate costs based on direct labor or machine hours, which now represent a relatively small share of costs. Where these inputs have been minimized through automation, companies need to adopt a new "activity-based" measurement system that can capture all relevant and significant customer-related expenses.

Part VI (Convert Customer Satisfaction into Profits) illustrates the importance of tracking cost to serve as a basis for enhanced profitability. "Measure Costs Right" provides specific guidelines for achieving that end. The authors stress that in designing an activity-based cost system, three rules should be applied: (1) focus on expensive resources, (2) emphasize resources whose consumption varies significantly by product or product type, and (3) focus on resources whose demand patterns are uncorrelated with traditional allocation measures like direct labor, processing time, and materials. The authors illustrate how these assumptions can yield radically different results, compared to traditional accounting systems, concerning the profitability of products and the efficiency of process technologies. These new accounting principles are indispensable for determining accurate costs. This knowledge in turn is vital for achieving long-term profitability.

The final article, "The Performance Measurement Manifesto," by Robert Eccles, is a call to action for managers everywhere to look beyond the narrow confines of existing systems to a set of controls that includes customer- and competition-based measures. "What quality was for the 1980s, customer satisfaction will be for the 1990s . . . As competition continues to stiffen, strategies that focus on quality will evolve naturally into strategies based on customer service."

Management's challenge is to translate these ideas into measur-

Exhibit I. The Importance of Measurement in Building Profitability

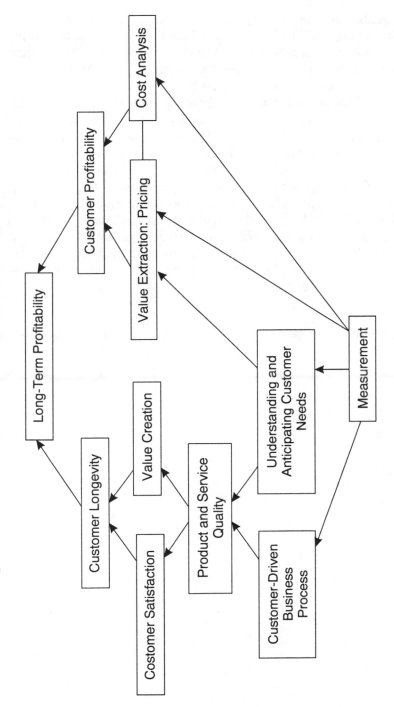

able goals that can be targeted, achieved, and monitored. Some leading companies have already taken the bold step of putting customer satisfaction measures on a par with return on investment in their compensation and incentive systems. The focus must grow in order to keep customers profitably.

Overall, the measurement challenge is tremendously important for all facets of keeping customers (see Exhibit I). Measures of the business process (such as those detailed in Part II) are vital. Statistical and qualitative assessments of customer satisfaction and perceived quality of products and services indicate today's price sensitivity and tomorrow's repeat purchase behavior.

Measurement provides both ongoing feedback and important symbolic value in keeping the organization continually focused on and invigorated by the process of serving customers. Together, each of these influences helps increase customer longevity and customer profitability, both of which reinforce the long-term profitability of the enterprise.

1

How to Measure Yourself Against the Best

Frances Gaither Tucker, Seymour M. Zivan, and Robert C. Camp

One way to judge the performance of an organization is, of course, to compare it with other units within the company. But these measurements often merely reinforce complacency or generate "not invented here" excuses. Comparisons with outsiders, however, can highlight the best industry practices and promote their adoption. This technique is commonly called "benchmarking," a term taken from the land-surveying practice of comparing elevations.

When Xerox started using benchmarking in 1979, management's aim was to analyze unit production costs in manufacturing operations. Uncomfortably aware of the extremely low prices of Japanese plain-paper copiers, the manufacturing staff at Xerox wanted to determine whether their Japanese counterparts' relative costs were as low as their relative prices. The staff compared the operating capabilities and features of the Japanese machines, including those made by Fuji-Xerox, and tore down their mechanical components for examination.

The investigation revealed that production costs in the United States were much higher. Discarding their standard budgeting processes, U.S. manufacturing operations adopted the lower Japanese costs as targets for driving their own business plans. Top management, gratified with the results, directed that all units and cost centers in the corporation use benchmarking.

But distribution, administration, service, and other support functions found it difficult to arrive at a convenient analogue to a product. These nonmanufacturing units began to make internal comparisons, including worker productivity at different regional distribution centers and per-pound transportation costs between regions. Next, they looked at competitors' processes. In logistics that meant comparing the transportation, warehousing, and inventory management of Xerox's distribution function with those of the competition.

Benchmarking against the competition, however, poses problems. For one thing, comparisons with competitors may uncover practices that are unworthy of emulation. For another, while competitive benchmarking may help you meet your competitors' performance, it is unlikely to reveal practices for beating them. Moreover, getting information about competitors is obviously difficult. Finally, we have observed that people are more receptive to new ideas that come from outside their own industry. Noncompetitor benchmarking, then, is the method of choice.

A noncompetitor investigation can give management information about the best functional practices in any industry. These may include technological advances unrecognized in your own industry (like bar coding, which originated in the grocery industry but has since been widely applied). Adoption of these practices can help you achieve a competitive advantage.

The first step in the process is to identify what will be benchmarked—expense-to-revenue ratios, inventory turns, service calls, customer satisfaction—whatever the "product" of the particular function is. Then pinpoint the areas that need improvement.

In Xerox's experience, managers tend to concentrate first on comparative costs. But as they become more knowledgeable about benchmarking, managers discover that understanding practices, processes, and methods is more important because these define the changes necessary to reach the benchmark costs. Moreover, as managers become more confident about benchmarking, they can readily extend it beyond cost reduction to profit-producing factors like service levels and customer satisfaction.

L&D and L.L. Bean

Where do you find well-run noncompetitors for the purpose of comparison? Annual reports and other easily available publications can uncover gross indicators of efficient operation. Universally recognized measures like ROA, revenue per employee, inventory turns, and percent SG&A expenses will help identify the well-managed companies.

To identify superior performance in particular functions, Xerox relies especially on trade journals, consultants, annual reports and other company publications in which "statements of pride" appear, and presentations at professional and other forums. The same well-run organizations keep turning up.

Getting a noncompetitor's cooperation in the venture is usually easier because professionals in a function are eager to compare notes. They want to know how their system stacks up. Indeed, several noncompetitors have agreed to share the expense of benchmarking studies with Xerox.

One of Xerox's most valuable benchmarking experiences, with L.L. Bean, Inc., the outdoor sporting goods retailer and mail-order house, illustrates well how these ventures work. It was carried out by the Xerox Logistics and Distribution unit, which is responsible for inventory management, warehousing, and transport of machines, parts, and supplies.

Historically L&D's productivity increases had been 3% to 5% per year. By 1981 it was clear that improvement was necessary to maintain profit margins in the face of industry price cuts.

The inventory-control area had recently installed a new planning system, and the transportation function was capitalizing on opportunities presented by deregulation. Warehousing was next in line for improvement, and the distribution-center managers wanted a change. They identified the picking area as the worst bottleneck in the receiving-through-shipping sequence.

A new technology, automated storage and retrieval systems (ASRS) for materials handling, had appeared on the scene and was the subject of hot debate in Xerox's distribution function. The company had just erected a high-rise ASRS warehouse for raw materials and assembly parts in Webster, New York, in the same complex as a large finished-goods distribution center. Internal benchmarking evaluations by L&D showed that heavy investment in capital equipment for ASRS could not be cost justified for finished goods. They needed a different way to boost warehousing and materials handling productivity, but what?

In January 1981 L&D assigned a staff member half time to come up with a suitable noncompetitor to benchmark in the warehousing and materials handling areas. The staff member combed trade

journals and conferred with professional associations and consultants to find the companies with the best reputations in the distribution business. He then targeted those companies with generic
product characteristics and service levels similar to Xerox repro-
graphic parts and supplies.

By November the staff member had singled out L.L. Bean as the
best candidate for benchmarking. Of particular interest were
Bean's warehouse operations. The staff member summed up his
impressions in a memo to his boss:

"I was particularly struck with the L.L. Bean warehouse system
design. Although extremely manual in nature, the design minimized the labor content, among other benefits. The operation also
did not lend itself to automation [of handling and picking]. The
design therefore relied on very basic handling techniques, but it
was carefully thought out and implemented. In addition, the design
was selected with the full participation of the hourly work force. It
was the first warehouse operation designed by quality circles."

To the layperson, L.L. Bean products may bear no resemblance
to Xerox parts and supplies. To the distribution professional, however, the analogy was striking: both companies had to develop
warehousing and distribution systems to handle products diverse
in size, shape, and weight. This diversity precluded the use of
ASRS.

Three months later a Xerox team visited Bean's operations in
Freeport, Maine. Besides the person in charge of benchmarking in
L&D, the team consisted of a headquarters operations manager and
a field distribution-center manager. These two people represented
the line employees who would ultimately make any changes.

Analysis of the findings back home in Rochester, New York,
revealed a broader range of computer-directed activities than Xerox
had. These activities included:

Arranging materials by velocity—that is, fast movers were stocked
closest to the picking route.

Storing incoming materials randomly to maximize warehouse space
utilization and minimize forklift travel distance.

Sorting and releasing incoming orders throughout the day to minimize picker travel distance (known as short-interval scheduling).

Basing incentive bonuses on picking productivity offset by error
rates.

Exhibit I.   Comparison of Key Performance Criteria in Two Distribution Centers

	L.L. Bean	Xerox
Orders per man-day	550	117
Pieces per man-day	1,440	2,640
Lines per man-day	1,440	497

Automating outbound carrier manifesting by calculating transportation costs ahead of time.

Plans for implementing automated data capture through bar coding.

Exhibit I compares the prospective performance of Xerox's most efficient warehouse then being planned with L.L. Bean's performance as of February 1982. Because of the nature of its operations, Xerox often picked several pieces per order, so Xerox had a higher figure for pieces per man-day. But L.L. Bean could pick almost three times as many lines per man-day. (A line, which represents picker travel distance for one trip to a bin, is the crucial measure of productivity.)

The report documenting the findings attracted wide interest within Xerox's L&D organization, particularly because Bean's was a labor-intensive system that could be adapted fairly easily to Xerox's purposes. As a result, L&D incorporated some of L.L. Bean's practices in a program to modernize Xerox's warehouses. These practices included materials location arranged by velocity, to speed the flow of materials and minimize picker travel distance, as well as enhancing computer involvement in the picking operation. Xerox is now putting together a totally computer-managed warehouse.

Further Experience

Benchmarking has become an ongoing practice at Xerox Logistics and Distribution. The requirement to carry on the procedure has been pushed down the organization to individual operations, which now do their own benchmarking rather than have a specialist per-

Exhibit II.   Practices Uncovered via Noncompetitive Benchmarking

Type of company	Practice
Drug wholesaler	Electronic ordering between store and distribution center
Appliance manufacturer	Forklift handling of up to six appliances at once
Electrical components manufacturer	Automatic, in-line weighing, bar-code labeling, and scanning of packages
Photographic film manufacturer	Self-directed warehouse work teams
Catalog fulfillment service bureau	Recording of item dimension and weight to permit order-filling quality assurance based on calculated compared with actual weight

form it. Because the process is well understood and because the people who undertake it are the ones who implement the findings, benchmarking is now much easier to carry out than before. L&D has taken the noncompetitor approach to benchmarking many times. Exhibit II shows some of the practices Xerox uncovered using this method.

From these efforts L&D has greatly increased its productivity. Before benchmarking, the organization was making annual productivity gains of 3% to 5%; now it strives for, and reaches, improvements of 10%. Of that figure, some 3% to 5% is derived from L.L. Bean-type investigations, using competitors as well as noncompetitors. In addition, the people involved in the benchmarking process often find that the work is broadening and furthers their professional growth. They become more useful to the organization.

L.L. Bean, incidentally, has benefited too. After seeing Xerox's success, the company adopted benchmarking as part of its own planning process.

2
Measure Costs Right: Make the Right Decisions

Robin Cooper and Robert S. Kaplan

Managers in companies selling multiple products are making important decisions about pricing, product mix, and process technology based on distorted cost information. What's worse, alternative information rarely exists to alert these managers that product costs are badly flawed. Most companies detect the problem only after their competitiveness and profitability have deteriorated.

Distorted cost information is the result of sensible accounting choices made decades ago, when most companies manufactured a narrow range of products. Back then, the costs of direct labor and materials, the most important production factors, could be traced easily to individual products. Distortions from allocating factory and corporate overhead by burden rates on direct labor were minor. And the expense of collecting and processing data made it hard to justify more sophisticated allocation of these and other indirect costs.

Today, product lines and marketing channels have proliferated. Direct labor now represents a small fraction of corporate costs, while expenses covering factory support operations, marketing, distribution, engineering, and other overhead functions have exploded. But most companies still allocate these rising overhead and support costs by their diminishing direct labor base or, as with marketing and distribution costs, not at all.

These simplistic approaches are no longer justifiable—especially given the plummeting costs of information technology. They can also be dangerous. Intensified global competition and radically new production technologies have made accurate product cost information crucial to competitive success.

We have written extensively on the shortcomings of typical cost accounting systems.[1] In this article we present an alternative approach, which we refer to as activity-based costing. The theory behind our method is simple. Virtually all of a company's activities exist to support the production and delivery of today's goods and services. They should therefore all be considered product costs. And since nearly all factory and corporate support costs are divisible or separable, they can be split apart and traced to individual products or product families. These costs include:

Logistics
Production
Marketing and Sales
Distribution
Service
Technology
Financial Administration
Information Resources
General Administration

Conventional economics and management accounting treat costs as variable only if they change with short-term fluctuations in output. We (and others) have found that many important cost categories vary not with short-term changes in output but with changes over a period of years in the design, mix, and range of a company's products and customers. An effective system to measure product costs must identify and assign to products these costs of complexity.

Many managers understand intuitively that their accounting systems distort product costs, so they make informal adjustments to compensate. But few can predict the magnitude and impact of the adjustments they should be making.

Consider the experience of a leading manufacturer of hydraulic valves whose product line included thousands of items. About 20% of the valves generated 80% of total revenues, a typical ratio for multiproduct organizations. Of even greater interest, 60% of the products generated 99% of the revenues. Nonetheless, management remained enthusiastic about the 40% of its products that generated only 1% of revenues. According to its cost system, these specialty items had the best gross margins.

An analysis using activity-based costing told a very different story. More than 75% of this company's products (mostly the low-volume items) were *losing* money. The products that did make money (fewer than one in four) generated more than 80% of sales and 300% of net profits.

Top executives may be understandably reluctant to abandon existing product cost systems in favor of a new approach that reflects a radically different philosophy. We do not advocate such an abrupt overhaul. The availability of cheap, powerful personal computers, spread sheets, and data-base languages allows businesses to develop new cost systems for strategic purposes off-line from official accounting systems. Companies don't have to commit their entire accounting system to activity-based costing to use it.

Indeed, activity-based costing is as much a tool of corporate strategy as it is a formal accounting system. Decisions about pricing, marketing, product design, and mix are among the most important ones managers make. None of them can be made effectively without accurate knowledge of product costs.

What Distorts Cost Data?

Product cost distortions occur in virtually all organizations producing and selling multiple products or services. To understand why, consider two hypothetical plants turning out a simple product, ball-point pens. The factories are the same size and have the same capital equipment. Every year Plant I makes one million blue pens. Plant II also produces blue pens, but only 100,000 per year. To fill the plant, keep the work force busy, and absorb fixed costs, Plant II also produces a variety of similar products: 60,000 black pens, 12,000 red pens, 10,000 lavender pens, and so on. In a typical year, Plant II produces up to 1,000 product variations with volumes ranging between 500 and 100,000 units. Its aggregate annual output equals the one million units of Plant I, and it requires the same total standard direct labor hours, machine hours, and direct material.

Despite the similarities in product and total output, a visitor walking through the two plants would notice dramatic differences. Plant II would have a much larger production support staff—more people to schedule machines, perform setups, inspect items after setup, receive and inspect incoming materials and parts, move inventory, assemble and ship orders, expedite orders, rework defective items, design and implement engineering change orders, negotiate with vendors, schedule materials and parts receipts, and update and program the much larger computer-based information system. Plant II would also operate with considerably higher levels of idle time, overtime, inventory, rework, and scrap.

Plant II's extensive factory support resources and production inefficiencies generate cost-system distortions. Most companies allocate factory support costs in a two-step process. First, they collect the costs into categories that correspond to responsibility centers (production control, quality assurance, receiving) and assign these costs to operating departments. Many companies do this first step very well.

But the second step—tracing costs from the operating departments to specific products—is done simplistically. Many companies still use direct labor hours as an allocation base. Others, recognizing the declining role of direct labor, use two additional allocation bases. Materials-related expenses (costs to purchase, receive, inspect, and store materials) are allocated directly to products as a percentage markup over direct materials costs. And machine hours, or processing time, are used to allocate production costs in highly automated environments.

Whether Plant II uses one or all of these approaches, its cost system invariably—and mistakenly—reports production costs for the high-volume product (blue pens) that greatly exceed the costs for the same product built in Plant I. One does not need to know much about the cost system or the production process in Plant II to predict that blue pens, which represent 10% of output, will have about 10% of the factory costs allocated to them. Similarly, lavender pens, which represent 1% of Plant II's output, will have about 1% of the factory's costs allocated to them. In fact, if the standard output per unit of direct labor hours, machine hours, and materials quantities are the same for blue pens as for lavender pens, the two types of pens will have *identical* reported costs—even though lavender pens, which are ordered, fabricated, packaged, and shipped in much lower volumes, consume far more overhead per unit.

Think of the strategic consequences. Over time, the market price for blue pens, as for most high-volume products, will be determined by focused and efficient producers like Plant I. Managers of Plant II will notice that their profit margin on blue pens is lower than on their specialty products. The price for blue pens is lower than for lavender pens, but the cost system reports that blue pens are as expensive to make as the lavender.

While disappointed with the low margins on blue pens, Plant II's managers are pleased they're a full-line producer. Customers are willing to pay premiums for specialty products like lavender pens, which are apparently no more expensive to make than commodity-type blue pens. The logical strategic response? De-emphasize blue pens and offer an expanded line of differentiated products with unique features and options.

In reality, of course, this strategy will be disastrous. Blue pens in Plant II are cheaper to make than lavender pens—no matter what the cost system reports. Scaling back on blue pens and replacing the lost output by adding new models will further increase overhead. Plant II's managers will simmer with frustration as total costs rise and profitability goals remain elusive. An activity-based cost system would not generate distorted information and misguided strategic signals of this sort.

Designing an Activity-Based Cost System

The first step in designing a new product cost system is to collect accurate data on direct labor and materials costs. Next, examine the demands made by particular products on indirect resources. Three rules should guide this process:

1. Focus on expensive resources.
2. Emphasize resources whose consumption varies significantly by product and product type; look for diversity.
3. Focus on resources whose demand patterns are uncorrelated with traditional allocation measures like direct labor, processing time, and materials.

Rule 1 leads us to resource categories where the new costing process has the potential to make big differences in product costs. A company that makes industrial goods with a high ratio of factory costs to total costs will want a system that emphasizes tracing manufacturing overhead to products. A consumer goods producer will want to analyze its marketing, distribution, and service costs by product lines, channels, customers, and regions. High-technology companies must study the demands made on engineering, product improvement, and process development resources by their different products and product lines.

Rules 2 and 3 identify resources with the greatest potential for distortion under traditional systems. They point to activities for which the usual surrogates—labor hours, material quantities, or machine hours—do not represent adequate measures of resource consumption. The central question is, which parts of the organization tend to grow as the company increases the diversity of its product line, its processing technologies, its customer base, its marketing channels, its supplier base?

The process of tracing costs, first from resources to activities and then from activities to specific products, cannot be done with surgical precision. We cannot estimate to four significant digits the added burden on support resources of introducing two new variations of a product. But it is better to be basically correct with activity-based costing, say, within 5% or 10% of the actual demands a product makes on organizational resources, than to be precisely wrong (perhaps by as much as 200%) using outdated allocation techniques.

The appendix "Allocating Costs under an Activity-Based System" shows how a company might calculate and assign the support costs of a common manufacturing overhead function—raw materials and parts control. The principles and methods, while illustrated in a conventional manufacturing setting, are applicable to any significant collection of corporate resources in the manufacturing or service sector.

The Impact of Activity-Based Costing

An activity-based system can paint a picture of product costs radically different from data generated by traditional systems. These differences arise because of the system's more sophisticated approach to attributing factory overhead, corporate overhead, and other organizational resources, first to activities and then to the products that create demand for these indirect resources.

MANUFACTURING OVERHEAD.   Let's look more closely at the manufacturer of hydraulic valves mentioned earlier. Cost information on seven representative products is presented in Exhibit I. Under the old cost system, the overhead charge per unit did not differ

Exhibit I.   How Activity-Based Costing Changes Product Profitability*

Valve Number	Annual Volume (units)	Manufacturing Overhead Per Unit			Gross Margin	
		Old System	New System	Percent Difference	Old System	New System
1	43,462	$5.44	$ 4.76	− 12.5%	41%	46%
2	500	6.15	12.86	+109.0	30	− 24
3	53	7.30	77.64	+964.0	47	−258
4	2,079	8.88	19.76	+123.0	26	− 32
5	5,670	7.58	15.17	+100.0	39	2
6	11,196	5.34	5.26	− 1.5	41	41
7	423	5.92	4.39	− 26.0	31	43

*We are not confident that the table's figures are exactly correct. For example, students of this case have estimated the appropriate overhead charge on valve 3 (listed at $77.64 per unit) to be as low as $64 and as high as $84. Whatever the exact figure, the difference between this activity-based cost and the original estimate ($7.30 per unit) suggests that the current labor-based system is seriously flawed.

much among the seven valves, ranging from $5.34 to $8.88. Under
the new system, which traces overhead costs directly to factory
support activities and then to products, the range in overhead cost
per unit widened dramatically—from $4.39 to $77.64. With four
low- to medium-volume products (valves 2 through 5), the overhead
cost estimate increased by 100% or more. For the two highest
volume products (valves 1 and 6), the overhead cost declined.

The strategic consequences of these data are enormous. Under
the labor-based cost system, valve 3 was considered the most profitable product of the seven, with a gross margin of 47%. The activity-based system, in contrast, revealed that when orders for valve
3 arrived, the company would have done better to mail its customers cash to buy the valves elsewhere than to make them itself.

Labor-based cost systems don't always underestimate the overhead demands of low-volume products. Valve 7, with the second
lowest volume in the group, shows a marked decrease in overhead
under an activity-based system. Why? Valve 7 is assembled from
components already being used on the high-volume products
(valves 1 and 6). The bulk of any factory's overhead costs are
associated with ordering parts, keeping track of them, inspecting
them, and setting up to produce components. For parts and components ordered or fabricated in large volumes, the per-unit impact
of these transaction costs is modest. Therefore, specialized products assembled from high-volume components will have low production costs even if shipping volume is not high.

MARKETING EXPENSES.   The redesign of cost systems should not
be limited to factory support costs. Many companies have selling,
general, and administrative (SG&A) expenses that exceed 20% of
total revenues. Yet they treat these costs as period expenses, not
charges to be allocated to products. While such "below the [gross
margin] line" treatment may be adequate, even required, for financial accounting, it is poor practice for measuring product costs.

We studied a building supplies company that distributed its
products through six channels—two in the consumer market and
four in the commercial market. Across all its products, this company had an average gross margin of 34%. Marketing costs for the
six channels averaged 16.4% of sales, with general and administrative expenses another 8.5%. (Exhibits II and III present information
on the four commercial channels.)

With operating profits in the commercial sector at only about

Exhibit II. OEM Changes from a Laggard . . .
Profits by Commercial Distribution Channel (Old System)

	Contract	Industrial Suppliers	Government	OEM	Total Commercial
Annual Sales (in thousands of dollars)	$79,434	$25,110	$422	$9,200	$114,166
Gross Margin	34%	41%	23%	27%	35%
Gross Profit	$27,375	$10,284	$136	$2,461	$40,256
SG&A Allowance* (in thousands of dollars)	$19,746	$6,242	$105	$2,287	$31,814
Operating Profit (in thousands of dollars)	$7,629	$4,042	$31	$174	$11,876
Operating Margin	10%	16%	7%	2%	10%
Invested Capital Allowance† (in thousands of dollars)	$33,609	$10,624	$179	$3,893	$48,305
Return on Investment	23%	38%	17%	4%	25%

*SG&A allowance for each channel is 25% of that channel's revenues.
†Invested capital allowance for each channel is 42% of that channel's revenues.

Exhibit III. . . . to a Solid Performer
Profits by Commercial Distribution Channel (New System)

	Contract	Industrial Suppliers	Government	OEM	Total Commercial
Gross Profit (from previous table)	$27,375	$10,284	$136	$2,461	$40,256
Selling Expenses* (all in thousands of dollars)					
Commission	$ 4,682	$ 1,344	$ 12	$ 372	$ 6,410
Advertising	132	38	0	2	172
Catalog	504	160	0	0	664
Co-op Advertising	416	120	0	0	536
Sales Promotion	394	114	0	2	510
Warranty	64	22	0	4	90
Sales Administration	5,696	1,714	20	351	7,781
Cash Discount	892	252	12	114	1,270
Total	$12,780	$ 3,764	$ 44	$ 845	$17,433
G&A (in thousands of dollars)	$ 6,740	$ 2,131	$ 36	$ 781	$ 9,688
Operating Profit (in thousands of dollars)	$ 7,855	$ 4,389	$ 56	$ 835	$13,135
Operating Margin	10%	17%	13%	9%	12%
Invested Capital*	$33,154	$10,974	$184	$2,748	$47,060
Return on Investment	24%	40%	30%	30%	28%

*Selling expenses and invested capital estimated under an activity-based system.

10% of revenues, the company was looking to improve its profitability. Management decided to focus on SG&A expenses. Previously, the company had allocated SG&A costs by assigning 25% of sales—the company average—to each distribution segment. A more sophisticated analysis, similar in philosophy to the overhead analysis performed by the hydraulic valve company, produced striking changes in product costs.

The OEM business was originally a prime target for elimination. Its 27% gross margin and laggard 2% operating margin put it at the bottom of the pack among commercial channels. But the OEM channel used virtually no resources in several major selling categories: advertising, catalog, sales promotion, and warranty. In the remaining selling categories, the OEM channel used proportionately fewer resources per sales dollar than the other major channels. Its marketing expenses were 9% of sales, well below the 15% average for the four commercial channels. A sounder estimate of OEM operating margin was 9%, not 2%.

The OEM segment looked even better after the company extended the analysis by allocating invested capital to specific channels. The OEM business required far less investment in working capital—accounts receivable and inventory—than the other commercial channels. Thus, even though the OEM channel had a below-average gross margin, its bottom-line return-on-investment turned out to be higher than the commercial average.

OTHER CORPORATE OVERHEAD. Virtually all organizational costs, not just factory overhead or marketing expenses, can and should be traced to the activities for which these resources are used, and then to the divisions, channels, and product lines that consume them. Weyerhaeuser Company recently instituted a charge-back system to trace corporate overhead department costs to the activities that drive them.[2]

For example, Weyerhaeuser's financial services department analyzed all the activities it performed—including data-base administration, general accounting, accounts payable and receivable, and invoicing—to determine what factors create demands for them. A division dealing with a small number of high-volume customers makes very different demands on activities like accounts receivable from a division with many low-volume customers. Before instituting the charge-back system, Weyerhaeuser applied the cost of accounts receivable and other functions as a uniform percentage of a division's sales—a driver that bore little or no relation to the activities that created the administrative work. Now it allocates costs based on which divisions (and product lines) generate the costs.

Similarly, companies engaged in major product development and process improvements should attribute the costs of design and engineering resources to the products and product lines that benefit from them. Otherwise, product and process modification costs will be shifted onto product lines for which little development effort is being performed.

Where Does Activity-Based Costing Stop?

We believe that only two types of costs should be excluded from a system of activity-based costing. First, the costs of excess capacity should not be charged to individual products. To use a simplified example, consider a one-product plant whose practical production capacity is one million units per year. The plant's total annual costs amount to $5 million. At full capacity the cost per unit is $5. This is the unit product cost the company should use regardless of the plant's budgeted production volume. The cost of excess or idle capacity should be treated as a separate line item—a cost of the period, not of individual products.

Many companies, however, spread capacity costs over budgeted volume. Returning to our example, if demand exists for only 500,000 units, a traditional cost system will report that each unit cost $10 to build ($5 million/500,000) even though workers and machines have become no less efficient in terms of what they could produce. Such a procedure causes product costs to fluctuate erratically with changes in assumed production volume and can lead to the "death spiral." A downturn in forecast demand creates idle capacity. The cost system reports higher costs. So management raises prices, which guarantees even less demand in the future and still higher idle capacity costs.

The second exclusion from an activity-based cost system is research and development for entirely new products and lines. We recommend splitting R&D costs into two categories: those that relate to improvements and modifications of existing products and lines and those that relate to entirely new products. The first category can and should be traced to the products that will benefit from the development effort. Otherwise, the costs will be spread to products and lines that bear no relationship to the applied R&D program.

The second category is a different animal. Financial accounting treats R&D as a cost of the period in which it takes place. The management accounting system, in contrast, should treat these costs as investments in the future. Companies engaged in extensive R&D for products with short life cycles should measure costs and revenues over the life cycle of their products. Any periodic assessment of product profitability will be misleading, since it depends on the arbitrary amortization of investment expenditures including R&D.

Strategic Implications

The examples we've discussed demonstrate how an activity-based cost system can lead to radically different evaluations of product costs and profitability than more simplistic approaches. It does not imply that because some low-volume products (lavender pens or valve 3) now are unprofitable, a company should immediately drop them. Many customers value having a single source of supply, a big reason companies become full-line producers. It may be impossible to cherry-pick a line and build only profitable products. If the multiproduct pen company wants to sell its profitable blue and black pens, it may have to absorb the costs of filling the occasional order for lavender pens.

Once executives are armed with more reliable cost information, they can ponder a range of strategic options. Dropping unprofitable products is one. So is raising prices, perhaps drastically. Many low-volume products have surprisingly low price elasticities. Customers who want lavender pens or valve 3 may be willing to pay much more than the current price. On the other hand, these customers may also react to a price increase by switching away from low-volume products. That too is acceptable; the company would be supplying fewer money-losing items.

More accurate cost information also raises strategic options for high-volume products. Plant II might consider dropping its prices on blue pens. The old cost system, which shifted overhead charges onto these high-volume products, created a price umbrella that benefited focused competitors like Plant I. Pricing its core product more competitively might help Plant II reverse a market-share slide.

Managers in the building supplies company we described took several profit-enhancing steps after receiving the revised cost data by distribution channels. They began emphasizing the newly attractive OEM segment and any new business where marketing costs would be well below the company average.

Information generated by an activity-based cost system can also encourage companies to redesign products to use more common parts. Managers frequently exhort their engineers to design or modify products so they use fewer parts and are easier to manufacture. But these exhortations will ring hollow if the company's cost system cannot identify the benefits to design and manufacturing simplicity. Recall valve 7, a low-volume product made from components fabricated in large volumes for other products. Now that the company can quantify, using activity-based techniques, the impressive cost benefits of component standardization, the entire organization will better understand the value of designing products for manufacturability.

Likewise, activity-based costing can change how managers evaluate new process technologies. Streamlining the manufacturing process to reduce setup times, rationalizing plant layout to lower material handling costs, and improving quality to reduce postproduction inspections can all have major impacts on product costs— impacts that become visible on a product-by-product basis with activity-based costing. A more accurate understanding of the costs of specialized products may also make computer-integrated manufacturing (CIM) look more attractive, since CIM is most efficient in high-variety, low-volume environments.

Activity-based costing is not designed to trigger automatic decisions. It is designed to provide more accurate information about production and support activities and product costs so that management can focus its attention on the products and processes with the most leverage for increasing profits. It helps managers make better decisions about product design, pricing, marketing, and mix, and encourages continual operating improvements.

Appendix

ALLOCATING COSTS UNDER AN ACTIVITY-BASED SYSTEM

The process of designing and implementing an activity-based cost system for support departments usually begins with interviews of the department heads. The interviews yield insights into departmental operations and into the factors that trigger departmental activities. Subsequent analysis traces these activities to specific products.

The following example illustrates the activity-based costing process for an inventory control department responsible for raw materials and purchased components. The annual costs associated with the department (mainly personnel costs) are $500,000.

Interview Department Head

Q: How many people work for you?
A: Twelve

Q: What do they do?
A: Six of them spend most of their time handling incoming shipments of purchased parts. They handle everything—from documentation to transferring parts to the WIP stockroom. Three others work in raw materials. After the material clears inspection, they move it into inventory and take care of the paperwork.

Q: What determines the time required to process an incoming shipment? Does it matter if the shipment is large or small?
A: Not for parts. They go directly to the WIP stockroom, and unless it's an extremely large shipment it can be handled in one trip. With raw materials, though, volume can play a big role in processing time. But there are only a few large raw material shipments. Over the course of a year, the time required to process a part or raw material really depends on the number of times it's received, not on the size of the shipments in which it comes.

Q: What other factors affect your department's work load?
A: Well, there are three people I haven't discussed yet. They dis-

burse raw material to the shop floor. Again, volume is not really an issue; it's more the number of times material has to be disbursed.

Q: Do you usually disburse the total amount of material required for a production run all at once, or does it go out in smaller quantities?
A: It varies with the size of the run. On a big run we can't disburse it all at once—there would be too much raw material on the shop floor. On smaller runs—and I'd say that's 80% of all runs—we'd send it there in a single trip once setup is complete.

Design the System

After the interview, the system designer can use the number of people involved in each activity to allocate the department's $500,000 cost:

Activity	People	Total Cost
Receiving purchased parts	6	$250,000
Receiving raw material	3	$125,000
Disbursing material	3	$125,000

In 1987, this company received 25,000 shipments of purchased parts and 10,000 shipments of raw materials. The factory made 5,000 production runs. Dividing these totals into the support dollars associated with each activity yields the following costs per unit of activity:

Activity	Allocation Measure	Unit Cost
Receiving purchased parts	Number of shipments per year	$10 per shipment
Receiving raw material	Number of shipments per year	$12.50 per shipment
Disbursing material	Number of production runs	$25 per run

We can now attribute inventory control support costs to specific products. Suppose the company manufactures 1,000 units of Product A in a year. Product A is a complex product with more than 50 purchased parts and several different types of raw material. During the year, the 1,000 units were assembled in 10 different production runs requiring 200 purchased parts shipments and 50 different raw material shipments. Product A incurs $2,875 in inventory control overhead ($10 × 200 + $12.50 × 50 + $25 × 10) to produce the 1,000 units, or $2.88 of inventory control costs per unit.

Product A also consumed 1,000 hours of direct labor out of the factory's total of 400,000 hours. A labor-based allocation system would allocate $1,250 of inventory control costs to the 1,000 units produced ($500,000/400,000 × 1,000) for a per-unit cost of $1.25. The 230% cost difference between the activity-based attribution ($2.88) and the labor-based allocation ($1.25) reflects the fact that the complex, low-volume Product A demands a much greater share of inventory control resources than its share of factory direct-labor hours.

Notes

1. See H. Thomas Johnson and Robert S. Kaplan, *Relevance Lost: The Rise and Fall of Management Accounting* (Boston: Harvard Business School Press, 1987) and Robin Cooper and Robert S. Kaplan, "How Cost Accounting Distorts Product Costs," *Management Accounting*, April 1988, p. 20.

2. See H. Thomas Johnson and Dennis A. Loewe, "How Weyerhaeuser Manages Corporate Overhead Costs," *Management Accounting*, August 1987, p. 20.

3
The Performance Measurement Manifesto

Robert G. Eccles

Revolutions begin long before they are officially declared. For several years, senior executives in a broad range of industries have been rethinking how to measure the performance of their businesses. They have recognized that new strategies and competitive realities demand new measurement systems. Now they are deeply engaged in defining and developing those systems for their companies.

At the heart of this revolution lies a radical decision: to shift from treating financial figures as the foundation for performance measurement to treating them as one among a broader set of measures. Put like this, it hardly sounds revolutionary. Many managers can honestly claim that they—and their companies—have tracked quality, market share, and other nonfinancial measures for years. Tracking these measures is one thing. But giving them equal (or even greater) status in determining strategy, promotions, bonuses, and other rewards is another. Until that happens, to quote Ray Stata, the CEO of Analog Devices, "When conflicts arise, financial considerations win out."[1]

The ranks of companies enlisting in this revolution are rising daily. Senior managers at one large, high-tech manufacturer recently took direct responsibility for adding customer satisfaction, quality, market share, and human resources to their formal measurement system. The impetus was their realization that the company's existing system, which was largely financial, undercut its strategy, which focused on customer service. At a smaller manufacturer, the catalyst was a leveraged recapitalization that gave the

CEO the opportunity formally to reorder the company's priorities. On the new list, earnings per share dropped to last place, preceded by customer satisfaction, cash flow, manufacturing effectiveness, and innovation (in that order). On the old list, earnings per share stood first and almost alone.

In both companies, the CEOs believe they have initiated a sea change in how their managers think about business performance and in the decisions they make. Executives at other companies engaged in comparable efforts feel the same—rightly. What gets measured gets attention, particularly when rewards are tied to the measures. Grafting new measures onto an old accounting-driven performance system or making slight adjustments in existing incentives accomplishes little. Enhanced competitiveness depends on starting from scratch and asking: "Given our strategy, what are the most important measures of performance?" "How do these measures relate to one another?" "What measures truly predict long-term financial success in our businesses?"

Dissatisfaction with using financial measures to evaluate business performance is nothing new. As far back as 1951, Ralph Cordiner, the CEO of General Electric, commissioned a high-level task force to identify key corporate performance measures. (The categories the task force singled out were timeless and comprehensive: in addition to profitability, the list included market share, productivity, employee attitudes, public responsibility, and the balance between short- and long-term goals.) But the current wave of discontent is not just more of the same.

One important difference is the intensity and nature of the criticism directed at traditional accounting systems. During the past few years, academics and practitioners have begun to demonstrate that accrual-based performance measures are at best obsolete—and more often harmful.[2] Diversity in products, markets, and business units puts a big strain on rules and theories developed for smaller, less complex organizations. More dangerously, the numbers these systems generate often fail to support the investments in new technologies and markets that are essential for successful performance in global markets.

Such criticisms reinforce concern about the pernicious effects of short-term thinking on the competitiveness of U.S. companies. Opinions on the causes of this mind-set differ. Some blame the investment community, which presses relentlessly for rising quarterly earnings. Others cite senior managers themselves, charging that their typically short tenure fosters shortsightedness. The important point is that the mind-set exists. Ask almost any senior manager and you will hear about some company's failure to make capital investments or pursue long-term strategic objectives that would imperil quarterly earnings targets.

Moreover, to the extent that managers do focus on reported quarterly earnings—and thereby reinforce the investment community's short-term perspective and expectations—they have a strong incentive to manipulate the figures they report. The extent and severity of such gaming is hard to document. But few in management deny that it goes on or that managers' willingness to play the earnings game calls into question the very measures the market focuses on to determine stock prices. For this reason, many managers, analysts, and financial economists have begun to focus on cash flow in the belief that it reflects a company's economic condition more accurately than its reported earnings do.[3]

Finally, many managers worry that income-based financial figures are better at measuring the consequences of yesterday's decisions than they are at indicating tomorrow's performance. Events of the past decade substantiate this concern. During the 1980s, many executives saw their companies' strong financial records deteriorate because of unnoticed declines in quality or customer satisfaction or because global competitors ate into their market share. Even managers who have not been hurt feel the need for preventive action. A senior executive at one of the large money-center banks, for example, grew increasingly uneasy about the European part of his business, its strong financials notwithstanding. To address that concern, he has nominated several new measures (including customer satisfaction, customers' perceptions of the bank's stature and professionalism, and market share) to serve as leading indicators of the business's performance.

Discontent turns into rebellion when people see an alternative worth fighting for. During the 1980s, many managers found such an alternative in the quality movement. Leading manufacturers and service providers alike have come to see quality as a strategic weapon in their competitive battles. As a result, they have committed substantial resources to developing measures such as defect rates, response time, delivery commitments, and the like to evaluate the performance of their products, services, and operations.

In addition to pressure from global competitors, a major impetus for these efforts has been the growth of the Total Quality Movement and related programs such as the Malcolm Baldrige National Quality Award. (Before a company can even apply for a Baldrige Award, it must devise criteria to measure the performance of its entire operation—not just its products—in minute detail.) Another impetus, getting stronger by the day, comes from large manufacturers who are more and more likely to impose rigid quality requirements on their suppliers. Whatever the stimulus, the result is the same: quality measures represent the most positive step taken to date in broadening the basis of business performance measurement.

Another step in the same direction comes from embryonic efforts to generate measures of customer satisfaction. What quality was for the 1980s, customer satisfaction will be for the 1990s. Work on this class of measures is the highest priority at the two manufacturing companies discussed earlier. It is equally critical at another high-tech company that recently created a customer satisfaction department reporting directly to the CEO. In each case, management's interest in developing new performance measures was triggered by strategies emphasizing customer service.

As competition continues to stiffen, strategies that focus on quality will evolve naturally into strategies based on customer service. Indeed, this is already happening at many leading companies. Attention to customer satisfaction, which measures the quality of customer service, is a logical next step in the development of quality measures. Companies will continue to measure quality on the basis of internally generated indexes (such as defect rates) that are presumed to relate to customer satisfaction. But they will also begin to evaluate their performance by collecting data directly from customers for more direct measures like customer retention rates, market share, and perceived value of goods and services.

Just as quality-related metrics have made the performance measurement revolution more real, so has the development of competitive benchmarking.[4] First, benchmarking gives managers a methodology that can be applied to any measure, financial or nonfinancial, but that emphasizes nonfinancial metrics. Second (and less obvious), it has a transforming effect on managerial mind-sets and perspectives.

Benchmarking involves identifying competitors and/or companies in other industries that exemplify best practice in some activity, function, or process and then comparing one's own performance to theirs. This externally oriented approach makes people aware of improvements that are orders of magnitude beyond what they would have thought possible. In contrast, internal yardsticks that measure current performance in relation to prior period results, current budget, or the results of other units within the company rarely have such an eye-opening effect. Moreover, these internally focused comparisons have the disadvantage of breeding complacency through a false sense of security and of stirring up more energy for intramural rivalry than for competition in the marketplace.

Finally, information technology has played a critical role in making a performance measurement revolution possible. Thanks to dramatically improved price-performance ratios in hardware and to breakthroughs in software and data-base technology, organizations can generate, disseminate, analyze, and store more information from more sources, for more people, more quickly and cheaply than was conceivable even a few years back. The potential of new technologies, such as hand-held computers for employees in the field and executive information systems for senior managers, is only beginning to be explored. Overall, the range of measurement options that are economically feasible has radically increased.

Veterans know it is easier to preach revolution than to practice it. Even the most favorable climate can create only the potential for revolutionary change. Making it happen requires conviction, careful preparation, perseverance, and a decided taste for ambiguity. As yet, there are no clear-cut answers or predetermined processes for managers who wish to change their measurement systems. Based on the experience of companies engaged in this revolution, I can identify five areas of activity that sooner or later need to be addressed: developing an information architecture; putting the technology in place to support this architecture; aligning incentives with the new system; drawing on outside resources; and designing a process to ensure that the other four activities occur.

Developing a new information architecture must be the first activity on any revolutionary agenda. Information architecture is an umbrella term for the categories of information needed to manage a company's businesses, the methods the company uses to generate this information, and the rules regulating its flow. In most companies, the accounting system implicitly defines the information architecture. Other performance measures are likely to be informal—records that operating managers keep for themselves, for instance—and they are rarely integrated into the corporate-driven financial system.

The design for a new corporate information architecture begins with the data that management needs to pursue the company's strategy. This may sound like a truism, but a surprising number of companies describe their strategies in terms of customer service, innovation, or the quality and capabilities of their people, yet do little to measure these variables. Even time—the newest strategic variable—remains largely underdeveloped in terms of which time-based metrics are most important and how best to measure them.

As part of this identification process, management needs to articulate a new corporate grammar and define its own special vocabulary—the basic terms that will need to be common and relatively invariant across all the company's businesses. Some of these terms (like sales and costs) will be familiar. Others, however, will reflect new strategic priorities and ways to think about measuring performance. For example, both a large money-center bank and a multidivisional, high-technology manufacturer introduced the use of cross-company customer identification numbers so they could readily track such simple and useful information as the total amount of business the company did with any one customer. It sounds elementary and it is—as soon as you start to look at the entire measurement system from scratch.

Uniformity can be carried too far. Different businesses with different strategies require different information for decision making and performance measurement. But this should not obscure the equally obvious fact that every company needs to have at least a few critical terms in common. Today few large companies do. Years of acquisitions and divestitures, technological limitations, and at times, a lack of management discipline have all left most big organizations with a complicated hodgepodge of definitions and variables—and with the bottom line their only common denominator.

Developing a coherent, companywide grammar is particularly important in light of an ever-more stringent competitive environment. For many companies, ongoing structural reorganizations are a fact of life. The high-technology company described above has reorganized itself 24 times in the past 4 years (in addition to a number of divisional and functional restructurings) to keep pace with changes in its markets and technologies. Rather than bewail the situation, managers relish it and see their capacity for fast adaptation as an important competitive advantage.

A common grammar also enhances management's ability to break apart and recombine product lines and market segments to form new business units. At a major merchant bank, for example, the organization is so fluid that one senior executive likens it to a collection of hunting packs that form to pursue business opportunities and then disband as the market windows on those opportunities close. The faster the company can assemble information for newly formed groups, the greater the odds of success. So this executive (who calls himself the czar of information) has been made responsible for developing standard definitions for key information categories.

How a company generates the performance data it needs is the second piece of its information architecture. Not surprisingly, methods for measuring financial performance are the most sophisticated and the most deeply entrenched. Accountants have been refining these methods ever since double-entry bookkeeping was invented in the fifteenth century. Today their codifications are enforced by a vast institutional infrastructure made up of professional educators, public accounting firms, and regulatory bodies.

In contrast, efforts to measure market share, quality, innovation, human resources, and customer satisfaction have been much more modest. Data for tracking these measures are generated less often: quarterly, annual, or even biannual bases are common. Responsibility for them typically rests with a specific function. (Strategic planning measures market share, for example, while engineering measures innovation and so on.) They rarely become part of the periodic reports general managers receive.

Placing these new measures on an equal footing with financial data takes significant resources. One approach is to assign a senior executive to each of the measures and hold him or her responsible for developing its methodologies. Typically, these executives come from the function that is most experienced in dealing with the particular measure. But they work with a multifunctional task force to ensure that managers throughout the company will understand the resulting measures and find them useful. Another, less common, approach is to create a new function focused on one measure and then to expand its mandate over time. A unit responsible for customer satisfaction might subsequently take on market share, for example, or the company's performance in human resources.

Unlike a company's grammar, which should be fairly stable, methods for taking new performance measures should evolve as the company's expertise increases. Historical comparability may suffer in the process, but this is a minor loss. What matters is how a company is doing compared with its current competitors, not with its own past.

The last component of a corporate information architecture is the set of rules that governs the flow of information. Who is responsible for how measures are taken? Who actually generates the data? Who receives and analyzes them? Who is responsible for changing the rules? Because information is an important source of power, the way a company answers these questions matters deeply. How open or closed a company is affects how individuals and groups work together, as well as the relative influence people and parts of the company have on its strategic direction and management. Some companies make information available on a very limited basis. At others, any individual can request information from another unit as long as he or she can show why it is needed. Similarly, in some companies the CEO still determines who gets what information—not a very practical alternative in today's world. More often what happens is that those who possess information decide with whom they will share it.

Advances in information technology such as powerful workstations, open architectures, and relational data bases vastly increase the options for how information can flow. It may be centralized at the top, so that senior executives can make even more decisions than they have in the past. Or it may be distributed to increase the decision-making responsibilities of people at every level. The advantages of making information widely available are obvious, though this also raises important questions that need to be addressed about the data's integrity and security. In principle, however, this portion of the information architecture ought to be the most flexible of the three, so that the company's information flows continue to change as the conditions it faces do.

Determining the hardware, software, and telecommunications technology a company needs to generate its new measurement information is the second activity in the performance revolution.

This task is hard enough in its own right, given the many choices available. But too often managers make it even harder by going directly to a technology architecture without stopping first to think through their information needs. This was the case at a high-tech manufacturing company that was growing more and more frustrated with its information systems planning committee. Then the CEO realized that he and the other senior managers had not determined the measures they wanted before setting up the committee. Equipped with that information, the committee found it relatively easy to choose the right technology.

Once the information architecture and supporting technology are in place, the next step is to align the new system with the company's incentives—to reward people in proportion to their performance on the measures that management has said truly matter. This is easier said than done. In many companies, the compensation system limits the amount and range of the salary increases, bonuses, and stock options that management can award.

In companies that practice pay-for-performance, compensation and other rewards are often tied fairly mechanically to a few key financial measures such as profitability and return on investment. Convincing managers that a newly implemented system is really going to be followed can be a hard sell. The president of one service company let each of his division general managers design the performance measures that were most appropriate for his or her particular business. Even so, the managers still felt the bottom line was all that would matter when it came to promotions and pay.

The difficulty of aligning incentives to performance is heightened by the fact that formulas for tying the two together are rarely effective. Formulas have the advantage of looking objective, and they spare managers the unpleasantness of having to conduct truly frank performance appraisals. But if the formula is simple and focuses on a few key variables, it inevitably leaves some important measures out. Conversely, if the formula is complex and factors in all the variables that require attention, people are likely to find it confusing and may start to play games with the numbers. Moreover, the relative importance of the variables is certain to change more often—and faster—than the whole incentive system can change.

For these reasons, I favor linking incentives strongly to performance but leaving managers free to determine their subordinates' rewards on the basis of all the relevant information, qualitative as well as quantitative. Then it is up to the manager to explain candidly to subordinates why they received what they did. For most managers, this will also entail learning to conduct effective performance appraisals, an indirect—and invaluable—benefit of overhauling the measurement system.

Outside parties such as industry and trade associations, third-party data vendors, information technology companies, consulting firms, and public accounting firms must also become part of the performance measurement revolution. Their incentive: important business opportunities.

Industry and trade associations can play a very helpful role in identifying key performance measures, researching methodologies for taking these measures, and supplying comparative statistics to their members—so can third-party data vendors. Competitors are more likely to supply information to a neutral party (which can disguise it and make it available to all its members or customers) than to one another. And customers are more likely to provide information to a single data vendor than to each of their suppliers separately.

Consulting firms and information technology vendors also have important roles to play in forwarding the revolution. Firms that specialize in strategy formulation, for example, often have well-developed methods for assessing market share and other performance metrics that clients could be trained to use. Similarly, firms that focus on strategy implementation have a wealth of experience designing systems of various kinds for particular functions such as manufacturing and human resources. While many of these firms are likely to remain specialized, and thus require coordination by their clients, others will surely expand their capabilities to address all the pieces of the revolution within a client company.

Much the same thing is apt to happen among vendors of information technology. In addition to helping companies develop the technological architecture they need, some companies will see opportunities to move into a full range of services that use the hardware as a technology platform. IBM and DEC are already moving in this direction, impelled in part by the fact that dramatic gains in price-performance ratios make it harder and harder to make money selling "boxes."

Finally, public accounting firms have what may be the single most critical role in this revolution. On one hand, they could inhibit its progress in the belief that their vested interest in the existing system is too great to risk. On the other hand, all the large firms have substantial consulting practices, and the revolution represents a tremendous business opportunity for them. Companies will need a great deal of help developing new measures, validating them, and certifying them for external use.

Accounting firms also have an opportunity to develop measurement methods that will be common to an industry or across industries. While this should not be overdone, one reason financial measures carry such weight is that they are assumed to be a uniform metric, comparable across divisions and companies, and thus a valid basis for resource allocation decisions. In practice, of course, these measures are not comparable (despite the millions of hours invested in efforts to make them so) because companies use different accounting conventions. Given that fact, it is easy to see why developing additional measures that senior managers—and the investment community—can use will be a massive undertaking.

Indeed, the power of research analysts and investors generally is one of the reasons accounting firms have such a crucial role to play. Although evidence exists that investors are showing more interest in metrics such as market share and cash flow, many managers and analysts identify the investment community as the chief impediment to revolution.[5] Until investors treat other measures as seriously as financial data, they argue, limits will always exist on how seriously those measures are taken inside companies.

GE's experience with its measurement task force supports their argument. According to a knowledgeable senior executive, the 1951 effort had only a modest effect because the measures believed to determine the company's stock price, to which incentives were tied, were all financial: earnings per share, return on equity, return on investment, return on sales, and earnings growth rate. He believed that once the financial markets valued other measures, progress within companies would accelerate.

Investors, of course, see the problem from a different perspective. They question whether managers would be willing to publish anything more than the financial information required by the SEC lest they reveal too much to their competitors. Ultimately, a regulatory body like the SEC could untie this Gordian knot by recommending (and eventually requiring) public companies to provide nonfinancial measures in their reports. (This is, after all, how financial standards became so omnipotent and why so many millions of hours have been invested in their development.) But I suspect competitive pressure will prove a more immediate force for change. As soon as one leading company can demonstrate the long-term advantage of its superior performance on quality or innovation or any other nonfinancial measure, it will change the rules for all its rivals forever. And with so many serious competitors tracking—and enhancing—these measures, that is only a matter of time.

Designing a process to ensure that all these things happen is the last aspect of the revolution. To overcome conservative forces outside the company and from within (including line and staff managers at every level, in every function), someone has to take the lead. Ultimately, this means the CEO. If the CEO is not committed, the revolution will flounder, no matter how much enthusiasm exists throughout the organization.

But the CEO cannot make it happen. Developing an information architecture and its accompanying technology, aligning incentives, working with outside parties—all this requires many people and a lot of work, much of it far less interesting than plotting strategy. Moreover, the design of the process must take account of the integrative nature of the task: people in different businesses and functions including strategic planning, engineering, manufacturing, marketing and sales, human resources, and finance will all have something to contribute. The work of external players will have to be integrated with the company's own efforts.

Organizationally, two critical choices exist. One is who the point person will be. Assigning this role to the CEO or president ensures its proper symbolic visibility. Delegating it to a high-level line or staff executive and making it a big piece of his or her assignment may be a more effective way to guarantee that enough senior management time will be devoted to the project.

The other choice is which function or group will do most of the work and coordinate the company's efforts. The CEO of one high-tech company gave this responsibility to the finance function because he felt they should have the opportunity to broaden their perspective and measurement skills. He also thought it would be easier to use an existing group experienced in performance measurement. The president of an apparel company made a different choice. To avoid the financial bias embedded in the company's existing management information systems, he wanted someone to start from scratch and design a system with customer service at its core. As a result, he is planning to combine the information systems department with customer service to create a new function to be headed by a new person, recruited from the outside.

What is most effective for a given company will depend on its history, culture, and management style. But every company should make the effort to attack the problem with new principles. Some past practices may still be useful, but everything should be strenuously challenged. Otherwise, the effort will yield incremental changes at best.

Open-mindedness about the structures and processes that will be most effective, now and in the future, is equally important. I know of a few companies that are experimenting with combining the information systems and human resource departments. These experiments have entailed a certain amount of culture shock for professionals from both functions, but such radical rethinking is what revolution is all about.

Finally, recognize that once begun, this is a revolution that never ends. We are not simply talking about changing the basis of performance measurement from financial statistics to something else. We are talking about a new philosophy of performance measurement that regards it as an ongoing, evolving process. And just as igniting the revolution will take special effort, so will maintaining its momentum—and reaping the rewards in the years ahead.

Notes

1. Ray Stata, "Organizational Learning—The Key to Management Innovation," *Sloan Management Review*, Spring 1989, pp. 63–74.

2. Donald A. Curtis, "The Modern Accounting System," *Financial Executive*, January–February 1985, pp. 81–93; and H. Thomas Johnson and Robert S. Kaplan, *Relevance Lost* (Boston: Harvard Business School Press, 1987).

3. Yuji Ijiri, "Cash Flow Accounting and Its Structure," *Journal of Accounting, Auditing, and Finance*, Summer 1978, pp. 331–348.

4. Robert C. Camp, *Benchmarking* (Milwaukee, Wisconsin: ASQS Quality Press, 1989).

5. "Investors: Look at Firms' Market Share," *The Wall Street Journal*, February 26, 1990, pp. C1–2.

About the Contributors

Robert C. Camp is manager, benchmarking competency, Quality Office for Xerox Corporation's U.S. Customer Operations. After joining Xerox in 1972, he was responsible for creating the benchmarking program for its Logistics and Distribution (L&D) department. Mr. Camp has served on the Executive Committee for the Council of Logistics Management, as an adjunct professor at the Rochester Institute of Technology, and has published *Benchmarking: The Search for Industry Best Practices That Lead to Superior Performance*.

Robin Cooper is professor of management in the Management Program, Claremont Graduate School. He was previously an associate professor at the Harvard Business School. His research interests include examining how firms determine product costs and how the design of cost systems affects the way firms enact their chosen strategies. He is a contributor to several publications, including the *Journal of Cost Management* and *Management Accounting*.

F. Stewart DeBruicker is a marketing consultant and executive seminar leader, based in California. He specializes in developing demand-driven marketing strategies for corporations burdened with excess capacity and changing customer environments. Since the original publication of his article he has consulted to companies in the defense, aerospace, automobile, securities, and biotechnology industries. Mr. DeBruicker is a former faculty member of the Harvard Business School and currently serves as an adjunct associate professor of marketing at the Wharton School of the University of Pennsylvania.

Robert G. Eccles is professor of Business Administration and chairman of the Organizational Behavior/Human Resource Management area at the Harvard Business School. His recent research has focused on the contribution that the humanities can make to the study, teaching, and practice of management. Recent publications include co-authorship of *Beyond the Hype: Rediscovering the Essence of Management* and co-editorship of *Networks and Organizations.*

Dan Finkelman is a principal in the Cleveland office of McKinsey & Company and a leader of the firm's worldwide customer satisfaction and service practice.

David A. Garvin is the Robert and Jane Cizik Professor of Business Administration at the Harvard Business School, where he teaches in the MBA and Advanced Management programs and has led seminars on teaching by the case method. He is a frequent contributor to the *Harvard Business Review;* recent books include *Operations Strategy: Text and Cases* and *Education for Judgment* (co-editor).

Tony Goland is a principal in the Cleveland office of McKinsey & Company, where he leads the worldwide customer satisfaction practice, the firm's marketing center, and the North American financial institutions group.

Christopher W. L. Hart is president of The TQM Group, Ltd., a consulting firm specializing in total quality management. Dr. Hart, who was previously a professor of production and operations management at the Harvard Business School, has focused on quality and productivity improvement, particularly in service organizations. His publications include the best-selling *Service Breakthroughs: Changing the Rules of the Game* (with former Harvard colleagues James L. Heskett and W. Earl Sasser, Jr.), *The Baldridge: What It Is, How It's Won, How to Use It to Improve Quality in Your Company,* and numerous articles in both academic and management journals.

James L. Heskett is the UPS Foundation Professor of Business Logistics and professor of production and operations management at the Harvard Business School. He has published widely on service management, including several *Harvard Business Review* articles and *Managing in the Service Economy.*

William M. Hutchison, Jr. was an associate with the management consulting firm of Booz, Allen & Hamilton, when his article was published.

Robert S. Kaplan is the Arthur Lowes Dickinson Professor of Accounting at the Harvard Business School. His research interests include developing new management accounting systems for the rapidly changing environment of manufacturing and service organizations. In addition to numerous articles he has published several books, including *Relevance Lost: The Rise and Fall of Management Accounting* (with H. Thomas Johnson) and *Measures for Manufacturing Excellence* (editor). He is currently involved in production of an on-site management video program to be based on new performance measurement systems.

Uday S. Karmarkar is Xerox Professor of Operations Management, director of the Center for Manufacturing and Operations Management and faculty director of Executive Seminar Programs at the William E. Simon Graduate School of Business Administration at the University of Rochester. His research interests include manufacturing planning and control, industrial marketing, and operations strategy. Consulting engagements have included projects in manufacturing, technology management, industrial marketing, and supply chain and distribution management. Dr. Karmarkar was a founding editor of the *Journal of Manufacturing and Operations Management* and has published in a wide variety of journals.

Milind M. Lele is founder and managing director of SLC Consultants, Inc., a strategy consulting firm with offices in Chicago and Los Angeles. The practice concentrates on marketing, distribution, and general business strategy issues for medium and large industrial and service companies. Dr. Lele is also a senior lecturer at the Graduate School of Business, University of Chicago, where he teaches courses in marketing, production and operations management, and business policy. Recent publications include the books, *The Customer Is Key* and *Creating Strategic Leverage,* as well as several technical reports and journal articles.

Theodore Levitt is an internationally recognized expert in marketing and the Edward W. Carter Professor of Business Administration, Emeritus, at the Harvard Business School. He has taught for more than 30 years, has published numerous articles (he is a four-time winner of the *Harvard Business Review* McKinsey Award), as well as books, including *Thinking about Management,* and a collected volume of *Harvard Business Review* articles, *Levitt on Marketing.* He is a former editor of the *Harvard Business Review.*

Regis McKenna is chairman of Regis McKenna Inc., an international high-technology marketing consulting firm, where he has helped launch several important technological innovations, including the first microprocessor, the first personal computer, and the first retail computer store. Mr. McKenna is also a general partner of the venture capital firm Kleiner Perkins Caufield & Byers, and serves on several technology advisory boards. He is the author of several books, including *The Regis Touch, Who's Afraid of Big Blue?,* and *Relationship Marketing.*

Rowland T. Moriarty is chairman of Cubex Corporation, an international management consulting firm based in Boston. Prior to founding Cubex, Dr. Moriarty was professor of Business Administration at the Harvard Business School, where he taught a variety of marketing courses in the executive and MBA programs. He has consulted to more than 75 companies worldwide, and has written extensively on the subject of marketing.

Randy Myer is chief executive officer of Windsor Pet Care, an emerging chain of up-scale pet care facilities around the United States, launched in 1990. At the time of his article's publication Mr. Myer was a vice president of Booz, Allen & Hamilton, responsible for the firm's operations practice serving domestic consumer product and service industries.

George W. Potts is founder and chairman of Occam Research Corporation, a microprocessor software development company in Wellesley, Massachusetts. The firm has recently developed MUSE, a data analysis software product for the Macintosh and Windows environments.

John A. Quelch is a professor of marketing at the Harvard Business School, where his interests include issues of international marketing. His numerous publications include *Sales Promotion Management* and *How to Market to Consumers,* as well as articles in a wide variety of professional and academic journals.

V. Kasturi Rangan is a professor of marketing at the Harvard Business School, specializing in distribution management. A member of the HBS faculty since 1983, he teaches a variety of courses in the executive and MBA programs. His industrial distribution research has been published in two books, *Going to Market: Distribution Systems for Industrial Products* and *Cases in Industrial Distribution.*

Frederick F. Reichheld is vice president and director of Bain & Company, where he leads the firm's customer retention practice and serves as a member of its worldwide policy committee. Most recently he has pioneered research on the quantitative relationships between service quality and profitability. He has also served as founder and director of two venture capital start-ups.

Elliot B. Ross is co-chairman of Inverness Partners, an LBO firm founded in 1988 to acquire and improve operations of mid-sized industrial manufacturing and distribution businesses. He is also co-chairman of Inverness Castings Group, a rapidly growing die casting supplier to the automotive, furniture, and appliance industries. Prior to founding Inverness, Mr. Ross spent 14 years as a member and partner in the Cleveland office of McKinsey & Company, where he was leader of the firm's worldwide marketing practice.

W. Earl Sasser, Jr. is the UPS Foundation Professor of Service Management and chairman, Advanced Management Program at the Harvard Business School. Among his publications are *Service Breakthroughs: Changing the Rules of the Game* and *The Service Management Course,* both developed with his *Harvard Business Review* co-authors, Christopher W. L. Hart and James L. Heskett.

Benson P. Shapiro, Malcolm P. McNair Professor of Marketing at the Harvard Business School, is a well-known authority on marketing and sales management. In more than 20 years on the HBS faculty, he has taught a wide variety of MBA courses and executive programs, and has held several administrative positions, including senior associate dean for Publications and faculty chair for Strategic Marketing Management. Professor Shapiro is the author or co-author of six books and numerous *Harvard Business Review* articles.

G. Lynn Shostack is chairman and president of Joyce International, Inc., a private company engaged in office products distribution and manufacturing. From 1981 to 1986, she was a senior vice president at Bankers Trust Company, where she created and managed the Private Clients Group. Ms. Shostack has spoken before numerous conferences, writes a regular column for the *Journal of Business Strategy,* and has been published in several journals and books, including *The Service Encounter* and *The AMA Handbook of Marketing for the Service Industries.*

John F. Stolle was vice president in charge of the Operations Research Division of Booz, Allen & Hamilton at the time of his article's publication.

Gregory L. Summe is general manager of the commercial motors business for General Electric in Fort Wayne, Indiana. Previously, he was a partner at McKinsey & Company in Atlanta, where he specialized in business strategy for technology-based companies.

John J. Sviokla is an assistant professor in Management Information Systems and Control at the Harvard Business School. His most recent research has focused on how to drive sales increases, higher prices, or superior quality through efficient management of information technology and organizational innovation. He has published widely and consulted to more than 50 organizations worldwide.

Hirotaka Takeuchi is a professor at the Institute of Business Research, Hitotsubashi University in Tokyo. At the time of his article's publication he was an assistant professor of marketing at the Harvard Business School.

Frances Gaither Tucker is an associate professor of marketing and logistics at Syracuse University, where she specializes in research on and consulting for companies involved in the strategic realignment of their operations and customers. She is a member of the editorial review boards for the *Journal of Business Logistics, International Journal of Logistics Management,* and *Journal of Macromarketing.*

Seymour M. Zivan is a management consultant, based in New York, assisting corporations in developing strategies, plans, and programs to ensure that their performance is tailored to end-user needs. An expert in benchmarking, Mr. Zivan retired from Xerox Corporation in 1987, after 23 years with its U.S. marketing organization, where he served as vice president of Logistics and Distribution.

INDEX